Witch Hunt

Books by George Seldes

You Can't Print That
Can These Things Be?
World Panorama
The Vatican
Iron, Blood & Profits
Sawdust Caesar
Freedom of the Press
Lords of the Press
You Can't Do That
The Catholic Crisis
Witch Hunt
The Facts Are . . .
Facts and Fascism
One Thousand Americans
The People Don't Know
Tell the Truth and Run
The Great Quotations
Never Tire of Protesting
Even the Gods Can't Change History
The Great Thoughts
Witness to a Century

WITCH HUNT

The Technique and

Profits of Redbaiting

by
GEORGE SELDES

COPYRIGHT ©, 1940, BY GEORGE SELDES

THIS BOOK HAS ENTERED THE PUBLIC DOMAIN IN THE UNITED STATES

WWW.EBOOK-DEPOSITORY.COM

"Fella named Hines—got 'bout thirty thousan' acres, peaches and grapes – got a cannery an' a winery. Well, he's all a time talkin' about 'them goddam reds.' 'Goddam reds is drivin' the country to ruin,' he says, an' 'We got to drive these here red bastards out.' Well, they were a young fella jus' come out west here, an' he's listening' one day. He kinda scratched his head an' he says, 'Mr. Hines, I ain't been here long. What is these gaddam reds?' Well, sir, Hines says, 'A red is any son-of-a-bitch that wants thirty cents an hour when we're payin' twenty-five!'"
—JOHN STEINBECK, *Grapes of Wrath*

"Guard against the impostures of pretended patriotism."
—GEORGE WASHINGTON

To

HELEN SELDES

For Collaboration with Eight Books

Foreword

This book concerns itself chiefly with the baiting of men, organizations, and ideas; the use of the word *red* as a weapon; and the bloodshed, terrorism, and profits which may result from name-calling.

There are very few Communists, that is, real reds in America; but there are millions of Americans who are liberal, democratic, progressive—and it is among these that the reactionary forces often find their victims. "The reactionaries," says John Dewey, "are in possession of force, in not only the army and police, but in the press and the schools." And where they cannot use guns they can call names, frequently with equally devastating effect.

Redbaiting may lead to individual murder—as in Centralia, Washington, where members of an American Legion post lynched a veteran who belonged to the Industrial Workers of the World; as in Aberdeen, in the same state, where Laura Law, a union leader, was recently murdered in an atmosphere of lynch incitement inspired by business leaders and the press. It may also lead to national murder, which is called war, it led to the murder of the Spanish Republic, of which the liberal Catholic weekly *The Commomweal* wrote on January 15, 1937, "the decision which brought Moorish troops to fight down radicalism may prove to be the most ill-advised patriotic maneuver in all history."

With the use of the word *red* for members of the Communist Party, this volume will concern itself very little, since Communists have raised a banner of that color over their philosophy and actions. But when *red* is used as a smear-word; when it becomes a systematically used weapon for diverting attention from real issues; when it is, for example, applied to a Joad who asks for thirty cents an hour for picking fruit—that is another matter. It is, in fact, the matter of this book.

Evidence will be presented to show that anything—from a modern painting to a new system of philosophy—may today be attacked as *red* to prevent its being discussed on its own merits, and that the representatives of the established system have always commanded this device. Bernard Shaw observes that whenever in history a forceful leader has arisen to protest against impostures, "the masters in parliaments, in schools, and in newspapers make the most desperate efforts to prevent us from realizing our slavery." Shaw names Voltaire, Rousseau, Tom Paine, and Karl Marx as examples of men who have been so abused. But it is only since 1917, when the Bolsheviks came to power in Russia, that parliaments, schools, and newspapers have all concurred upon the term *red* to denote the worst features of atheism, libertinism, murder, and brutality. Since then they have consistently applied it to every man and every idea that does not conform, that they do not like, and that they want to destroy.

"A large part of the American public," Heywood Broun once said, "has been so riddled with propaganda that it is willing to believe that any group which asks for fifty cents a week more in pay or an hour less of work a week is under the direct leadership of Stalin. As far as this particular public goes, the issues in any dispute are immediately lost to sight once the cry of *red* is raised." Broun was himself a victim of redbaiters, and since his own field was the newspaper business, he was particularly hated by those most responsible for maintaining the impostures of which Bernard Shaw speaks.

Simeon Strunsky of the *New York Times*, a conservative journalist against whom such terms of reproach will certainly never be leveled, says, in referring to the trend in liberalism since the Russian Revolution, that "*liberal* has been a word of confusion. Everybody who was not a

Conservative became a Liberal or Radical or Red, whichever came first to the mind. In the newspapers it was often a matter of headline convenience."

Two types of persons thus indiscriminately use the word *red:* the ignorant, for whom it is a synonym for nonconformity; and the very wise in malice, who know that sticks and stones may break your bones but that names can inspire massacres.

When he threatens to tamper with the *status quo,* not even the President of the United States is immune to the charge of being a red. From the 1934 days of the Blue Eagle until 1940, when Mr. Roosevelt began to make peace with his critics, the campaign against the President and his advisers was a redbaiting campaign. There was not one Communist, not even a real Socialist, in the administration; nor was one of the planks of the Marxian manifesto or even one idea of Marx's *Capital* employed in the liberal reformist program which came out of Washington. Nevertheless, that program was redbaited into compromise and failure.

It is impossible to estimate the influence of the smearing use of such words as *red* upon the failure of progressive ideas in America. Dr. George W. Hartmann has conducted some illuminating tests of the effect of labels upon many groups of people. He asked two series of questions eliciting opinions on social issues, in the first of which he labeled the possible responses as Socialist, Republican, etc.; the answers of the majority of his guinea pigs reflected conventional indoctrination. But when he removed the labels, and asked a similar series of questions, he found that the majority of his subjects were, by the same criteria, liberal or even radical! If Dr. Hartmann's test is fair —and similar ones conducted in various places confirm it —it is evident that the mere matter of a label is important in American affairs. The Institute for Propaganda Analysis issues a bulletin every month showing how the public mind is constantly being influenced, and frequently perverted, by seven propagandist devices, of which the misleading use of labels is a favorite.

> bait. l. v.t. & i. Worry (badger, chained bear, etc.) by setting dogs at it, (of dogs) worry (animal); torment (person) . . .
> —*Pocket Oxford Dictionary*

Usually it is the majority, or at least a group firmly entrenched in power, that resorts to baiting, and usually it is a minority—religious, political, economic—that is baited, for it takes wealth and power to unleash with impunity the badgering dogs of journalism. But if the majority is weak and hesitant, and the minority is backed by force, the usual roles may be reversed. Thus the Brownshirt minority in Germany first baited the Republic, and finally destroyed it. Thus the Spanish Republic, with its population of 24,000,000, only 25,000 of whom were Communists, was labeled red by Franco, Hitler, Mussolini, and the Catholic hierarchy, and was destroyed.

In America, the chief use of redbaiting is as a weapon against the labor movement, as a means of breaking strikes. It is, moreover, a big business itself, as well as being the policy of big business; and its profits, both for its practitioners and its beneficiaries, can be counted in millions of dollars, in economic power, in social control.

A race, a nationality, a religious sect, a political or economic group may be baited with a compound of lies, half-lies, forgeries, and distortions, and yet there may be no legal redress. For under the American tradition of free speech and a free press, there can be no law against propaganda. But surely there ought to be some resort to the American spirit of fair play in combating underhanded smearing campaigns. The press, the radio, the movies, and the other means of public communication should be required to adhere to their own widely advertised codes of ethics. The radio station or newspaper that makes itself a party to such attacks should be made to provide equal free time or space for rebuttal and for the denial of proved misstatements, as is now required in some countries.

Most redbaiting does not consist in the baiting of reds. Not only labor, but also progressive individuals in the tradition of Jefferson or Lincoln, may be silenced when Jeffersonian or Lincolnian ideas are branded Marxian. "One of the best ways to get yourself a reputation as a dangerous citizen these days," writes Senator La Follette's *Progressive,* "is to go about repeating the very phrases which our founding fathers used in the great struggle for independence."

Redbaiting does not depend on reason, logic, consistency, or truth for its effectiveness, for it is essentially obscurantist and anti-intellectual. In one section of the country it may be directed against the Catholics; and in another it may be led by Catholics and directed against the Jews. But everywhere it is anti-liberal and anti-labor; its chief aim is to stem the movement of the great mass of the American people for better living, working, and cultural conditions. This statement may stand despite the fact that so much redbaiting is conducted by labor unions themselves, by working men and women, and by so-called intellectuals, such as newspaper columnists and college professors.

A man named Coughlin may smear the President of the United States by calling him a radical, a Socialist, or a Communist. A congressman named Dies may undermine the entire liberal and progressive movement in the nation by publicizing falsifications, distortions, and propaganda against every organization formed to uphold the Bill of Rights, protect minorities and the consumer, and promote the "general welfare" of the the people as provided in the Constitution. (Since a congressman may make statements which from a private citizen would be considered criminal libel, Mr. Dies has been challenged to repeat as a layman the charges he has made as a congressman, so that he might be sued for libel, defamation, and slander; he has not to date accepted this challenge.)

Perhaps political baiting in modern times fulfills a psychological need that in other days was provided by the baiting of bears in pits. A man who would not himself attend a bloody cockfight in a secret arena may publicly gloat on the radio over reports of Christian Fronters beating up "reds" on the streets of New York. It must not be forgotten that the purpose of baiting is the incitement of hatred, which in turn makes for violence.

"The forces seeking repression are active and voluble," says the 1937 report of the American Civil Liberties Union; "the Red Label is pasted on all kinds of progressive movements. Chief offenders are the American Legion, the Catholic Church, chambers of commerce, the D.A.R., Klan and Nazi agencies, and of course reactionary employers."

Behind many of the repressive movements against civil liberties, it becomes clearer every year, is the profit motive. Ever since the First World War the profit motive has been happily combined with the impulse to sadism to develop the technique of redbaiting. In the ever-present conflict between property rights and human rights, redbaiting has emerged as the chief weapon—short of force—of one side; a weapon, moreover, that prepares the ground for future violence.

The following pages were written to illustrate specifically some of the foregoing generalities.

GEORGE SELDES

Contents

Foreword ix

Part I
Background

1 Personal History: Marshal Foch and Woodrow Wilson 3
2 European Panorama 19
3 A Short History of American Redbaiting 33
4 A Decade of Witch Hunts 47

Part II
Case Histories: Some Victims

5 Star Salesman 67
6 The Wages of Redbaiting 81
7 Two Children and a Witch Trial 91
8 Just Around the Corner 97
9 Small-Town Fascism 103

Part III
Sample Redbaiters

10 Easley: America's No. 1 Redbaiter 115
11 George E. Sokolsky 125
12 Matthews: Convert to Redbaiting 133
13 From Capone to Coughlin 149
14 In Congress and Out 171

Part IV
Big Business As Usual

15 Business Patriotism	191
16 The Chambers of Commerce	211
17 The National Association of Manufacturers: Power and Corruption	229
18 Associated Farmers: Tom Joad, That Red	237
19 The Johnstown Plan: Big Business as Vigilante	245
20 The Liberty League and Its Offspring	257

Part V
Marching As To War

21 The Triumph of Dies	269
22 Who Are the Real Fifth Column?	279
23 Conclusion: War of Words and Worlds	289

Part I

BACKGROUND

CHAPTER 1
Personal History
Marshal Foch and Woodrow Wilson

During the World War, I was a member of the press section of the United States Army in France and Germany and I was later present at the peace-making at Versailles. Accompanying Woodrow Wilson on his grand tour of Europe, I saw the beginnings of what is today the great game of redbaiting throughout the world, though I was at the time totally unaware of what was going on. Years later I realized that the great men of that time were also the founding fathers of redbaiting.

Marshal Foch, victor of the World War, was magnanimous enough to receive us, the twenty members of the press corps of the American Army in France, and to confide to us the greatest secret of all, the planned attack of November 14., 1918, which was to have rolled up and through the Germans, flooded the Rhine, and ended with bannered victory on Unter den Linden. . . .

"The Yankees would have led the attack," explained the hero, beaming on us. "The Yankees throughout the war were superb . . . vigorously idealistic . . . admirably gallant. . . . You brought youth, virility, morale . . . hastened victory. General Pershing"—he nodded to our chaperon, whom he called "Pairshan"—"wanted to concentrate on an American sector. The Argonne and the Meuse were the hardest. 'All right,' I said to him, 'you Americans have the devil's own punch. You overcome everything. *Allons*-y. Go to it.'"

When it came to my turn, I said: "*Monsieur le maréchal*, we have heard rumors that you are dissatisfied with the armistice, that you thought it premature. . . ."

"I could not be otherwise," replied Marshal Foch; "the

Germans gave everything we demanded. Naturally a general would have preferred to give battle. . . .

"Germany surrendered because the German command knew what we had planned for November 14—three days after the armistice—if the armistice had been broken. General Pershing that day would have led six American divisions, more than 160,000 men, and I would have commanded twenty French, 200,000 men, in an attack in Lorraine, while Marshal Haig would have made a supporting in Flanders. Nothing would have stopped us from breaking into Germany and opening the road to Berlin. Meanwhile the British bombers were concentrated in your (American) territory with planes capable of bombing Berlin with the new big bombs."

(It is more than twenty-one years since I heard Marshal Foch tell us this story, on January 17, 1919, and I can feel again the tingle of journalistic excitement that comes to those rare moments when one knows one is getting something that will go down in history. Meeting Foch was itself a thrilling event, but getting the innermost secret of the war was tremendous.)

"The Germans were lost," continued Foch. "They capitulated. And now we must make a peace which will answer to the magnitude of our victory. . . . France has a right to effective measures of protection after the formidable effort which she put forth to save civilization. The Rhine is the guarantee of peace. . . ."

He went to the map and showed us how the river and the land formed an Indian bow. The string could be the river, the bow either in Alsace-Lorraine or in the German Rhineland, depending on whether or not the Allies occupied both banks of the river.

"Let us watch on the Rhine," he continued. "Democracies never attack . . . but who can say that Germany, where the democratic ideals are so recent and perhaps so very superficial, will not quickly retrieve itself from its defeat and within a very few years attempt a second time to crush us?

"Russia is temporarily *hors de combat*. . . . But France must always be ready to safeguard the general interests of mankind. These interests are at stake on the Rhine. We must prepare to obviate a painful surprise in the future. Let us watch lest we lose the fruits of our common victory. . . ."

Eight years later I learned why Foch had come to see us, why he had given us one of the great stories of our times, why he had launched through us his plan for the permanent occupation of Germany's side of the Rhine, why the dark hints of German recuperation and the mention of Russia.

At that very time Marshal Foch was moving heaven and earth—and attempting to move Wilson, Clemenceau, Lloyd George, and Orlando also—to get authorization for the Allied invasion of Bolshevik Russia. The world was in arms and there was already a small attempt at co-operative attack in Archangel and in Siberia. Japan, he knew, could be paid to attack in the Far East; and with the Rhineland as an Allied base, with Germany completely subjected to military occupation, he felt sure that he could march a big army all the way to Moscow and drown in blood the newborn socialist state. That was his hope, his plan. He came to Trier and used the American press corps for floating his *balloon d'essai,* and we had been only too glad to puff it up in the press of the world. In August 1927, Marshal Foch confessed that immediately after launching this trial balloon he had tried the plan on the Big Four.

"In February 1919, in the early days of Leninism," he said, "I declared to the Ambassadors' Conference meeting in Paris that, if the states surrounding Russia were supplied with munitions and the sinews of war, I would undertake to stamp out the Bolshevik menace once and for all. I was overruled on the ground of war-weariness, but the sequel soon showed I was right." In 1920 he had spoken with one of the chief statesmen of the Versailles treaty-making—Clemenceau no doubt, although he did not identify him.

This leader, according to Foch, said: "You were quite right and I greatly regret the short-sightedness I then displayed. I trust you will make no mention of it when you write your memoirs."

In the years of the Long Armistice—1918 to 1939—there were many plans to unite all Europe for an invasion of Russia to save civilization from the Red Menace. The most noted of these was the attempt by General Hoffmann of Brest-Litovsk fame; but, historically, Marshal Foch must be listed as first in this movement. He was a deeply religious man, the brother of a priest, but he was also among the first to advocate the bloody adventure against the Soviets in the name of the gentle Jesus. He had held back in October 1918 from a too-enthusiastic advocacy of a march into Berlin, because that battle of November 14 would entail the loss of another 200,000 men; and although this figure was small compared to the millions already slaughtered, it was on the grounds of humanitarianism that he finally consented to call off the war.

"The father of a family, I could not help thinking of the blood that would be shed on the road to Berlin," he told us. "A victory, however easy, costs the lives of men. We had victory without any further sacrifice. We took it as it came."

That sounded quite noble. In fact we marveled at this display of the heart on the sleeve of a military leader. We had not found it elsewhere. Certainly if General Pershing had a heart that beat for humanity he kept it so tightly concealed under his icebound exterior that no one expected anything but military efficiency from him, regardless of human costs. But Foch was a southern Frenchman, a smiling-eyed, voluble, easy, kindly man; the very antithesis of the military type of most German officers and of "Von" Summerall, Mangin "the Butcher," and the impassive Pershing. Yet when it came to Russia, godless Russia, which had raised the banner "Religion Is the Opium of the People" and had expropriated the British oil companies and defaulted on the bonds held in France, kindly Marshal Foch was ready to lead a "Christian Crusade" which would result in the deaths of millions of Christians on both sides in the snows around Moscow. And the press of the world, which we represented, was this time slated to play an unwitting role in one of the bloodiest conspiracies in history.

In the seventeen years I spent in Europe as a correspondent, this was, of course, the most sensational episode in my personal relationship to anti-red conspiracies, but there were many other times when I was expected to play my part as a redbaiter. Some of these I was conscious of, in others I was an innocent victim or a mere journalistic bystander. There were, for example, my dealings with General Ludendorff.

During armistice week, with three other members of the press section of the American Army, I had gone across the line, in violation of the treaty, to see Hindenburg, who had withdrawn to the town of Cassell. The gruff, stern-faced old man actually wept for his Fatherland as he told us that there were two things that won the war—the British blockade and the American attack in the Argonne. "The British blockade made it impossible for us to win . . ." he said. "The American attack broke the balance of power, won the war." But, after 1920, when I was head of the Berlin bureau of the *Chicago Tribune*, there were frequent interviews and much correspondence with General Ludendorff, and during all the years I was in Germany, Ludendorff kept repeating the same phrases:

"We did not lose the war in the field."

"The German army was stabbed in the back by the Socialists."

"The German army was stabbed in the back by the Jews."

"The German army was stabbed in the back by the Jesuits."

"The German army was stabbed in the back by the Freemasons."

"The German army was stabbed in the back by *Bolschevismus.*"

When Woodrow Wilson made his grand tour of the Allied countries, he was hailed everywhere as the greatest man in history since Jesus. At that same time, however, a strange mood pervaded the American army. Our soldiers were still convinced of the idealism and nobility of their leader—but they were just beginning to taste disillusionment about the purposes of the war. The Russians had opened the secret archives which proved conclusively the real war motives of the Allies. If Italy had been promised territory, Russia Constantinople, Japan slices of China, was it perhaps also true, the doughboys asked, that the United States, as German propaganda had so frequently charged (and as the Nye Committee was to prove to the next generation), had entered the war to save the Morgan loans?

The soldier had already learned that it was not true that the Germans cut off the hands of Belgian babies, that the Germans boiled soldiers' corpses for axle-grease, that they crucified prisoners. Many of the doughboys were now stationed in Germany and were discovering that the Germans were like other people. The American soldiers were not mutinous, but in their sudden learning of the truth, they were becoming uneasy, confused, nervous.

Then General Pershing and his aides acted: the still fresh specter of Bolshevism was raised in the Rhineland. The army was kept on the *qui vive:* Bolshevism was in Germany. "The American army on the Rhine must hold the frontier of civilization against Bolshevism," said the general to the war correspondents; "there will be no let-up in discipline."

It became a crime to talk to a German girl, though the hospitals of Coblenz were soon full of doughboys who in violation of military discipline had "talked" to German girls. The hospitals were known as "soap and chocolate," these two commodities being the scarcest in starving Germany and the quickest and cheapest way to a lady's heart, and, alas, frequently, to the institutions presided over by my friend, Major Jenner.

Morals and morale, thought the command, were breaking down. So the intelligence department of the American army, taking on the services of a propaganda bureau, suddenly began to find evidence of Bolshevik plots in every vineyard of the Rhineland. I remember that it fed us one tall story of a great "Bolo-inspired German uprising against the American Army of Occupation," a plan to slit the throat of every soldier, murder every officer, rid Germany of its foreign invader. We did not stop to think how ridiculous this propaganda was but sent the sensation to America. It did double duty: it continued to make bad blood between America and starving Germany, and it fed the flames of hate against Russia.

We who were on the periphery at Versailles while Wilson and the elder statesmen concocted their "peace" treaty did not then know that it was signed in haste, in fear of the lengthening
red shadow of the Kremlin.

The statesmen had come to Paris after having prepared their peoples for a better world. "Do not be content," Lloyd George had said, addressing labor during the war, "with anything less than a new world." In England and France they spoke of their countries after the war as "lands fit for heroes." The Pan-American Labor Conference had met in Laredo, Texas, with Samuel Gompers presiding, and it had been decided that the future America would provide industrial freedom and social justice for labor. Labor was about to come into its own. That was its reward for winning the war. In the agricultural countries the politicians promised the peasants land; in the industrial countries the politicians promised participation in control, even co-operative ownership.

It was Lloyd George who had coined the phrase "a new deal for everybody" in his promises to soldiers and workmen. The soldier would return to civil life, a workman, and would be honored for his sacrifices. Nowhere in the victorious democracies in those early days was there a fear that labor would take if nothing was given, that the Russian example might have an effect on other people. But the change came early in 1919.

Woodrow Wilson won all the preliminary battles of Versailles. The first fight was over the plan for a League of Nations, and the American delegate succeeded in having that put first on the agenda. (Later he was to explain to a disillusioned people that all the compromises and surrenders would be made good through the functions of the League.) His second battle was for the recognition of Russia, which was to be followed by a conference at which all factions, Bolshevik and anti-Bolshevik, monarchist and émigré, would be invited. The Associated Powers, read the official announcement, "recognize the absolute right of the Russian people to direct their own affairs without reservation. . . ." (At that very time Marshal Foch was secretly urging the Allies to military intervention.)

But Woodrow Wilson, the American idealist, humanitarian, liberal, was in the hands of the cleverest politicians in Europe, several of them ex-Socialists and pseudo-liberals. Clemenceau persuaded Wilson to keep the Versailles meetings secret; M. Poincaré persuaded Wilson to agree to the punishment of the Germans as the one guilty party in the war. Everywhere in Europe liberals, Socialists, labor parties, were already active in begging the American President—the Prince of Peace, the "new messiah," the "king of humanity," as he was actually described in the press—to co-operate with them in giving life to all the promises of the wartime leaders, to make the world a better place for the masses of its inhabitants.

The rulers of Europe had, of course, no intention of reforming the world, and now that they were victorious their promises meant nothing. They were merely continuing in 1919 where they had left off in 1914. On December 15, 1918, for example, the working people of Paris, united in Socialist and labor organizations, asked for a permit to march by Woodrow Wilson's home, in homage to the world's greatest leader and hero; but Clemenceau and Poincaré not only refused to permit this demonstration but also refused to tell Mr. Wilson, who had waited at his window all morning, why the workmen of the capital had failed to appear. Nor did they tell him that they had sent both the police and the army to frighten and subdue the "pacifists" who had asked to march.

President Wilson went on to London and Rome. In London he lived in the palace and did not meet the people. While occupying berths on sleepers, he failed to get the report from the Archangel Front where, months after the World War was over, American troops together with French and British, were assisting Russian monarchists in attacking the Russian Bolsheviks; nor was he told that the American Army of Occupation in Germany, which had been warned not to talk to German men and women, had now received orders "not to fraternize with German children." And we who were in that Army of Occupation thought the orders were intended to keep us from becoming friendly to a late enemy, not to a potential "red" enemy, a Soviet Germany.

From the balcony of the Palazzo Venezia, overlooking the noble square where a few years later Mussolini was to address the Blackshirts, President Wilson planned to make the greatest speech of his life: an appeal to all the common people of Europe to join the American people in a pact of friendship which could never be broken by dissension and wars. A committee of notable citizens, which included a prince and many Italian officers wearing the gold and silver medals of war heroism, had discussed the speech with the President and promised that all Rome would be in the square the next day to hear it; but the crowd never came, the speech was never made. Wilson did not know until years later that the Italian government had repudiated the committee by labeling it "red" and "Bolshevik," and had sent regiments of soldiers to frighten the thousands who might come to the Venetian Square. The monarchy was afraid for its life. Mr. Wilson was restrained from speaking.

The Socialists and the labor unions, joined by the Liberal Party and the Catholic Party of Don Sturzo and by other liberals—who were immediately afterwards to be denounced as radicals—dominated the Italian scene. In Milan the government permitted free speech for one day and there was a roaring demand that Wilson smash the imperialisms of the world—British, French, and Italian imperialism as well as German. Forty mayors of large Italian cities, carrying the red flags of their Socialist Party, called on Wilson to help Italy in its appalling industrial situation: the owners rolling in war profits and the workers starving. Mr. Wilson made his usual promise: the League of Nations would take care of everything. The Italian monarchy immediately clamped on the censorship and stopped parades.

Mr. Wilson apparently knew nothing about all this ferment which was going on in Europe. I traveled with him those fateful weeks, spoke to him, heard him speak and explain, and I cannot believe ill of him. The ferment was only in part Bolshevism, although the Russian Revolution had already unleashed a force which was from then on to make itself felt in the world; the ferment at that time was simply the desire of the great masses of people for a better world. It was merely a demand that the promises of the leaders be kept. Socialist and Left Socialist groups and parties everywhere, being most articulate, naturally joined labor unions in leadership of the millions. Only in Germany, however, was there a noticeable Bolshevik organization, and that was immediately drowned in blood by the Social-Democrats with the help of their "enemies," the monarchists.

In America, Professor Woodrow Wilson's doctrine of

"industrial democracy" was about to become a living fact. The soldiers who were returning from France and Germany knew nothing about Bolshevism—they had not even heard the word because the censorship abroad had been stricter than that at home—but they knew what they wanted. They had lived through a terrible disillusionment, they had vaguely realized that they had not "made the world safe for democracy" but they felt that they had earned a share in the better future which was certain in America. The daily press had promised them that. In the "new freedom" there would be nothing but friendship, cooperation between capital and labor, participation of the workmen in the control and ownership of the works. Even an old reactionary like Charles M. Schwab, who had fought labor all his life (while selling the American government battleship armor that was full of blowholes), now announced that capital and labor were "partners in the future of America. We have entered upon a social era in which the aristocracy of the future will be men who have done something for humanity and their nations. There will be no rich and no poor."

Naturally the whole world felt that awakened labor would dominate the peace conference of Paris. Its purpose, everyone agreed, was first of all to settle the political problems of the world to the satisfaction of all—with the aid of the Christlike "Fourteen Points," which had been publicly accepted by everyone—and then to accomplish something even more important: to provide for a decent standard of living throughout the world. Although America at that time had not yet realized that one-third of the American people did not have enough clothes, shelter and food to live decently, all Europe knew that a third or a half or three-quarters of its population was ill-clad, ill-housed, ill-fed. Samuel Gompers, president of the American Federation of Labor, came to Paris to co-operate with President Wilson, not merely to advise him but actually to organize the International Labor Federation, which was to embody all the good points of all labor organizations, including the Second and Third Internationals, and even supersede them, thus introducing a utopian era in world affairs.

That was the world of December 1918 and January 1919.

We did not then know that British business interests had sold arms and munitions to the Germans during the war; that the French de Wendel family owned coal and iron interests on both sides of the front; that war munitions were being routed through Switzerland and Italy by both sides, to the benefit of a small group of merchants of death. We did not then have the phrase "The Two Hundred Families" for the little group which owned and controlled the Bank of France, the Briey Basin, the munitions industry, and big business; nor the words, "Cliveden Set" for the reactionaries who frequented Lady Astor's country estate and ran the British empire to suit the British merchants and imperialists; nor the term "Sixty Families" in the United States—nor the knowledge that there were analogous groups in all the powerful countries. They were silent in January 1919. They felt the ferment, the rising tide, the movement of the people reaching out for a better world. And they kept quiet and worked together to save themselves.

When Wilson surrendered to Clemenceau, the cause of this better world was lost. There would be no open covenants openly arrived at, and eventually no land fit for heroes. Within three months, while the conspirators met at Versailles—and laid the base for the Second World War—the ruling families, the armies and police which they controlled, and the press which they owned, were able to change mental attitudes and political outlooks everywhere. Within three months the labor movement in every country was being attacked by the politicians, the press, and the armed forces, and the first world-wide campaign to destroy the hopes the First World War had engendered was well under way. The victors were grabbing the imperialist spoils of the world and fighting the agitated and groping populations at home with all their weapons: police, press, platform, and the smear-words—*red, Socialist, Communist, Bolshevik, radical, alien, and un-American.* . . .

And what did Woodrow Wilson read in his morning newspaper in those fateful days of 1919? He read these headlines:

(*January* 8)
TROTSKY ARRESTS LENIN AND MAKES
HIMSELF SOLE DICTATOR
(*January* 15)
TROTSKY FLEES PETROGRAD
(*January* 16)
TROTSKY CAPTURED WITH KRYLENKO
(*Helsingfors, January* 23)
BOLSHEVIKI KILL 3000 IN KIEV
(*Almost any day; in fact, 91 times*)
FALL OF BOLSHEVIKI BELIEVED CERTAIN

Wilson was worried. He sent Lincoln Steffens, the noted "muckraker," and William C. Bullitt, the rich young man from Philadelphia temporarily slumming in social politics, on a mission to Russia. When Steffens got back he said, "I have seen the future and it works." Bullitt brought the peace terms which Lenin had given him and which Lloyd George had requested, They were:

Lifting of the food blockade against Russia.
Non-interference with Russian sovereignty.
Reciprocal rights of entry into all nations' territories.
Release of all political and war prisoners.
Withdrawal of foreign troops from Russia.

The trip had been suggested by Colonel House; the technicalities of travel had been smoothed out by the British Foreign Office at the request of Lloyd George. The

Allies, meeting in Paris, had listened to Wilson's suggestion that Russia be invited to join the "civilized" nations (which were then and there preparing the barbaric destruction of Germany) and discuss terms for a rapprochement.

But when Bullitt came home, a new White Russian was about to conquer the Reds: Kolchak, who was advancing daily with the help of British and French money and arms. Bullitt was refused an interview by the President, and British leaders actually lied about their part in his mission. Bullitt protested. He demanded that he be heard. The result of it all was that some newspapers turned the Bullitt disclosures into attacks against President Wilson.

Was it true, the State Department and Secretary Lansing were asked, that Lenin and Trotsky had really opposed the Brest-Litovsk treaty and had signed it only because the Allies had not come to Russia's aid? Was it true that the Russian leaders had given Colonel Raymond Robins a letter to the President which said that the Russians would not sign, but would continue to fight Germany, if Wilson promised moral support, food, and guns? Was it true that Lansing had suppressed the letter and Wilson had never seen it? Was it true that as a result of this trickery Colonel Robins was refused an interview by Wilson, and that Robins was silenced by his employer, the American Red Cross, through the agency of the State Department?

Robins had come out of Moscow to say that the report that Lenin and Trotsky were German agents was untrue, and that the sending of American troops to Archangel to fight Russia was a crime. For telling these truths Robins was immediately attacked by officialdom, superpatriots, and the press, denounced as a red, and silenced. His factual reports were replaced by propagandist announcements from the State Department having no correspondence to the facts.

It was not the Espionage Act and the State Department which prevented the American people from hearing anything from Russia except tales of terror and horror.

There was no official censorship, but the voluntary pledge of the publishers was even more effective. All the men and institutions which held power exerted it to deceive and suppress; in America, as in Europe where the ruling families and the premiers and chancellors gave overt orders, the forces which represent the *status quo* determined that the new challenging force, Marxian Socialism, should never be mentioned except by way of falsification and slander.

The words *radical, liberal, socialist, anarchist,* and *Bolshevik* were used indiscriminately by the American press and later by the American people; and because it was so easy to use the three-letter word *red* in a headline, the newspapers—which of course had no red advertisers who might object—used it almost exclusively. One had but to apply the terms *red* or *Bolshevik* to a person, a thing, an idea, a movement, a party, an organization, and these were eternally damned. Philosophers, humanitarians, politicians, were among the victims. The redbaiting words became the most powerful weapons of constituted authority, wealth, the entrenched, and the satisfied.

The years of noble words were over. The universal craving for a new world, political and industrial democracy, lands fit for heroes, a new deal for everyone, was turned, in 1919 and 1920, into a hunt for the international scapegoat; it was diverted into red hysteria, or it was destroyed with fire and sword. As times grew worse in the earlier 1920's, the red witch hunts grew more intense. The link between redbaiting and political and financial profits became a little more apparent.

CHAPTER 2
European Panorama

GERMANY

In January 1919, President Wilson joined Herbert Hoover in an effort to lift the blockade that was starving the men, women, and children of Germany, but Clemenceau and the British Admiralty replied that their warships would not permit a loaf of bread to enter the defeated nations. Hoover said that "hunger is the mother of anarchy," and Wilson pleaded that food, not guns, would cure the world of Bolshevism, but the victorious Allies were unmoved.

Karl Liebknecht, the Socialist leader who had defied the war-makers in 1914 by refusing his vote to the Reichstag's war budget, and Rosa Luxemburg, second leader of the Independent Socialists, tried to lead the hungry, disillusioned, unhappy people of Berlin into a revolt. For two weeks there was fighting in the streets, in trenches in the Tiergarten, at the Silesian station; and then the Social-Democratic government and its monarchist officers not only suppressed the Spartacus uprising, as it was later known, but lynched Liebknecht and Luxemburg.

In March 1920 the counter-revolution began in Germany. It had only one objective: to overthrow the democratic republic and restore the monarchists, the Junkers, the men responsible for the World War but who wanted to hold on to their profits after it was lost. But Dr. Kapp and General von Lüttwitz, who led the Kapp Putsch, announced their aims in these words: "We consider it urgent to take this action for the protection of Europe against danger from the East. Nothing is being done by the Allies to stay the advance of Bolshevism."

As a matter of fact it was freely rumored that the

Kappists had received word from occupied Rhineland that Marshal Foch regarded their efforts benevolently. The Kapp Putsch was finally defeated by a general strike of the German workers, but even the German Republic, governed by Social-Democrats, employed redbaiting when it was opportune—as in the case of the American, Paul De Mott. De Mott, a youth of the highest ideals, a Quaker, a pacifist and humanitarian, was arrested by some officers in the Essen district, during the last days of the civil war between the people and the monarchists. The German soldiers shot him.

In April 1920, I came to the town of Wesel just in time to attend a sort of military coroner's inquest. Thick-necked, be-monocled Prussian officers sat in a courtroom and took evidence, while on a desk there lay the bloody garments and all the personal belongings of the murdered youth.

The Germans said Paul De Mott was a red. They also said he took the wrong door while ostensibly going to the prison latrine, so they shot him. They testified that he had fraternized with the armed workmen of the Rhineland uprising, and they sent on to the American diplomatic mission in Berlin a lot of letters found in De Mott's pocket.

A month later I called on Ellis Loring Dresel, our representative in Berlin, and his secretaries, who had handled the case. "De Mott?" they said. "Oh, he was a Bolshevik. Nothing to bother about." And so the American government did not bother. Reds were not considered human beings or Americans.

The evidence: De Mott had gotten an assignment to do some magazine stories in Germany and Russia, and among his effects were two letters, one addressed to Trotsky, the other to Lenin. But the red flag had been raised; the American State Department surrendered. (And that very week the French government got a million francs in gold and a salute because the Germans had killed one of their nationals in a brawl.)

Just before Hitler was arrested for the Bürgerbrau

Putsch of 1923, he said to the press: "I did what I did because Bolshevism was brewing in Germany. Let not France rejoice in Germany's downfall; when Bolshevism destroys Germany it will envelop France as well. This will be the curse which follows Poincaré's victory in the Ruhr." For the benefit of American correspondents he said the man he most admired was Theodore Roosevelt; for the benefit of Italian journalists he said he had read all of Mussolini's speeches.

Facing, with Ludendorff, the charge of treason, Hitler said: "I joined the National Socialist Labor Party and organized the movement because of my desire to exterminate Marxism and drive the Jews out of Germany."

Between Armistice Day, 1918, and May Day, 1924, when he died in delirium, screaming that there were reds under his bed, Hugo Stinnes bestrode the German Fatherland like a colossus. He was one of the wealthiest men the world has ever known, having at one time been worth more than a billion dollars; he employed 600,000 men, built an industrial empire that had ramifications everywhere, and spoke in favor of the capitalist system in his own sixty-three newspapers. He was also one of the most fanatical redbaiters the world had ever known, and damned progressive labor, socialism, the Soviets, and progressive ideas in the same scared breath.

Isaac F. Marcosson made Hugo Stinnes a *Saturday Evening Post* hero. It is true that Hugo Stinnes paid better wages than any other employer in Germany; it is true that he was patriarchal. He said that his men loved him, and when he forbade them to join the unions of the Social-Democratic Party many of them cheered him. But the story the writers in the popular magazines did not tell was that it was Stinnes who looted Belgium, it was Stinnes who got the Kaiser to approve his plan of forced labor of the Belgian people, it was Stinnes who later looted Germany and was more than any other man responsible for the starvation years after the war, for the spread of Marxian ideas, and for the reaction to Hitlerism.

In 1924, in the McKenna report to the House of Commons, it was shown that between $1,808,000,000 and $2,070,000,000 in German marks had been sold to foreigners; that about one million persons who had bank accounts in German banks had lost everything; that every German patriot who had bought war bonds instead of industrial stocks was bankrupt; that Americans had lost about one billion dollars in mark investments.

For every dollar lost in Germany there was a dollar gained by someone. The Hitlerites and the big industrialists, of whom Stinnes was the first leader, blamed the inflation and the profiteering on immigrant Polish Jews, or on all the Jews, but the facts were otherwise: the money was gained by the big industrialists and bankers of Germany, and the one who profited most was Hugo Stinnes. The "higher wages" he paid his workmen were paid in worthless marks borrowed from the Socialist government of Germany, while he kept his profits abroad in golden pounds and golden dollars. Frequently he repaid with one dollar a loan of millions of marks made a few months previously. He paid his workmen only three or four cents a day in gold but gave them thousands of paper marks, and thus he fooled the world and won the accolade of brass-check journalists. It was a monstrous piece of irony: looting the Socialist German Republic and with the loot keeping down the Socialist idea among workingmen.

"It was a harvest for the vultures, for those patriots of Germany fattening on the carcass of national credit," Irving Bush, president of the Chamber of Commerce of New York State, said at that time, adding: "Men like Stinnes did not start the inflation but saw where it was heading. They grew wealthy and powerful. The shadow of Stinnes sits at every council table. It is the greatest danger to the world today. Stinnes' power is a danger to the world because it is certain to bring discredit to honest business leaders."

Before his death Stinnes laid down the law of "family,

factory, nation"—in the order of importance of the trinity he worshiped, although nation to him meant an appendage to factory, and factory was part of family. "There shall be no divergent interests," he ordered; "if any question arises, your mother shall be the sole judge and final arbiter. You are united to build. What I have created consider solely the foundation for the structure you and those who come after you will erect. Let nothing keep you from the goal."

Stinnes believed in the autocracy of the industrial capitalist; he fought labor all his life, combatted the Socialist movement of the republic, and trembled at the growing strength of the Communist movement. He so worded his will and made such arrangements that the German government got nothing in taxation. He went to his grave clutching his millions; but just before he died, he shrieked, in delirium, of the reds, whom he saw as spirits, all around him and even under his bed.

ITALY

In Italy, from September 1 to 19, 1920, the men in the metallurgical works staged a sit-down strike; they also attempted to operate the factories, buy and sell, with nonchalant disregard of the owners. There was not a skull cracked or a face slapped. There was not a sword drawn or a pistol fired. All was serene. But the world's commercial press was outraged. Having yelled revolution on September 1, it had to supply something to its readers, and so it faked the news.

I was an eyewitness to one of the big frauds of the time. It was all very well for the foreign correspondents to cable news which had no foundation in fact, but the press photographers had to supply the evidence, and this presented a pretty dilemma. Hearst photographers were equal to it. It was Hearst men in Milan and Turin who painted *"Viva Lenin"* on the automobile and typewriter works, supplied the red flags to the sit-downers, posed them with old blunderbusses and wartime officers' swords, and otherwise faked up a pretty Bolshevik revolution for the news reels and picture pages. It is true that most of the boys and girls waving the red flags, swords, and guns were smiling and shouting their laughter, but the public would not notice that, and grim and bloody revolution it would remain.

General Charles H. Sherrill, who later was to be an American ambassador, reported that "At Turin a Red Tribunal, composed partly of women, caused men to be thrown alive into blast furnaces. . . . Some sailors were ambushed by a band of Socialists, men and women, and literally torn to pieces, every last one of them, with all the excesses of the French Revolution—the women ripping off ears with their teeth. . . ." It was a tremendous story, but unfortunately for the press, it didn't happen. General Sherrill got it from the same source which reported that these same Socialists had burned "Signor Fiat" in his own automobile factory furnace. There was of course no Signor Fiat, the company's name being derived from the initials F.I.A.T., but that falsehood also was never repaired by the press.

Among those who approved violently of the occupation of the Italian factories was a journalist named B. Mussolini, who had once been a member of the Socialist Party and had been expelled for accepting from the French government 50,000 francs for starting a pro-Ally newspaper and a monthly subsidy all through the war. Mussolini now tried to rejoin the Socialists. He called on Signor Buozzi, head of the Italian Federation of Labor, and offered to make the sit-down strike into a political weapon, to furnish a Blackshirt militia, march on Rome, and establish a radical government. Buozzi, however, did not believe in violence and mistrusted a renegade. He declined the invitation. That same week Mussolini sold his idea to Secretary-General Olivetti and other members of the Confederazione dell' Industria, the equivalent of our National Association of Manufacturers.

Nevertheless, Mussolini was honest enough to admit (on June 2, 1921, in an editorial in his paper, *Popolo d'Italia*) that "the Italy of 1921 is fundamentally different from that of 1919. . . . To say that the Bolshevik danger still exists in Italy is equivalent to trying to exchange, for reasons of self-interest, fear against the truth. Bolshevism is conquered. More than that, it has been disowned by the leaders and the people."

It is important to note that Mussolini never did any redbaiting until 1925. Before and after taking power he cursed the parliamentary system, denounced democracy, wrote that famous piece about not being afraid "to pass once more over the more or less decayed corpse of the Goddess of Liberty"; but he never attacked radicals, Socialists, or Communists before 1925.

Why then did Mussolini start redbaiting later? The answer is known to Wall Street. In 1925 the natural economic course, which the liberals and radicals planned after the World War and which brought reductions in debt and a raising of the standards of living even into Mussolini's reign, came to its end, and the Fascist "economy" was already a failure. The process of double budgeting and faking the national statistics began, and foreign loans were necessary to keep up the Fascist bureaucracy. Money could be had in America. But America had up to then had an honest report about Fascism, and it was not good. American public opinion had to be changed before the House of Morgan could float its loans of hundreds of millions in Wall Street, before Dillon, Read and Company could supply $30,000,000 to the shady Fascists who ran the city of Milan.

And so the press agents were hired; the Bolshevik legend was created. It was spread by such journalists as Isaac F. Marcosson, Kenneth L. Roberts, Irvin S. Cobb; it was repeated by Thomas W. Lamont, Morgan partner, in the reputable magazine, *The Survey*, in 1927; it was broadcast by all the Italian journalists who worked for the

Associated Press, the *New York Times*, the London *Daily Mail*, Reuters, and the corrupt French press. Against this flood of propaganda the reports of Hiram Kelly Motherwell, Percy Winner, David Darrah, and a dozen others—most of whom were deported from Rome—could not prevail. The myth that Mussolini had conquered Bolshevism or communism, or even radicalism, remains to this day. What Mussolini did conquer, and boasted of conquering at the time, was the Catholic Populari of the great priest, Don Sturzo, Mussolini's real rival for Italian rule-—and the Goddess of Liberty.

The world-wide myth that Mussolini came to save Italy from Bolshevism is, therefore, in the first instance an American and British invention—an invention of foreign monopolists and bankers, who gained direct profit from it, and of their spokesmen in the press. Chiefly responsible are Sir Percival Phillips, Lord Rothermere, Lord Beaverbrook, Otto Kahn, and the House of Morgan. As late as the summer of 1940, Frank Gervasi, writing in *Collier's Weekly*, repeated the story that Mussolini came to power in a struggle with communism in Italy. Incidentally, the House of Morgan is still represented in the board of directors of the Crowell Publishing Company, owners of Collier's, and it was Thomas W. Lamont himself, then a director of the company, who at the time of the flotation of Morgan loans for Mussolini wrote that when the Duce came into power "Italy seemed to be tottering on the brink below which lay Communism and Bolshevism. . . ."

Simultaneously, of course, Mussolini began to make good at home the foreign-made myth about his role as a bulwark against Bolshevism, spurred on by another deal he was negotiating with an American concern for an oil monopoly. He spoke in parliament on "The Crimes of the Reds," whereupon the Socialist leader Matteotti came before parliament with a speech in which he showed Mussolini to be both a hypocrite and liar. He said:

I have investigated all these cases, I have not consulted a single Socialist because we are such notorious liars and because we are beyond the law, but I have taken testimony from the newspaper of the Honorable Mussolini and neutral sources. What have I found? The victims almost always belong to the same class which the Honorable Mussolini accuses of furnishing the aggressors.

Take the conflict at Castelfranco. The two wounded in the battle the Honorable Mussolini described as due to the "reds" are Marriotti and Serri. I find their names in the premier's own paper, and Marriotti and Serri are Socialists, and the men who shot them, according to Mussolini's paper, are *carabiniari*.

At the battle during the strike at Decima di Persiceto; five dead, many wounded, listed as "Red aggression" by the premier. In his newspaper I find: "A sergeant of police upset a table upon which a Socialist orator was speaking. Rioting. The sergeant fired into the crowd. All the dead and wounded are among the strikers." Well, if this is red aggression, it is red aggression against reds, and this same Mussolini wrote an editorial saying: "The sergeant should not have tried to stop the orators."

Matteotti went through the entire list of cases. There were no Socialists, Anarchists, Bolshevists or other Left elements to blame for the violence and murder: it was all the work of the Fascists. Matteotti also announced three further speeches in which he would prove that the elections of 1924 were stolen, and that the Fascist hierarchy was involved in a tremendous piece of corruption in the oil monopoly negotiations. Mussolini gave orders to do away with Matteotti, and he was murdered by Mussolini's own bodyguard and closest associates.[1]

---

1 Cf. George Seldes, *Sawdust Caesar* (Harper & Bros., 1935), Chapter 14.

Eastern Europe

On June 28, 1919, Lieutenant-Colonel Warwick Green, chief of the American Mission to the Baltic Provinces, informed the American Peace Mission in Paris (as the State Department archives reveal) that "the Baltic provinces and Lithuania have an importance out of all proportion to their size and population, due to their geographical position which makes them the western and at present the most important key to the Russian problem."

The American chargé d'affaires in Denmark cabled the State Department: "In interview with naval attaché yesterday morning, General Mannerheim stated that his army is willing to and capable of defeating the Bolsheviki in Northern Russia. They need neither men nor ammunition but merely moral support of the Allies. Mannerheim stated that he was willing to commence hostilities immediately if encouraged to do so by the Allies and assured that the United States would hasten sending food supplies to Finland."

Frank L. Polk, acting Secretary of State, informed Secretary of War Baker that the American Peace Mission had approved "the sale of rifles to Finland, and to those parts of Esthonia and Latvia which are non-Bolshevik." Herbert Hoover made a contact with the so-called Provisional Government of Russia (i.e., the Tsarists) whereby the monarchist Northwestern Army would receive enormous supplies of foodstuffs.

And President Wilson, on October 22, endorsed plans for economic relief . . . the most effective means of limiting the bread of Bolshevism and of protecting, thereby, the Government of the United States from the dangers of subversive propaganda." The American Red Cross promised to feed the people of Petrograd—provided the Whites captured the capital. On September 9, by order of Mr. Polk and with the approval of Wilson, 45,000 tons of supplies were transhipped from British and French ports to General Yudenich.

European Panorama

The United States thus joined with all the reactionary forces in the world in an attempt to upset the Soviets before they were actually on their feet. To justify this war, the foreign offices and state departments as well as the newspapers engaged in the greatest campaign of redbaiting in history. It was at this time that the myth of the "nationalization of women" in Russia, the forged documents purporting to show Lenin and Trotsky as German agents, and a million other false stories were disseminated for the purpose of misleading the common people of the whole civilized world. They succeeded.

One of the great injustices of Versailles was the decision to take territory from Hungary in addition to that already seized by the victors, and award it to Romania. Count Karolyi, the head of the Hungarian government and a true democrat, had tried to ride down the middle of the road, but now that was impossible; no government could survive having agreed to such treatment. He resigned.

When Bolshevism came into Budapest the newspaper men were there; they could see it and report it. They reported that the revolution of Kun Bela was bloodless, but that one of its first "crimes" was to seize the homes of the super-wealthy and convert them into homes for children, and that another was to abolish tips in restaurants and barber shops.

Said Bela Kun: "The continued refusal to send food and raw materials by the Entente Powers after the Armistice was signed has done more to cause the ruin and bankruptcy of the capitalist system of Hungary than the war itself."

Within a few weeks the Allies, acting under orders from the renegade Socialist, Clemenceau, sent Hungary an ultimatum: it demanded that "the people" destroy their "tyrant," Bela Kun, immediately; otherwise they would be starved to death by the World War Victors. On the very day the ultimatum was sent out, a press campaign of redbaiting was begun in the Paris newspapers, and it spread throughout the world. The red terror was invented in France weeks before anything occurred in Budapest which could warrant even a rumor of such events.

Eventually the Kun regime did defend itself, and there was shooting, death, and capital punishment; though, all told, the extent of the violence was not much worse than that of the race riots in Chicago—which happened at about the same time—with its "looting, arson and murder, fourteen dead the first day, and a total of thirty-three dead, a thousand wounded, in three days of terrorism."

The food blockade finally defeated communism in Hungary. Herbert Hoover's aide in Budapest, Captain Gregory, claims the credit for the Hoover policy and practice. General Bandholtz, who had "taken" the capital by buying up all its gold and precious stones with inflation money, telegraphed to Washington that "the reign of terror which began in March is ended." Three days later the Rumanian Army, which the Allies permitted to replace Kun, entered the city and pillaged it.

On the morning of the day on which he was to be named national governor, to have his dictatorship legally accepted, Admiral Horthy of Hungary received me at his palace in Buda and said: "So long as I am alive, Bolshevism will never raise its head in my country. At its first sign of life, I will suffocate it in blood. I will not tolerate another red terror and my armies are ready to fight.

"The time will come when the Entente leaders will go down on their knees and plead with me to save Europe from Bolshevism."

Admiral Horthy restored "law and order." That meant a "white terror" in which were murdered many times the number of men and women whose deaths were charged to the "red terror." Thousands of Jews were killed because Catholic Hungary was intensely anti-Semitic and because Bela Kun was a Jew. Horthy's officers indulged in sadistic orgies of torture as well as killings. Horthy re-established feudalism. Money was safe. The nobility and the landowners were well repaid for their campaign against the reds.

When a bomb exploded in the Cathedral of Svetl Kral in Sofia, Bulgaria, during the funeral of General Georghieff, who had been assassinated in April 1925, the world was told that the two hundred dead were the victims of the reds. Thousands of radicals, liberals, and labor leaders were imprisoned as "Moscow agents." But later a man about to commit suicide in a Luxembourg prison confessed to having planted the bomb, and he was neither a Communist nor a liberal. He simply hated religion.

CHAPTER 3
A Short History of American Redbaiting

Thomas Jefferson, whom President Roosevelt denounced as a radical as recently as the Jackson Day Dinner of 1940, was not only the founder of our democracy but was so strongly under the influence of the French Revolution that his enemies called him an agent for a foreign government, the spreader of an alien "ism." Tom Paine actually was a foreign radical agitator, although he was not deported by the F.B.I. of his time. And the historian will tell you that from 1806 to 1843 strikes were considered criminal conspiracies—a situation we have not entirely outgrown when one considers the present use of the Sherman and Clayton Acts, originally passed to curb monopolistic trusts, against labor unions. On August 2, 1828, the military was first used to smash labor, and at about this time there was a general attack against the Freemasons.

In the early nineteenth century another minority accused of alienism was made a scapegoat: for twenty years the Roman Catholics were not only baited in the press but attacked in riots (a curious fact for Father Coughlin and Christian Fronters to ponder). In 1830 the Know Nothings controlled five states, just as almost a hundred years later the Ku Kluxers controlled five states, and in both instances the Catholics, the Irish, the aliens, were the victims of an intolerant movement.

In 1886 German-Americans in Chicago striving for an eight-hour day were the victims of police brutality equaled only by the police brutality in Chicago in 1937. The Haymarket bomber was never found; the men executed and imprisoned for the bombing were labor leaders, "foreign agitators" preaching a "foreign doctrine" (that is, shorter working hours, more pay, better living standards, and human dignity). Six years later the Governor of Illinois declared the Chicago anarchists innocent. History regards them as martyrs who helped make the eight-hour day possible.

In 1916, Mooney and Billings, two labor leaders, were charged with planting a bomb in a preparedness parade in San Francisco. Accused of being reds and therefore capable of any kind of murder, these two men were convicted on the perjured testimony of men who later, but in vain, confessed their perjury. President Wilson saved their lives in 1918 but could not free them. The judge who sentenced Mooney said later it was a "dirty job," and nine of the ten surviving members of the jury publicly regretted their verdict. In 1931 the Wickersham report was to clinch the matter by denouncing the judicial process in California as "shocking to one's sense of justice."

Why had Mooney and Billings been arrested, found guilty, kept in jail, when the intelligent world knew they were innocent? The answer, as given by a reporter who had covered the trial in his youth and who sixteen years later wrote up the whole story in *What Happened in the Mooney Case,* was that in 1916 there was a wave of red hysteria in San Francisco—red hysteria and red-white-and-blue hysteria—because the country was being drummed into a war. Ernest Jerome Hopkins of the San Francisco *Bulletin* wrote: "Sixteen years of printed poison have convinced Californians that, evidence or none, it is better to keep two radicals in prison than remove a nation-wide stimulus to radicalism." That was Hopkins's conclusion. And it was fear of the press of California that prevented governor after governor—and eventually Franklin Roosevelt, who was expected to do it—from pardoning two innocent men. The Mooney-Billings case remains one of America's most alarming instances of the accomplishments of redbaiting.

Similar was the case of the Industrial Workers of the

World who had defended themselves in Centralia, Washington, and had been shot, murdered, and lynched by a mob led by American Legionnaires. The National Catholic Welfare Council and the Federal Council of Churches issued a report which showed that the I. W. W.'s had not conspired, that they had not fired on the Legion paraders, that the paraders had attacked them, and that therefore the sentence of the court had been "very severe." But redbaiting by the "best citizens" prevailed.

In 1917, when we went to war, an espionage act was passed by which the American people were denied all their usual liberties, despite the Civil War decision of the Supreme Court (*ex parte Milligan*) that the Constitution holds good in war as in peace, that nothing may be changed to curtail or diminish, weaken or abolish, a comma of the Bill of Rights.

In March of that same year there was a revolt against the Tsar, and in November the Bolshevik Party of Russia seized power, and for the first time in history an attempt was made—in an agrarian and illiterate country—to put into practice the theories of Karl Marx and Friedrich Engels, the theory of socialism. This philosophy marched under a red banner, and from that day on, redbaiting became a world activity.

So long as the war lasted, the hysterical enthusiasm lasted and only a tiny minority had to be sent to prison for being immune to it. But when the soldiers came home and the great disillusionment began, when times grew hard because of the war that had been won, when jobs grew scarcer, wages lower, and the cost of living higher—then the real redbaiting campaigns began, aided in spirit and action by the national government.

The name-calling grew fiercer. For example, when Senator Bob La Follette told Congress that the American troops should be withdrawn from Archangel (generals had done the same, leading reactionary statesmen in Europe had realized the expediency of such an action), his opponents saw a God-given opportunity to harm him. He was denounced everywhere as "the Bolshevik spokesman in America." And again, when the workmen on the Stone & Webster lines struck for a decent living wage, Mayor Ole Hanson of Seattle denounced them as Bolsheviki, crushed them, and became nationally notorious. In every strike of the era the first thing done was to bring out the red label. Sometimes it won the strike for the employers by itself; always it was the fulcrum on which the police, the press, and the men of big business worked their powerful levers. In Butte, Montana, veterans who had formed the Sailors and Soldiers Association, one of the several non-reactionary organizations antedating the American Legion, were met by the 44th Infantry, with Major A. M. Jones calling them I. W. W.'s and Bolsheviki and threatening them with machine-gun fire.

In the great hysteria of 1919 the superpatriots shouted that there were a million foreign reds in America—or at least 600,000—and one of the many anti-alien deportation waves spread through the country. The government promised to take action. It did. It found that instead of a million, or even 600,000, deportable alien reds there were only some 30,000 who answered a redbaiter's description of "undesirable," and of these only a handful were subject to deportation. The "Soviet Ark," the S.S. *Buford*, finally sailed on December 21, 1919, carrying a total of 246 men and three women, among them Emma Goldman, and Alexander Berkman, anarchist leaders.

All the liberal-intellectual publications were smeared as radical. Such magazines as the *World Tomorrow*, the *Nation*, the *Dial*, the *New Republic*, the *Liberator*, and the newspaper *The Call* were attacked, and one of the leading patriotic crusaders deplored the fact that intellectual leaders, "the different editors connected with these various publications, Norman Thomas, John Haynes Holmes, Oswald Garrison Villard, Henry Raymond Mussey, Lincoln Colcord, Martin Johnson, Herbert Croly, Walter Weyl,

A Short History of American Redbaiting

Walter Lippmann, Signe Toksvig, and H. W. L. Dana," were Americans and therefore could not be deported to Soviet Russia.

In March 1919 the New York legislature appointed the notorious Lusk Committee to investigate "subversiye" activities. The committee collected many volumes of testimony, most of which has been thoroughly discredited by the leading jurists of our time but which still serves succeeding generations of redbaiters. The Federal Government under Attorney-General A. Mitchell Palmer indulged in illegal raids and mass arrests, deporting many foreign-born residents and violating with impunity the constitutional rights of citizens.

In April 1919 a score of bombs were found in the mails addressed to leading men of the country, including the "Fighting Quaker," Mr. Palmer, and when this plot failed, a man threw a bomb. It blew the porch off Mr. Palrner's house and killed the thower. Curiously enough a radical publication, *Plain Words*, was found near the dead man. This "radical" publication was one of the many frauds in which the government engaged at the time; it was actually published by the government, through a certain Andrea Salsedo, who was later to figure in a mysterious way in the Sacco-Vanzetti case.

This was the year of great strikes, as well as of the first great American red scare. On the west coast the shipyard workers and the seamen went out. In Lawrence, Massachusetts, scene of a bloody labor battle in 1912, and in Paterson, New Jersey, scene of endless struggles of the silk-workers, there were textile strikes. Four hundred thousand coal miners (in John L. Lewis's union) asked for more wages, shorter hours.

Early American redbaiting ran the gamut from humor to tragedy. The actors went on strike in New York and Marie Dressler organized the chorus girls. The press then called Equity a "soviet" and Broadway laughed. But it was a different story in Pittsburgh, where the great steel strike—a really important event in American labor history—for an eight-hour day and a few cents more an hour was smashed when the owners, who had made billions in the war, succeeded in smearing the labor leaders as "un-American" and "red."[1]

President Wilson himself used his high office to attack labor. He characterized the coal strike, called for October 1919, as "a fundamental attack, which is wrong both morally and legally, upon the rights of society and upon the welfare of the country." These are the familiar words of exploiters of labor, but when a President uses them, they can be a powerful weapon. Palmer translated them into action under the claim that the Lever Act, passed in wartime to prevent the breakdown of the supply of food and resources to the government, was still in force; and he succeeded in having Federal Judge A. B. Anderson in Indianapolis issue an injunction against the coal miners, forbidding them to strike.

Since this was a violation of the coal miners' rights, there was an outcry of protest, whereupon the Department of Justice, instead of presenting a bill of particulars, raised a red scare. The press immediately leaped to the aid of the Justice Department with headlines like:

> REDS PLANNING TO OVERTHROW AMERICAN GOVERNMENT

The evidence proved to be a circular which apparently had not circulated and which was signed by "The Federation of Russian Workers," an organization which either did not exist or which had so few members that not one could be found. But that was only the beginning of the co-operation of government bureaus in fraudulent redbaiting.

In the West, American infantry drove striking miners back to work at the point of bayonets. Leading officers of

---

[1] Fully documented in the Interchurch World Movement report. Cf. *Freedom of the Press*, pages 374-5.

the United Mine Workers, notably President Lewis and Secretary William Green, were cited for contempt, arrested, and tried. In Pennsylvania the "Black Cossacks" rode down the assemblies of workers, shooting and clubbing. At Breckenridge they killed Fanny Sellins, an organizer for the U.M.W.

The hysteria became nation-wide. In New York City the Rand School was raided, and in one day no less than a thousand persons were arrested as aliens, foreign agents, reds, enemies of society. That furnished more scare-lines for the press. But when, within a few hours, 953 of these persons had been released because there was not even a suspicion of a real charge against them, there were only little paragraphs on inside pages to announce that fact. In Bogalusa, Louisiana, the forces of law, order, and mob hysteria massacred five union men in the saw-mill strike. "Criminal syndicalism" laws were passed in many states.

So hysterical was the public mind that the arrest of three Poles who were caught "red-handed" reprinting the 1848 manifesto of Karl Marx became "Alien Reds Plot Overthrow of American Government" in the day's headlines. And there were even stranger happenings.

As the Anti-Saloon League rode from triumph to triumph in the several states of the nation, the liquor interests, rather belatedly, realized their danger and united their ranks. The Drys, they heard, had been spending $2,000,000 a year, and were raising the fund to $5,000,000 for 1919 with the slogan, "America bone dry by 1920." The saloon and liquor men pledged a billion dollars, but this sum never materialized; what did materialize was an alarming series of newspaper advertisements which had a triple purpose: (1) to buy the support of the press; (2) to attract readers to their cause; and incidentally to take a crack at the ubiquitous reds! Booze was linked with personal freedom, with rugged individualism, with the American Dream—and prohibition with the antitheses of these, including Bolshevism. "Will Bolshevism come with

National Prohibition?" read one flaming headline in a paid advertisement, and the answer was that it would. To save America from red socialism all that was necessary was to support good old "red-eye"; a vote for John Barleycorn was a vote against Karl Marx.

On January 2, 1920, G-men began raiding the clubs as well as political headquarters of radicals, liberals, and trade unionists; they hacked, burned, tore, and destroyed property and maltreated men and women. If ever an organization merited the terms *Cheka* and *Gestapo* as scornfully used by people who believe "it can't happen here," it was the Federal Bureau of Investigation of 1920. Altogether it arrested 10,000 persons.

One explanation of the brutal and lawless actions of the enforcers of the law was the onward march of labor following the World War. It is true that in certain industries wages were high in wartime; but it is also true that the cost of living was high. In 1919 the cost of living continued rising, but wages came down, and 4,160,348 union and non-union men protested their lot in strikes in that year. The most important, and most threatening, event of 1919 was the great steel strike led by William Z. Foster, of the American Federation of Labor.

When the five duly elected Socialist members of the New York State Legislature were thrown out of their seats —because Socialist meant red, and red meant Bolshevik, and Bolshevism, the American people had been told by their press, meant everything that was un-American— Bernard Shaw cabled: "It is time for the *Mayflower* to put to sea again. My old label, 'A Nation of Villagers,' still holds. When is the Bartholdi statue to be pulled down?" The press thought Shaw was clowning as usual; and, besides, no damned foreigner had a right to criticize the august New York legislature.

Every crime of violence involving a bomb is usually laid to a radical. Every assassination is laid to an anarchist, a socialist, or a communist the moment after it happens, the

A Short History of American Redbaiting 41

press of the world forgetting all about the rules of evidence in the breathless moment. The report has spread until it is generally believed throughout America that foreigners commit more than their proportional quota of crime, whereas just the opposite has been proven by the Wickersham investigation.

For May Day, 1920—traditional labor day of workingmen the world over—A. Mitchell Palmer, attorney-general of the United States, promised a fine, first-class red revolution, during which the American Bolsheviki would attempt to "plant the red flag on the Capitol in Washington," after incidentally murdering all prominent gentlemen holding high office or large bond portfolios.

Inevitably, May Day came to Washington as it did to London, Paris, and Berlin, and not a shot was fired in all four capitals, nor was a drop of red blood, or blue blood, shed anywhere; and for the first time in the years of Mr. Palmer's hysterical redbaiting he was greeted with laughter and a little derision.

On September 16, 1920, a bomb was thrown in Wall Street, and to this day reds are accused of the deed despite the lack of an iota of evidence.

In the first ten years after this bombing there were many arrests, twenty-eight publicly announced; many persons were tortured to make a confession; and a dozen announcements were made by the police and the Burns detective agency that they had proof that "the Reds plotted the crime and sent a man with a horse and wagon and much dynamite into the street opposite the offices of J. Pierpont Morgan"—where the dynamite exploded and killed both man and horse. The police refused to open their ears to the explanation that the crime was that of an individual, a maniac, or a terrorist; they insisted that reds were behind it. In 1922 when one, Wolfe Lindenfeld, confessed" in Warsaw that he and Moscow were responsible for the crime, the press and police indulged in a three-day orgy of redbaiting. Later, the United States Government deported

Mr. Lindenfeld as a fraud—he had invented the story as a means of getting free transportation to America—but the press did not give the public three-day headlines repairing the damage it had done.

1920 was a depression year, a red-scare year. It was also the year of the great exposure of the fraud of the 1919 World series baseball games. It had been a secret; Comiskey of the White Sox had kept quiet; but when the indictments came, Eddie Cicotte, the star pitcher, confessed that "eight or ten of us got together before the game . . . talked about throwing the series . . . decided we could get away with it. I was thinking of my wife and kids and how I needed the money. I told them to have the cash ready . . . ten thousand dollars. . . . All the runs scored off me were due to my own deliberate errors. . . ."

The scandal was too horrible for the mind to encompass. And so the press said that what the incident showed was that "the Bolshevik virus had entered the national sport."

Alfred Noyes immediately came to the front page with the statement that the Bolshevik virus had also entered the minds of the intellectuals, even poets. The new free-verse poetry was Bolshevism. (In London, the American sculptor Epstein was called "an artist Lenin, bolshevizing art" in a popular paper, because of his modern, unconventional style.)

Mr. Calvin Coolidge was shocked to find radicalism in the women's colleges. He wrote for *Delineator*, at a great price per word, the story of how a Miss Smith of Vassar, attending the trial of the Soviet representative Martens in Washington, had said out loud that Mr. Martens had more intelligence than the committeemen trying him. In Radcliffe, Mr. Coolidge discovered there was a Socialist Club. And he had also been informed that a lecturer in a college had had as his topic "The United States of the World." What was the world coming to!

When, in 1923, Charles Lindbergh, father of the "Lone

Eagle," ran for the governorship of Minnesota on the Farmer-Labor ticket, he was attacked by the press as a "red-hot radical," a "Bolshevik," a "dangerous red." Had he not opposed our entry into the war, and, worse, had he not publicly said: "l am an enemy of Wall Street," urging Congress to investigate the "Money Trust"?

Three sample headlines from the American press of 1925 were:

> CHINESE UPRISINGS ATTRIBUTED TO RUSSIAN COMMUNISTS
>
> RED SPIES BETRAY FRENCH TROOPS IN THE RIFF
>
> SOVIET AGITATORS FOMENTING REBELLION IN AFGHANISTAN

Governor Al Smith named Colonel Haskell major-general in command of the National Guard of New York. The colonel, as Hoover's agent, had saved ten million people from starvation in Russia, had spoken to Lenin several times, and had hinted that the Russian leader was a great man. He had also said in 1922 that the Russian regime would not fall in six months, thus flying in the face of the world press. And so in 1925 the American Defense Society, one of the professional patriotic groups, demanded that the governor cancel the appointment because "it has been alleged that Colonel Haskell's sympathies are for Soviet Russia."

In 1919 this same outfit of self-styled patriots had announced a red revolution for June: the opening of jails, the seizure of government by "an autocratic minority of anarchists." The organization had objected to the restoration of German opera after the war and favored the recognition of the terrorist Kolchak in Russia. It had also decided on how much indemnity Germany was to pay and generally tried to dictate patriotism to the American people from 1919 to 1925.

In 1925, however, good times were at hand. The red hysteria was waning; so it was no wonder that, in coming to the support of Colonel Haskell, the New York *World* called the attack upon him "foolish words from the American Dementia society, which has the brains of an ostrich, the courage of a rabbit, and the manners of a polerat."

As the world advanced towards the catastrophe of 1929, times looked so good that there was no necessity for redbaiting, and a liberal glow settled over America. Free speech, free press, free assembly, were little interfered with by the chambers of commerce, the Legion and other military associations, and the professional or dollar patriots. When Eugene Debs died in 1926 this Socialist, labor leader, pacifist, radical, and spreader of "alien doctrine" was called by the press "distinctly American, of the frontier or colonial type, alas now vanishing"; to save themselves from criticism, the same newspapers said editorially that Debs really was not a Communist, but a pure Yankee non-conformist of the Washington and Franklin type, and more like his own hero, John Brown. (In 1921 the New Jersey convention of the American Legion had held a "Keep Debs in Prison" demonstration, and the New York *Times* had said editorially when President Harding commuted Debs's prison sentence: "Certainly the majority will not approve; a shallow howling, whining minority had its way.")

In 1926 the Illinois commander of the American Legion, accused "this person, Jane Addams" of working to abolish all military training and of turning Hull House into "a hotbed of Bolshevism."

In the great boom days of 1927 in America, news came that there were riots and demonstrations throughout the civilized world because a poor fish-peddler and a shoemaker had been electrocuted on August 23 in the death house at Charlestown, Massachusetts. The men were radicals, and that, apparently, was enough to justify their death, at least in the mind of men like Judge Webster Thayer, who, during the time he was sitting as judge in this

A Short History of American Redbaiting

famous Sacco-Vanzetti case, referred to the accused men as "anarchist bastards" in conversation at his club.

In 1929 the stock market crashed and, though very few knew it then, a world collapsed with it. As, in the early thirties, the extent of the disaster, politically, economically, socially, and morally, became known, and as this led to a search for a better social-economic system, the endangered rulers of society began to exert themselves in every way to hold on. In this effort there was unloosed throughout the world the second great red hysteria, which is so virulent now, in the first days of the 1940's.

CHAPTER 4
A Decade of Witch Hunts

Our own decade, the fourth of this century, has been one of unbroken depression. The cycles of panic and breakdown seem to be getting more frequent while the periods of hard times seem to be lasting longer. I leave it to the economists to explain. But what is evident, and relevant to the subject of this book, is the coincidence of hard times with tremendous assaults on civil liberties—and the use of the powerful weapon, redbaiting, to shout down the appeals of the unemployed, the hungry, the dispossessed.

By May Day, 1930, there were fear and apprehension throughout the world. It was "Red Labor Day." The police of all nations where such celebrations were still permitted predicted revolutionary uprisings and cleaned their guns; but there were only marches and speeches: not a shot was fired, not a bomb thrown.

But later, in Budapest, food riots broke out and hungry people smashed the doors of bakeries and restaurants shouting "Long live Kun Bela," reviving the name of the "red tyrant" of 1919. The Horthy police killed two, wounded two hundred, and silence again descended upon feudal Hungary.

In American cities, with winter approaching, there were demonstrations (immediately called red) of the unemployed, and sometimes riots in which hungry men were killed and wounded. Instead of providing work, the politicians pinned the communist label on the jobless.

Professor and Mrs. Einstein landed in New York on December 11, 1930. "Politically," said Mrs. Einstein, "we are Socialists." "The ideals which have always shone before me and filled me with the joy of living," Einstein wrote as his credo, "are goodness, beauty, and truth." But being the combination of Jew, Socialist, and pacifist made one of the greatest scientists of the modern world the subject of redbaiting. In the American consulate in Berlin, Professor Einstein had been asked such ridiculous questions about his trip to America that he was forced to say to the vice-consul: "Are you doing this on supreme authority or for your own amusement?" But the so-called diplomat continued to hammer away with questions about socialism, anarchism, communism, and pacifism. When Einstein prepared to go to Princeton, the Woman Patriot Corporation protested and called him a Communist. When he was invited to make a visit to California, the organizer of the Los Angeles branch of the American Legion, Dr. A. D. Houghton, called on the ex-soldiers to prevent the scientist's visit.

In 1932 Georg Grosz, one of the great among German artists, was engaged to teach at the Art Students League of New York only to arouse a storm of protest: Jonas Lie, American academician, thought Grosz was not "healthy," and others whispered "Communist."

Congressman Hamilton Fish investigated communism in America and reported that there were 12,000 dues-paying members of the party in 1930, that it had 82,000 votes and half a million sympathizers. Congressman Nelson said that "the best defense against the red shirt of the Communist and the black shirt of the Fascist is the blue shirt of the American workingman"—but millions of workmen had no money for blue shirts, or shirts of any color. Congressman Jerry O'Connell declared that the best way to fight Communist propaganda was "to put something in the soup besides statistics," but the two chickens Hoover promised for every pot had not materialized. Mrs. Hearst opened a soup kitchen amidst great publicity in Times Square.

The Pope in 1931 made two declarations against the reds. "'Religious Socialism,' 'Christian Socialism,' are expressions implying a contradiction in terms," he said, denying what every Christian Socialist in America takes as a fundamental of the teachings of Jesus Christ. "No one can be at the same time a sincere Catholic and a true Socialist." And again, in an encyclical:

> One section of Socialism has degenerated into Communism. Communism teaches and pursues a twofold aim: merciless class warfare and complete abolition of private ownership. . . . We do not think it necessary to warn upright and faithful children of the Church against the impious and nefarious character of Communism.
>
> Whether Socialism be considered as a doctrine, or as a historical fact, or as a movement, if it really remain Socialism it cannot be brought into harmony with the dogmas of the Catholic Church.

A whispering campaign against the banks in March 1932 was denounced as a dirty job of the reds. The newspapers and magazines took up the subject, explaining to their readers how delicate was the matter of confidence in financial institutions and how villainous were those who questioned what went on in the solid temples of gold. When, however, in February 1933 an epidemic of bank holidays swept the United States, it was proved that the whisperers—red or not—had been right. It was the banks who were "in the red," and on March 6 the President of the United States had to close them all.

But the great event of 1933 was the burning of the German Reichstag in February and the first remark that Adolf Hitler made when he was told about it. *"Dar ist das Werk der Kommunisten,"* said Hitler.

But it was not the work of the Communists. The Nazis did produce a moron named Van der Lubbe, whom they tried and executed, but he had been expelled from the Communist Party years earlier. The Nazis accused Georgi Dimitroff, a Bulgarian Communist, of being one of the plotters, but Dimitroff made a fool of Goering and the others at the Leipzig hearings, and even the Nazi legal machinery, frankly announcing itself as serving the ends of the party rather than justice, was unable to convict him or to find new victims. Meanwhile the evidence mounted that the inflammable materials found in the Reichstag had been carried there over a period of weeks by several persons who entered the meeting place of the old parliament through the residence of none other than Herr Goering. The whole affair was a fraud and both the fire and the fraud were the work of the Hitler party.[1] Blame on the reds was, of course, the declaration of the war of extermination against all opposition parties—red, pink, and even royal purple—which far out-numbered the Nazis.

Within a year of taking office President Franklin Delano Roosevelt had succeeded in producing a program which aroused unthinking emotion in friends and enemies alike. The stock market went down, big business men began talking about the menace of red revolution, and several even went so far as to talk about the benefits of assassination. "Roosevelt is a red." "Roosevelt is following the Communist Party line." That was the sort of talk heard in Wall Street and in the citadels of the *status quo.*

A great strike wave began. Strikes were the natural answer of millions of workers who had been told the government would maintain their inalienable rights, provide minimum-wage and maximum-hour regulations, better working conditions, a nobler life—and who were unmistakably informed by their employers that they had no such rights. Thus was introduced a new era of anti-labor violence and espionage, renewed redbaiting and heresy hunting, pressure by so-called patriotic organizations for bigger and better repressive legislation and gag laws.

The press, as the slightest study of American labor history will show, has always been on the side of the

---

[1] See *The Storm Breaks* by the New York *Times* correspondent, Frederick T. Birchall (Viking, 1940), Chapter III.

employers, but not until 1934 did publishers deliberately unite to strangle the labor movement. Instead of remaining as usual in the background, "agitating" public opinion through editorials, flaming headlines, and distorted news, a group of editors and publishers, inspired by William Randolph Hearst, actually met and planned an attack on the general strike in San Francisco.

The strike had been peaceful, and the press should have known better when it said that the city's infants had been deprived of milk and the city's doctors of gasoline. The strike had had the sympathy of the public—until the owners of the press conspired to break it by fair means or foul. The foul means consisted almost entirely in spreading the magnificent lie that reds, Communists, and foreign agitators were the instigators, leaders, and potential beneficiaries of the strike.

The falsehoods were spread so thoroughly that General Hugh Johnson, arriving in San Francisco to mediate, said (or was quoted in the press as saying) that "when the means of food supply—milk for children—necessities of life to the whole people are threatened, that is bloody revolution." The San Francisco *Chronicle* said: "The radicals have seized control by intimidation. . . . What they want is revolution." The Los Angeles *Times* said: "What is actually in progress there is an insurrection, a communist-inspired and led revolt." The Sacramento *Bee* said the strikers sought to overthrow the United States government. The Oakland *Examiner* accused "the small group of communists" of trying to extend their power over the maritime unions, and then over California. The Portland *Times* said the strikers were refusing to give the public the necessities of life, and blamed "rampant radicalism."

It was one of the best-organized campaigns of universal redbaiting ever witnessed in America. Although it was founded largely on falsehood, it resulted in mass hysteria. The press of the rest of the country naturally reprinted the news and the editorial views of the Pacific coast newspapers. This flood drowned out the few sane voices (as, for instance, Evelyn Seeley's in the *New Republic*, accusing San Francisco publishers of "deliberate journalistic malpractice"; and Will Rogers's, remarking that all was quiet in California and "I hope we never live to see the day when a thing is as bad as some of our newspapers make it").

The New York *Times* was proud to say that public opinion broke the strike. A vigilante reign of terror followed in which hundreds of innocent persons accused of being reds were jailed and beaten, and private homes, offices, and labor union headquarters robbed and destroyed by ax and fire. Violence in the strike, which began with the police killing two innocent men, ended with a newspaper-inflamed mob running wild in the streets.

Some time later it became known that behind the scenes the co-operators in the red scare had been: John Francis Neylan, general counsel for Hearst, acting on his orders; Clarence Lindner of the *Examiner;* George Cameron of the *Chronicle;* Robert Holliday of the *Call-Bulleti*n; Joseph Knowland of the Oakland *Tribune,* and Richard Carrington of the Oakland *Post-Inquirer.* Hearst had telephoned from London telling the editors how the British government had beaten the general strike of 1926, and urging them to wave the red flag in order to divide labor into two camps, conservative and radical, and to attack the radicals; and, most important of all, to enlist public opinion on the side of business by insisting that the strike was a red revolution.

A congressional committee, chaired by John W. McCormack, for the purpose of investigating Nazi and other propaganda, issued a report confirming an alleged conspiracy of Wall Street men and agents to establish a fascist dictatorship in Washington under the guise of saving the country from Bolshevism. The report stated:

> In the last few weeks of the committee's official life it received evidence showing that certain persons had

A Decade of Witch Hunts

made an attempt to establish a fascist organization in this country. . . .

There is no question but that these attempts were discussed, were planned, and might have been placed in execution when and if the financial backers deemed it expedient.

This committee received evidence from Major General Smedley D. Butler (retired), twice decorated by the Congress of the United States. He testified before the committee as to conversations with one Gerald C. MacGuire [employed by Grayson M.-P. Murphy, director of the New York Trust Co.] in which the latter is alleged to have suggested the formation of a fascist army under the leadership of General Butler. . . . Your committee was able to verify all the pertinent statements. . . . [One] was corroborated in the correspondence of MacGuire with his principal, Robert Sterling Clark. . . .

Two most important facts relating to the foregoing conclusions must be noted: first, that the news weekly *Time*, the New York *Times*, and the press of the country generally (with the exception of the Philadelphia *Record* and the New York *Post*) tried to destroy the sensational story as "fantastic" when General Butler first exposed the Wall Streeters; and, second, that the congressional committee itself suppressed testimony involving important persons and organizations, refused to call outstanding bankers for questioning—notably Grayson M.-P. Murphy, one of the men who originated and financed the American Legion and later became head of a Morgan house in Wall Street.

So angry was General Butler over the congressional committee's suppression of the facts that he repeated his testimony over the radio:

> MacGuire showed me a check for thousands of dollars, made out by Grayson Murphy to MacGuire. These thousands of dollars were to promote this super-army. . . . A man named Clark told me he had

$30,000,000 . . . he was ready, if necessary, to spend half of that thirty million to save the other half. . . . This was no piker set-up. . . . MacGuire, who was the agent of Wall Street bankers and brokers who proposed this organization, told me that $3,000,000 was "on the line" and that $300,000,000 . . . was in view. . . .

Paul Comley French, the newspaperman who broke the story, testified that MacGuire stated: "We need a fascist government in this country to save the nation from the communists who want to tear it down and wreck all that we have built in America." MacGuire had sent reports to another of his superiors, Robert Sterling Clark, the multimillionaire who was willing to spend half his fortune for fascism to save the other half from the reds, describing the excellence of the fascists in Europe and how dangerous the reds were in France, Austria, and elsewhere. Thanks to General Butler's giving the story to the two liberal papers, which in turn forced the congressional committee to take testimony, the plot was destroyed before it became a serious menace to the American system of government. It did one thing. It showed clearly the fascist pattern here as elsewhere: big business and big money getting together to spend millions backing a Hitler or a Mussolini—or an American general, if he would take the job—to seize power, overthrow a government, and safeguard wealth at the expense of the population. And as always in the fascist pattern the red scare, the threat of bolshevism, was to be used as the banner under which greed and corruption and violence could join and fight.

These elements made of 1935 (as they were later to make of 1940) a year of red scares and witch hunts. Hearst, owner of gold mines and vast farming enterprises as well as newspapers, reached the apogee of redbaiting (and the nadir of journalism) at the same time. Scores of repressive bills were introduced into the House and Senate; seven sedition acts were pending, and among the military bills one, H.R. 4845, went far beyond the 1917 wartime espionage act in depriving the American people of their civil liberties and the numerous enjoyments of freedom listed in the Bill of Rights. Hearst, the American Legion, the chambers of commerce, and all those who stood to profit by repression, backed all this proposed legislation.

Of the red scare of 1935 Roger Baldwin, head of the American Civil Liberties Union, wrote:

> Hunting reds is so ancient a pastime of patriots and scoundrels hiding their own misdeeds that a new drive just seems familiar repetition. But the new pack of hounds on the trail is more blood-thirsty, and the hunt more promising than in years. I have been through them all, since the first big drive just after the war and the Russian Revolution. I have not, in all that time, witnessed so powerful an alliance as today is in full cry for the complete annihilation by federal and state law of the Communist movement, and with it ultimately, the parties of the left and the militants of labor. . . .
>
> The New Deal aroused hope among the workers, farmers, and the sinking middle class. It promised the forgotten man his "rights" and a larger share in the national wealth. It has failed to deliver. Disillusionment is a dangerous reaction. The Huey Longs and the Father Coughlins capitalize it. But they can be brought into line, and anyhow, they cannot be suppressed.
>
> But the reds are fair game, and easy marks. . . . They threaten to be a source of opposition to capitalism from which wide-spread revolt may grow. The San Francisco general strike struck terror into the whole ruling class, slight as was the participation of the reds, and the response in raids, prosecutions, and general hysteria was unmatched in recent years. It was from that that the Hearst drive got its inspiration. It fanned into flames the sparks of Fascist vigilantism and of that "patriotism" organized in a score of commercial and military leagues which does the high-minded stuff for the business rulers. . . .
>
> They now come to the front with a program designed, they say, to outlaw only "those who advocate

the overthrow of the government by force and violence." Ignoring the Fascist advocacies of violence, they confine their attack largely to the left. The report of the United States Chamber of Commerce, by an anonymous special committee, and recently widely circulated, wholly ignores any "subversive activities" except by anti-capitalist parties. That Fascists can be "subversive" simply does not occur to them. Their concept is precisely in line with the traditional behavior of the authorities and of the big business crowd behind them. Crimes of violence by reactionaries against strikers or reds go without punishment, while the slightest suggestion of violence by strikers or reds is met with hysterical publicity and prosecution.

The Congressional Committee investigating un-American activities has just reported that the Fascist plot to seize the government, exposed by General Smedley Butler, was proved; yet not a single participant will be prosecuted under the perfectly plain language of the federal conspiracy act making this a high crime. Imagine the action if such a plot were discovered among Communists!

Which is, of course, only to emphasize the nature of our government as representative of the interests of the controllers of property. Violence, even to the seizure of the government, is excusable on the part of those whose lofty motive is to preserve the profit system. But on the part of those who would upset it in the interests of the producers and consumers of wealth, it is a crime.

If a chart could be made showing the rise and fall of red witch hunting activities, their intensity and their violence, it would undoubtedly prove to be an exact reversal of the stock-market or business barometer. Bad times have always brought persecution of the scapegoats. President Roosevelt arrived at a bad time, but from the day of his inauguration until the end of 1936 times grew better, and 1936 was quite a good year on the market. It is no wonder then that civil liberties also had a good year in 1936, and that for a while it seemed the red scare of 1934-35 would not be repeated for a long time. Hearst almost alone was screaming "agents of Moscow" as the labor and liberal movement marched forward.

On August 5 there occurred a very important event in American history—the expulsion of 1,000,000 members from the American Federation of Labor because of their affiliation with the Committee for Industrial Organization. The C.I.O. now began a march which in four years gave it parity in membership with the A.F. of L. From this time on, the professional redbaiters, all of them enemies of labor, could no longer contain themselves. It was now possible to attack militant union labor in the C.I.O. while hypocritically pretending that one was not opposed to "American" trade unionism, as exemplified in the A.F. of L.

The pink glow over the stock-market and over industry faded in 1937. It was the great year of the sit-down strikes, and the C.I.O. went from success to success in unionizing new industries, notably auto and steel. Governor Frank Murphy of Michigan refused to order troops to Flint to fight the Chevrolet No. 4 plant workingmen and enforce Judge Gadola's injunction ordering evacuation. Peace came with victory for labor. In Pittsburgh, 27,000 workers at Jones & Laughlin's chose the C.I.O. In New York, Mike Quill's transport workers carried the subways. In Chicago, however, the police murdered ten picketing C.I.O. strikers of the Republic Steel Corporation's plant. In Youngstown, Ohio, Governor Davey sent troops to break the steel strike in that district, but in Johnstown, Pennsylvania, Governor Earle stood on the side of labor.

Testifying in Washington on June 24, Tom M. Girdler, chairman of the board of Republic Steel, said he would never sign a contract with an "irresponsible, racketeering, violent, communist body like the C.I.O." unless forced to by law. The police had killed Girdler's employees. The police, and not the C.I.O., had initiated violence. The C.I.O. had no reputation for containing racketeers; it was the old and now respectable A.F. of L. that had some racketeering in certain trades. Nor was the C.I.O. communist and irresponsible, for its leading unions were among the oldest, biggest, and most disciplined. But Mr. Girdler's words were trumpeted in the press; and when a former radical writer named Stolberg wrote articles in the Scripps-Howard papers smearing the C.I.O., Mr. Girdler quoted him, and the press again quoted Mr. Girdler.

In its 1937 report, the Civil Liberties Union noted that the redbaiting campaign was again a prominent part of the general attack by the defenders of the *status quo* (and their brass-check spokesmen) against the forces of democracy; the usual red smear was being applied to everything progressive, the usual offenders being the Legion, the chambers of commerce, the Catholic hierarchy, the D.A.R., the K.K.K., the Nazis, and the like.

Everything progressive, the Union report noted, was attacked as communist or *communistic* (a more cautious word designed to keep its users from being sued for libel). The Civil Liberties Union itself, whose philosophy made it defend Nazis as well as Communists and which finally expelled Communists from its board, again became the victim of the witch hunt.

The only newcomers on the list of suppressive organizations and red-smearers was the Catholic hierarchy, which throughout the history of the United States had been a victim of majority prejudices, name-calling, and persecution. This group, which now took up the cry that the reds were following a "line" from Moscow and a foreign philosophy, went into action when a foreign ruler—namely, the Pope—announced his "line" in an official encyclical issued in a foreign tongue and in a foreign country.

"Next to the Legion," concluded the Union report, "our correspondents cite the anti-communist drive of the Catholic Church and its lay organizations as responsible for the atmosphere in which repression of civil rights thrives."

The stock-market charts, Dun and Bradstreet, the New

A Decade of Witch Hunts

York *Times,* and *Time's* business indexes agree that the economic trend was downward in 1939, and the students of social economics note that the line of hysteria, alien-baiting, redbaiting, police and F.B.I. witch hunting mounted very high. In 1939 war broke out between Germany and Poland; it was followed within three days by a declaration of war on the former by Great Britain and France; and on November 30, negotiations for a peaceful settlement having failed, Soviet troops moved into Finland. The American people, who just twenty years earlier had realized they had been betrayed into the First World War, were now being betrayed into taking sides in the second; but whereas Wilson (perhaps hypocritically, perhaps from the noblest motives) had asked us to remain neutral in mind as well as in acts, Roosevelt encouraged an unneutral attitude in 1939 —and in 1940 practically pledged the country to aid Finland against the Soviets and Britain against Germany— all the time protesting he was not war mongering.

The *New Republic* for October 25, 1939, noted "with a sinking heart" the repetition of the 1917 and 1920 red scares. We could look back to the first wartime witch hunt with humiliation, but:

> Today, when the United States is not at war and when everyone declares a firm intention of staying out, we see an ominous return to these activities. Witch hunting is again in progress all over the country. Stimulated by an indiscreet public statement of Attorney-General Frank Murphy . . . zealous patriots everywhere have begun to look for spies, a term that is pretty much equivalent to anybody with a foreign accent whom you don't like. . . . The Dies Committee . . . is advancing its well-known aim, which is to "smear" the Roosevelt administration in every possible way, with a new burst of anti-Communist activity. . . . So serious is the situation all over the country that the ACLU and allied organizations felt it necessary to call in New York a few days ago a National Conference on Civil Liberties

in the Present Emergency.

In conclusion it was stated that "the Department of Justice under the liberal Frank Murphy is conscious of the dangers of the situation," but by November it became evident that Murphy himself was an instigator of the red hunt. At his press conference on the twenty-ninth of that month, Murphy said that in addition to the prosecution of Earl Browder, head of the Communist Party, there would be a round-up. He was asked by one of the correspondents, Adam Lapin, whether the round-up of subversive persons would include Father Coughlin. He replied that it would not.

As regards strikes and other labor activities, the attorney-general said there was "a lot of merit" to the Minnesota law which forces unions to give notice of intended walkouts. Mr. Murphy also said he had written a letter to William Green, head of the American Federation of Labor, supporting the contention of Assistant Attorney-General Thurman Arnold that labor could be prosecuted under the Sherman Anti-Trust Act.

This was the famous conference which marked the turn of Frank Murphy from a pro-labor liberal to a reactionary, anti-labor politician. Several of the correspondents sensed that. They asked about civil liberties, and Mr. Murphy replied with great passion that there would be no witch hunt, no redbaiting, no raids, no round-ups, nothing like the Palmer violations of personal rights, and that therefore "no one need be alarmed. . . . This department is not interested in what a man writes, or what he says or what he thinks."

Having thus restated his position as a libertarian, Mr. Murphy felt free to continue with an even more impassioned attack upon the Communists. He admitted that a systematic drive by the G-men had been on for some time and would continue. It is interesting to note that raids made in the course of the succeeding weeks (later admitted to be violations of civil liberties) and the prosecutions under

A Decade of Witch Hunts

technicalities were planned during the incumbency of this libertarian.

The war, the presidential campaign, and the deepening depression in the first months of 1940 undoubtedly added to the intensity of the campaign against minorities and progressives. One of the most flagrant of such actions was the raid on homes of persons who had helped send American volunteers to Loyalist Spain. In Detroit the agents of F.B.I. Chief J. Edgar Hoover, taking their lesson from the Hitler Gestapo treatment of Jews and non-Nazis, broke into bedrooms between four and five o'clock in the morning and took men and women, chained to each other, to jail.

Franz Boas, honorary chairman, and Alfred K. Stern, chairman of the National Emergency Conference for Democratic Rights, telegraphed to Attorney-General Jackson (successor of Murphy, who had been elevated to the Supreme Court) protesting "violations of the constitutional amendments" and calling the incident a "dangerous parallel to discredited 1919 raids condemned by nation." In a press release Chairman Stern said:

> . . . the Department of Justice must never become an agency for intolerance and hate-spreading. . . . In 1919-20 the Palmer raids became the national excuse for blackmailing attacks by vigilante groups and prejudice-ridden individuals. . . . In 1919-20 it was used by the large lumber monopolies in the west to jail, blacklist, and beat up trade union leaders. In the industrial midwest it was used as the major excuse for violent attempts to destroy the ever swiftly growing trade union movement.
>
> We not only remember what happened to democracy in America in 1919-20 when Palmer unloosed his deputized hordes on the country to violate almost every article in the Bill of Rights and every canon of human decency.
>
> We are acutely aware that in the country today major

violations of our fundamental laws are committed daily by men and groups who are more subversive than any of those ever caught in a witch hunt have proven to be.

The Wages and Hours Law is being surreptitiously and even openly violated in various parts of the country. . . .

Peonage—condemned by our Constitution as insufferable since it is the semi-enslavement of human beings—is rampant in scores of counties in a number of southern states. It would take the whole F.B.I. to root it out.

An increasingly powerful Ku Klux Klan working carefully these days to avoid too much publicity is spreading anti-Semitism, anti-Catholicism, and anti-unionism as far north as upstate New York.

Senator Reynolds's Vindicators Association, whose headquarters are a stone's throw from the Capitol Building in Washington, has a five-point program, four points of which are the quintessence of subversive un-Americanism.

Pelley's Silver Shirts, 20,000 strong, are admittedly a semi-military fascist organization.

Suddenly Attorney-General Jackson ordered the actions against the Friends of Loyalist Spain dropped. Then curious little bits of news began coming out of Washington to confirm the report that the raids had been ordered in December 1939 by Murphy. Jackson himself was reported indignant about the whole matter. This apparent piece of hypocrisy on the part of a supposed upholder of the Bill of Rights surprised and shocked the friends of civil liberties.

Why had Murphy organized a witch hunt? The answer now seemed clear to many. Murphy, it was said, had made a great reputation in Michigan as a liberal, even a radical. Being a Catholic, he could not (owing to Protestant prejudices still prevalent) hope to go as far up in Washington as many of his friends thought he should. And now the same spreaders of falsehood and innuendo who smeared every labor leader and every liberal had put the red

A Decade of Witch Hunts

stamp on Murphy, and with that in his eyebrows his career was limited. As an attorney-general hoping to enter the Supreme Court, it was argued, he was expected to give hostages to politics, and he set about doing exactly what up until then he had denounced as mean and vicious: he instigated a red hunt. The profit at any rate was immediate. Roosevelt placed the washed white lamb alongside the liberals in the highest tribunal of the land.

Still more startling were the accusations by Ludwell Denny of the Scripps-Howard papers and John T. Flynn of the *New Republic,* who named President Roosevelt himself as Murphy's partner in the 1939-to-date red hunt. Denny said bluntly that "the crusade against so-called subversive activities was not started last fall by J. Edgar Hoover but by Mr. Roosevelt"; Flynn wrote that Hoover's Gestapo "is so clearly traceable to the President that there can be no equivocation about it. And the liberals in groups in this country would do well to open their eyes and take a good honest look at this particular matter before it goes any further."

Part II

CASE HISTORIES: SOME VICTIMS

CHAPTER 5
Star Salesman

In the labor wars, too, as in imperialist wars, there are often commercial and industrial interests which are in conflict with humane interests, and there are also merchants of death who make good profit out of them. In these wars, too, patriotism may be turned to private gain. Machine-gun and gas-bomb salesmen know how to raise the red, white, and blue over themselves while they throw the red banner over labor. Publicly they declare that the interests of capital and labor are identical, that peace should reign in industry, while in private letters to agents and corporations they speak of the increasing conflict between capital and labor and recommend labor espionage and the "complete munitioning" of great plants.

The noblest patriot of them all is President John W. Young of Federal Laboratories; this chapter deals almost entirely with him, his nationwide redbaiting campaign, and the bloodshed brought on by one of his gas salesmen. The background is the San Franciseo strike of 1934. The rival is the Lake Erie Chemical Company, whose salesman in San Francisco was one Ignatius McCarty. A letter written by McCarty, discussing the rivalry of the two firms, contains the following paragraph (as published in the La Follette committee report):

> If we let Federal get away with this attempt here, they will give us the laugh throughout the state and we will be discredited, as the Chief, who is one of these fake flag-wavers who is always spouting about the danger of Communism, and what he is doing to combat it, will be

asked why he chose Federal instead of our gas.[1]

The police of California had been driven into a hysterical state by the red scare: they had been told by Hearst, Chandler, and the rest of the redbaiting press that every move by labor for higher wages, better living conditions, a decent wage, a better life, was dangerous to law and order because it was all a red plot instigated by Moscow. The Associated Farmers, the steamship companies, the chambers of commerce, the press, the police—in fact every man and organization that could be classed as representing power and wealth—were engaged in redbaiting and war preparations, while labor had none of the means of communication to state its case to the public.

Federal Laboratories instituted a vast campaign of redbaiting as a means of interesting every police chief and every National Guard officer in America in its main product: gas. Its plan is fully told in a government report published in 1939:

> Section I. Use of the "Red" Scare in Selling Munitions
>
> To prospective customers Federal Laboratories sends large amounts of antiradical and anticommunist literature. In all, it distributed over 1,500 copies of *The Red Network* by Elizabeth Dilling. These books were given to the National Guard of each State, to hundreds of police departments, and to all Federal Laboratories salesmen with the recommendation that they be distributed as widely as possible. Through an arrangement with the publishers, Federal Laboratories was able to obtain the book at half price. This compendium of misinformation, distortion, and absurdity was distributed as an authority on the American radical movement and as a handbook for the

---

[1] *Violations of Free Speech and Rights of Labor: Hearing: Before a Sub-committee of the Committee on Education and Labor,* United States Senate, Seventy-sixth Congress, 1st session (Washington, D. C.:

Star Salesman

purchaser of tear gas. On July 24, 1934, John W. Young, president of Federal Laboratories, wrote to all Federal Laboratories agents, enclosing a newspaper article on "the danger of revolution in this country," from one of the Washington, D. C., Hearst papers. After calling attention to the newspaper article, Mr. Young wrote:

"Couple this up with the account of communistic activity as given in a book entitled *The Red Network* by Elizabeth Dilling, copy of which we are sending to you, and you have a clear picture of the underlying cause of our present difficulty. We are heading for plenty of trouble and it is a time for all of the American patriotism you can manifest.

"This book sells for $1 each. It costs us $0.50 plus expressage, plus postage. Whatever you do, read this book when you get time. Carry it with you and get every police chief and sheriff you talk to to buy one; get each industrial leader to buy one. We should be glad to fill these orders at cost, which will run about $0.75 in an effort to stir up the American public to prepare for the things that are facing us."

In the next paragraph, Mr. Young makes clearer what he meant by the "things that are facing us."

"Police Departments in small communities can no longer say that they need not worry about trouble. Section 7-a of the National Recovery Act states that labor shall have the right to organize without interference on the part of the employer—but it does not state that labor shall not be interfered with from the outside. . . ."

. . . It is clear that Mr. Young sought to create, in the minds of his salesmen, an association between Russian Communism and the effort of employees in this country, through the American Federation of Labor, to avail themselves of the right of collective bargaining. Mr. Young's persistence in distributing the book through his sales force indicates that he must have felt that identifying labor organization with revolution would aid in the sale of his munitions.[2]

---
2 Op. cit., P. 3, p. 157.

In Los Angeles, George Cake, munitions salesman, delivered 150 copies of the "compendium of misinformation, distortion, and absurdity" to the Junior Chamber of Commerce; the Pittsburgh offices of the Burns detective agency took four copies; ten were given to an official of the Standard Oil Company in San Francisco; and Mr. Young dug down into his own pocket and mailed a copy gratis to the National Guard of every state in the Union, together with a letter saying that much of the trouble in the country could be traced to "radical agitators, who have boasted that they will not stop until they overthrow our constitutional government."

The Red Network is nonsense, vicious nonsense; Mr. Young made a fool of himself testifying before the La Follette committee; and the salesmen's plan to carry *The Red Network* with them to stir up customers when showing samples of gas and machine-guns may sound absurd, but the La Follette committee found that instead of being ludicrous, it was a most serious matter:

> It may be doubted that this book by itself would convince many employers that the workmen in their plants were plotting to tear them down or take them over. What is most significant . . . [is] the attitude and ideas which Mr. Young sought through it, to implant in his salesmen. . . . Mr. Young's efforts went a long way toward giving his agents the idea that all labor leaders or strikers were "reds" and fair game for the gas grenade or gas gun of any police officer, private guard, or munitions salesman.

Mrs. Dilling's misinformation was not enough for the Federal Laboratories' redbaiting campaign: it got out its own original publication, in which, while selling murderous weapons to use against labor, it made the charge that crime and civil disorder are due to the radicals. Government investigations have proven time after time that in the vast majority of cases of disorder, of clashes between workmen

Star Salesman

and military, the so-called forces of law and order are responsible for the initiation of violence—and the list of dead and wounded in all American labor history is sufficient proof that those who carry arms (police, vigilantes, militiamen) always take a toll in death and blood from those who do not carry arms (workingmen) and rarely have any casualties themselves.

But Mr. Young of Federal Laboratories is in business to make money. In order to make money the mere falsification of history or current fact is a little thing. The Young pamphlet, as read into the record by Senator La Follette himself, contained such statements as the following:

> During the past year from the east coast to the west coast those who advocate social change by violence have been confronted with and stopped by the Federal tear gas, but those people are not willing to take defeat so easily. . . .
> Those same leaders openly boast that they must disarm the country before they can successfully overthrow our government and establish the government built on the principles of Marx and Lenin.
> The enclosed booklet entitled *The Red Line of Crime and Civil Disorder* has been supplied to all leading newspapers in your territory. . . .

Mr. Young admitted he was not a writer. The pamphlet was merely his idea. Who actually did the writing? Asked Senator La Follette. Mr. Young disclosed the name of Ketchum, McCloud & Ketchum, advertising agents, in Pittsburgh. (Years ago James Rorty predicted that when fascism came to America the advertising fraternity would be the boys to put it over.)

> The absurdity of the [gas and machine-gun] company's emphasis on the revolutionary menace [said the La Follette report] is illustrated by the doctoring of a photograph on this bulletin's lurid cover. The picture

shows a crowd being routed by tear gas. Nearly every face which is visible to the camera has been obviously touched up in ink with the pointed beard, mustache, or horn-rimmed glasses of the caricatured "foreign agitator." The title and purpose of this pamphlet is calculated to confuse crime and labor activities.

Another fraud which Mr. Young, merchant of death, was willing to propagate was something called "The Communist Oath," which reads like this:

> I do solemnly swear that I hold in contempt all institutions of capitalism, including ecclesiastical and secular; its flag, its courts, its codes AND ITS CHURCHES AND ITS RELIGIONS. I will obey all summons of the elected officials of this order under penalty of death, and spare neither time, effort, nor money to obey, even to the last drop of blood.

Senator La Follette asked Mr. Young who had sent him the oath (printed on stickers) which he had distributed. Young named three possibilities—the Boy Scouts, the National Guard, and the American Legion—but at a later date informed the committee that it was the R.O.T.C. Association. Senator La Follette asked if Mr. Young had tried to verify the oath, if he had made any inquiry whatever to find out if it was a forgery or a fact. Mr. Young had not. He had merely distributed it.

He also sent out high-pressure sales talks to the distributors of gas bombs in the field, talks full of his philosophy of redbaiting and profit-making. Senator La Follette read typical extracts from them:

> Class struggle [wrote Mr. Young] has become more defined and more pronounced. Mediation boards are finding greater difficulty in holding the left wing in check. This is going to call for a heavy drain on police powers as shown in our sales record. Sales exceeded the million dollar mark by a healthy margin the first months

of this year. . . .

    We expect that this summer will see a continuation of labor unrest, and you have a real service to offer the police departments. . . .

Senator La Follette recalled the fact that the Pinkerton and other detective agencies "sell their labor espionage and strike-breaking service on the basis of combating Communism." Mr. Young said he was not familiar with that fact.

"For your information, a reading of the testimony before this committee," continued the senator, "will indicate that it is the practice of the detective agencies to cover up their strike-breaking and labor espionage work under the designation of combating Communism. Do you use any of the same tactics?"

"Well," replied Young, "I would go a step further, perhaps, and say that I use some of my personal time for that purpose."

He was asked if he had read any books. He replied that "most of them are pamphlets that come and go." He had learned all about the reds from literature sent him by phony patriotic societies, apparently, but he also read the newspapers. Asked to interpret the program of the Third International, he replied:

"Reading it from the New York *Times*, or I would say, from the newspapers, it is a world revolution to the communist form of government."

Whereupon Senator La Follette read Mr. Young's bulletin No. 14, dealing with this matter. In part, Mr. Young had written:

    A most significant thing has occurred, The Third International, which is comprised of 53 organizations of Communists . . . manifested a change in policy. They are no longer secretly planning revolution. They came out and openly boasted of the progress they are making in various countries, especially the United States, and urged greater activity in riots and civil disorder leading to the overthrow of our Government. Some of us have known of these activities for quite some time, but it is rather a shock to a large percentage of the American public. . . . The most attractive order of the week was one for 12 Thompson submachine guns from the city of Detroit, through George Greig.

Having established the background and general use of redbaiting, involving forgeries, fraud, distortion, and plain and fancy lying for the purpose of making more money, the La Follette committee then went on to its climax: the matter of the murder of workmen over whom the red flag had been dragged, and who were no longer to be regarded as human beings, let alone American citizens.

"Do you know," Senator La Follette asked, "whether your agents confine their anti-communist activities to propaganda, or whether they take active part sometimes in gassing Communists?"

Mr. Young said he did not know.

Did he know if his men had ever killed a Communist?

Again, he did not know.

Whereupon Senator La Follette offered for the record one of the most sensational cases of violence in American labor history.

On April 30, 1934, one of Young's salesmen named J. M. Roush wrote to another (Exhibit 920): "Well, I suppose you are going to have a good time tomorrow with all the Reds. . . . I hope all the Reds get sickening gas in L.A. I will do what I can about it up here [in San Francisco]." And he did.

In his next letter, which is Exhibit 921,[3] Salesman Roush begins by relating his tribulations and successes: he was a new man, he had to "break in," he "contacted" all law-enforcement agencies, "and when the strike came up I felt that I might at last get some business." But his

---

3   *Op. cit.*, P. 7, pp. 2724-2727.

Star Salesman 75

competitor had "connection . . . with the city fathers," so it was no dice. He made friends with Chief Quinn, Chief Wallman, Clarence Merrill, Sergeant McInerney, Officer Myron Gernea, and finally he was invited to demonstrate the effect of Federal Laboratories gas at a riot the police hoped for on a certain day and place. En route Mr. Roush noted his competitor in a car from the inspector's bureau, and soon the two of them were at work. "It was most interesting to see not only our grenades but our competitor's grenades tossing back to us as though they were so many apples," says the letter. But the wind was in their faces.

> I then started in with long range shells and believe me they solved the problem. From then on each riot was a victory for us. . . . It was most interesting as well as educational. . . . The Chief had become so sold on our equipment . . . he exercised his authority to buy emergency equipment. It was a landslide of business for us. . . . I was in seventh heaven. . . .

> I plan next week to get pictures of the San Francisco riot squads and of the riots themselves, which I shall forward to you. I might mention that during one of the riots, I shot a long range projectile into a group, a shell hitting one man and causing a fracture of the skull, from which he has since died. As he was a Communist, I have no feeling in the matter and I am sorry that I did not get more. The enclosed handbill shows a picture of me after I had just fired the shot. I imagine that this is the first time that one of your agents has had his picture posted all over town by Communists. . . .

> The effects of our selling Federal equipment to the city of San Francisco has had another interesting effect: our mutual friend, Mr. Lane of the Bank of America, to whom you and I tried so hard to sell our wares, has asked me to work out tear gas protection for the main vault. . . .

> Now let me at this time thank you from the bottom of my heart for the very wonderful cooperation that you gave me. . . . I can think of no greater inspiration to get out and get more business. . . .

When he read the part about the murder of a striker which Salesman Roush did not regret, Senator La Follette asked President Young if he agreed with those sentiments. President Young said he did not. Whereupon the senator produced a letter from B. H. Barker, vice-president of the corporation: "The report is splendid and we think enough of it to excerpt a large portion of it and send it to the men so you will be well known when you come in September 1st."

> SENATOR LA FOLLETTE: . . . I call your attention to the fact . . . that you sent him this laudatory comment on his report in which he brought your attention to the fact he was sorry he had only killed one Communist.
> MR. YOUNG: I think that was misguided enthusiasm.
> SENATOR LA FOLLETTE: That didn't make much difference to the man who died. (*Laughter.*) Did you, Mr. Young, take any steps to investigate this fatality?
> MR. YOUNG: I do not recall I did. . . .
> SENATOR LA FOLLETTE: It did not shock you very much, then, did it?
> MR. YOUNG: There was not anything to be done about it that I know of except to caution Mr. Roush when he came in, which we did.

Robert Wohlforth, secretary of the La Follette committee, told me that the investigators had reason to believe that several of the so-called riots in San Francisco were instigated by the police. This is a usual procedure, the distinguishing feature of those in California being that behind the police instigators were the munitions salesmen and munitions corporations. The merchants of industrial death—there were three companies contending for the police department orders—each wanted to try out its wares

Star Salesman 77

in actual practice. No sham battles would do.

And so Salesman Roush, convinced he had committed a murder, did not regret it because the murdered man was a radical; in fact, he did regret that he had not killed several radicals—and his report was mimeographed as a sales talk for other salesmen. The corporation did not bother to find out whether the supposedly dead man was a radical or a Republican. The La Follette committee did investigate.

Eyewitnesses testified that three men—one in police uniform, one (a policeman) in a brown suit, and one in a gray suit (identified by Vice-President Barker as his Mr. Roush)—came down the streets of San Francisco accompanied by a sound truck of a motion picture company, other photographers, and the press. This shooting was not only for the purpose of proving to the police that Federal's gas was good, but apparently was to be staged for the movies and the newspapers as well. But since there were no strikers on the streets at the moment, the Federal men and police fired gas into the Seaboard Hotel, gassing a number of strikers who were taking refuge in the lobby, and many innocent bystanders.

In the empty street walked James Engle, a member of the International Longshoremen's Association. "Engle was the only striker in the street," reads the sworn eyewitness testimony. As he walked around a parked automobile, Roush fired directly at his head. Engle slumped to the ground, and was left for dead. When the police and munitions salesmen with their motion picture outfit had moved on, workmen carried Engle into the hotel.

> It is absurd to state that he was a Communist [reads the eyewitness testimony which became Exhibit 923 in the La Follette report]. I know to a certainty that "Kentucky" [as Engle was called, after his native state] never had any contact with the radical labor groups on the waterfront. He was a loyal union man and a member of the International Longshoremen's Association. . . . The action of this group of three men in tiring those

shells was absolutely unjustified. There was no commotion or disturbance. . . . There was no crowd . . . no demonstration. . . . The only explanation which seems to me to make sense is that the whole thing was started for the benefit of the motion picture cameraman. My belief is based on experience of many years as a motion picture operator.

Senator La Follette then brought the case to a dramatic climax by producing evidence that Engle had not been killed. He had been taken to a hospital, operated on, and discharged as improved but permanently injured. The company was not interested. Nor was Roush ever arrested for felonious attack or attempted murder. The red label had been enough.

"There is no blinking the fact," said the La Follette report of 1939, "that Mr. Roush's expressed attitude was one of murderous intent. No justification exists in law or morals for an intent to kill people because of their political beliefs."

Nor did the case end there. As in the most marketable of fiction stories there was even an O. Henry twist in the last paragraph.

After all the testimony, which showed patriotism, redbaiting, and bloodshed intermingled, was taken, and just after President Young had declared that the "Communist literature" he had received—the pamphlets issued by the anti-communist patriots—indicated that the reds advocated the violent overthrow of the government, Senator La Follette asked an innocent question: was Mr. Young acquainted with any diplomatic or trade representatives of the Soviet Union?

"We do business with the Amtorg Trading Company," replied Mr. Young. That was the trade organization of the Soviets, he explained. The cross-examination continued:

> SENATOR LA FOLLETTE: Have you ever made any sales of gas or munitions through the Amtorg to the

Soviet Union?

Mr. Young: They bought our samples. (*Laughter.*)

Senator La Follette: I offer for the record a Federal Laboratories invoice to the Amtorg Trading Company for $339.43. . . . Now, Mr. Young, according to your testimony, the Soviet Union and the Third International are trying to bring about revolution by force and violence in the United States; why did you sell them munitions?

Mr. Young: Senator, the Soviet Union in Russia is one thing, and the communism in America is another thing.

Senator La Follette: What is the difference? You said just now you thought their policy for the party, including the Communist Party of the United States, was directed from Moscow.

Mr. Young: Are you quoting me correctly there?

Senator La Follette: And the literature of the Communist Party of America is advocating overthrow of this government by force and violence?

Mr. Young: Would you like to have some of their literature submitted to you, Senator, which does advocate that?

Senator La Follette: I want to have you explain to me why you feel it is all right, in view of your attitude toward communism, to sell munitions to the Amtorg sales representative of the Communist Government in Russia.

Mr. Young: That is the American buying representative, not selling.

Senator La Follette: Well, answer the question, if I made a mistake.

Mr. Young: The Russian background I think justified action in Russia to bring about a different form of government, but we do not have that background in America. I have no controversy with the Communist Government in Russia.

Senator La Follette: Have you any controversy with them if you think they are closely connected with the party in this country which is advocating overthrow of our Government by force and violence?

MR. YOUNG: I have controversy with any meddling in our Government affairs here, but I have no proof they are doing that.

SENATOR LA FOLLETTE: The feeling does not extend to the point of turning down their good hard dollars when they want to buy some of your stuff, does it?

MR. YOUNG: I think tear gas is properly used in any country, regardless of their political doctrines.

SENATOR LA FOLLETTE: In view of your feeling about communism, how can you be sure it is going to be properly used?

MR. YOUNG: It is pretty hard to improperly use tear gas. (*Laughter.*)[4]

The final judgment of the La Follette committee on the whole affair is one of the clearest indictments of the redbaiting-for-profit motive in American history. Whether there was sincere antipathy for the doctrines of communism or merely an attitude created largely by the profit motive, the committee found, was clearly shown by the testimony, which "throws considerable doubt on the sincerity" of Mr. Young's position:

> Where the forces of communism appeared as customers for his weapons, his crusading zeal seems to have flagged. . . .
>
> In other words, in sales arguments Mr. Young had no hesitation in urging employers to buy gas on the ground that their workers were being led astray by agents of Moscow bent on destroying the American Government. Nevertheless, he sold munitions to Russia because he had no proof that Russia was "meddling in our government affairs." Such an admission clearly demonstrates that Mr. Young's emphasis on the danger of communism sprang rather from mercenary motives than from honest convictions.

---

4   *Op. cit.*, pp. 2503, *f.*

CHAPTER 6

The Wages of Redbaiting

The public utilities of America form a vast empire whose wealth, lumped together, runs into billions of dollars and whose power for corruption has been felt in the Senate and House of Representatives, in almost all the newspaper offices of the nation, in the universities and public schools, in the pulpits of thousands of churches, in tens of thousands of meeting places—in fact, almost wherever there is oral, written, or graphic communication. No less than $25,000,000 a year was spent by the light, heat, and power companies on molding American opinion. One of the tactics employed was to redbait every liberal who believed in municipal or government ownership.[1]

The object of all this tremendous expenditure was to change the economic thinking of the nation to suit the corporations and monopolies. But what concerns us now is an episode which illustrates the special use of redbaiting by dollar patriots.

The story has a human-interest ending. Its principals were John B. Sheridan of St. Louis, director of the Missouri Committee on Public Utility Information, and John W. Colton of New York, editor of *Aera*, published by the American Electric Railway Association. Mr. Sheridan was one of the chief propagandists for the utilities, an employee

---

1 The whole story—which the newspapers of America generally suppressed—is told in 73 volumes which the Federal Trade Commission issued over a period of years. Concerning the corruption of the American press, I have summarized tens of thousands of words of testimony in a chapter in *Freedom of the Press* (Bobbs-Merrill, 1935), and Carl Thompson, Ernest Gruening, and Stephen Raushenbush have written books on the public utility end of the story.

of the propaganda bureau first proposed by Samuel Insull to combat the sentiment for public ownership of public utilities and which grew into a vast network spending huge sums of money on advertising and bribery. Sheridan and his colleagues deplored the fact that they had been able to win over only four-fifths of our dailies and weeklies—only 16,000 of America's 20,000 journalistic publications! (In one state—Missouri—they captured 699 out of 700 publications.)

How was the job done? In many ways. Country editors were easy, said Mr. Sheridan; all they needed was a little entertainment, an occasional drink, a little money. "All of them are God's fools, grateful for small and most insignificant services." Big newspapers got tens of thousands of dollars' worth of advertising, it is true, but more important than money, perhaps, was a sort of self-bribery that came from newspaper owners and utilities owners belonging to the same class of society. A newspaper owner who had a portfolio of $18,000,000 in stocks and bonds wrote editorials favoring private ownership of public utilities without being asked to do so by Mr. Sheridan and his colleagues.

But, when everything else failed, when there was public clamor for municipal ownership, then the method was "to pin the Bolshevist idea on the fellow that advocated anything against private ownership." That was the plan originated by Mr. Sheridan and adopted by his twenty-seven colleagues who operated in thirty-eight states of the Union with overwhelming success.

"Judge," said Mr. Sheridan when he was up before the Senate investigation committee, "as I recollect it, getting this rumor and gossip and things that came around, this was an idea to tie up any plan against private-owned utilities with the Bolshevist idea; see?"

Among Mr. Sheridan's colleagues who "saw" was Mr. Bernard J. Mullaney, past president of the American Gas Association, official of the Peoples Gas Light and Coke

The Wages of Redbaiting

Company, and director of the Illinois branch of the utilities information bureaus. "I did say," testified Mr. Mullaney, "that all advocates of red or communist information stood in behind every municipal ownership enterprise. . . ." In an address, appropriately delivered before the Associated Advertising Clubs of the World, Mr. Mullaney, servant of the Insulls, said: "Government ownership is the masked advance agent of communism—not merely 'socialization of basic industry for the common good' as the 'pinks' have it, but the communism of the 'reds' as the dictionary has it, abolition of all private property and state control of all labor, religion, social relations." Naturally the government projects at Muscle Shoals and Boulder Dam were condemned as Bolshevism at this meeting.

Still another angle of the method was divulged by Mr. Rob Roy McGregor, assistant director of the Illinois Committee. Here is the record:

> JUDGE HEALY: In this paper here Mr. Mullaney stated to you that if you were running for the nomination for United States Senator against a man whose speeches had indicated that he favored public ownership, and you had to get up a series of speeches tackling him on that line, what have we that you find pertinent and useful? That was the thing put up to you?
>
> MR. MCGREGOR: Yes, sir.
>
> JUDGE HEALY: In response to that you prepared this document here?
>
> MR. MCGREGOR: Yes, sir. . . .
>
> JUDGE HEALY: Read the last paragraph aloud for the record.
>
> MR. MCGREGOR (*reading*): This, of course, is not an attempt at writing a speech. My idea would be not to try logic or reason but to try to pin the Bolshevik idea on my opponent. I do not believe that the theory of government ownership would be much use except before a hand-picked audience.
>
> JUDGE HEALY: You were just simply trying to pin the Bolshevik idea on your opponent?

MR. MCGREGOR: Yes, sir.

JUDGE HEALY: Why didn't you discuss the reason or the logic of it?

MR. MCGREGOR: As I stated in the last paragraph, I did not think that it would be a political discussion; that the merits in an abstract way of government ownership would be of much use.

JUDGE HEALY: You simply tried to raise a prejudice against the man that proposed it and tried to pin the Bolshevik idea on him?

MR. MCGREGOR: Yes, sir.

JUDGE HEALY: That is all.[2]

Nineteen thousand copies of the Mullaney report advising the use of the red label instead of logic or reason were sent to the press, to college professors, to lecturers who argued for pay against government or municipal ownership, to college debaters, and to others especially interested. In this report the Mullaney logic and reason also shine. Says he: "Scratch any aggressive government ownership advocate, no matter in which guise he may appear, and the deeper you go the redder you will find him. He has to be fundamentally 'red.' If he is sincere, he knows all government ownership proposals lead logically to the ultimate 'red' objective, which is complete government ownership and Communism."

The utilities used many means for spreading their propaganda. One important one was advertising, another was the editorial and news columns of the press. "Advertising had a very distinct value in obtaining the support of newspapers for the private ownership theory which the industry strongly advocated," said the final government report on the subject. One redbaiting campaign was entrusted to E. Hofer & Sons, Portland, Oregon, which used the slogan: "To discourage radicalism in all forms." It

---

2 U. S. Congress, *Utility Corporations Report,* Seventieth Congress, 1st Session (Washington, D. C.: Government Printing Office, 1939), P. 2, pp. 68-72.

received about $84,000 a year for this work.[3]

Colonel Ernest Hofer had been the author of a book expressing his philosophy. It dealt with "the conservation of life for the greatest service," and of his ten rules for living, the best were:

> Drink plenty of pure water.
> Eat plain foods that are bulky, avoiding condensed foods. [He did not then have any canning company contracts.]
> Mentally live on a high plane of Good Will, Justice and Clean Thinking, holding no one in condemnation. Give the other fellow the best of it whenever you can without too great a sacrifice to yourself.

The concluding department of the philosophic work was devoted to a series of rules on "how to be popular," which included the following:

> 1. Seem always to listen to others
> 2. Do not oppose what others say.

Hofer established "The Manufacturers & Industrial News Bureau," which he described as "the Handmaiden of Good Government and Enduring Industrial Prosperity," and which was secretly subsidized by the utilities. It offered a weekly review to newspapers, but it did not tell them that the news was supplied by interested parties, that redbaiting was an essential part of its service (to its backers), that the whole business was mostly press-agentry, and that its objective was to destroy the movement for public ownership of public utilities. In one of his pamphlets, Hofer said he hoped "to stabilize the mass consciousness and crystallize it against the adoption of radical or unsound propositions. . . ." To the utility corporations he promised "straight from the shoulder arguments against socialistic propaganda of whatever nature, because socialism does not

---
3 *Utility Corporations Report*, P. 71-A, p. 93.

square with our American industrial system and is contrary to the very foundation principle of our constitutional form of government." In a letter he wrote that "the leading utilities of the country have made it possible for us to conduct this work." That work was fighting the United States government at Muscle Shoals, defending the Insull interests, denouncing the Ontario hydro-electric system, boosting rugged individualism (of the Hoover type), and attacking socialism. Fifty percent of the Hofer funds (says the government report) came from the privately owned public utilities, and yet the Hofer company announced it was "an independent publication dissociated from direct connection with any industry."

On the witness stand, Hofer stated his program as follows:

> First, to reduce the volume of legislation that interferes with business and industry; second, to minimize and counteract political regulation of business that is hurtful; third, to discourage radicalism by labor organizations and all sorts of agitators; fourth, a constant fight for reasonable taxation by state, city, and county government; fifth, a scientific educational campaign against all socialistic and radical propaganda of whatever nature.

Summing up the smear campaigns of the public utilities, the final government report says:

> Further to strengthen their position, the utilities have worked with considerable success, to secure the support of other industries in their opposition to municipal or public ownership. In this effort the assertion has been repeatedly made that municipal or public ownership of utilities is merely the opening wedge in the direction of public ownership of all industry. Reckless language carrying popular odium has been a part of this campaign. *Bolshevik* and *Bolshevists, Reds, Sovietized* and similar appellations, were often used. Such labeling was

apparently with the object of adding the element of fright in such recruitment of aid of private industry.[4]

> Attacks against those favoring public ownership of utilities were carried to the extent of labeling all those with such beliefs as Bolsheviks, Reds and Pinks of various shades.[5]

> A favorite method of attack was . . . not to meet the public-ownership arguments but to "pin the red label" on their proponents. Thus advocates of the right of the people to own and operate their own public utilities were labeled as "Bolsheviks," "reds," or "parlor pinks."[6]

Thus "the most perfectly organized, the best oiled, and the most effective machine for propaganda" in the United States, if not in the world, "backed by the pressure of millions of dollars of advertising annually expended through local papers," as the Federal Trade Commission characterized it, succeeded, largely through perverting the newspapers and to some extent the schools and colleges, in affecting the economic thinking of the American people; and one of its most effective methods was the method of smearing: of pinning the red label on anything that might hurt private profits though it might also aid the general welfare of the people of this country.

The man who thought up this brilliant attack, John B. Sheridan, had been for many years on Pulitzer's St. Louis *Post-Dispatch*, one of the few liberal, unbribable, crusading newspapers of our time. During the utility hearings, Judge Healy asked him about some letters he had written. Was it true that he had said: "For thirty years I spoke as I felt?" Mr. Sheridan answered affirmatively. Those were the years he worked on the *Post-Dispatch*. "And for five years you say," said the court, reading the letter, "you held your tongue." "Yes, sir," replied Mr. Sheridan. "And those were the five years during which you were employed by the

---
4 *Utility Corporations Report*, p. 13.
5 *Ibid.*, p. 43.
6 *Utility Corporations Report*, p. 393.

[public utilities propaganda] committee?" "Well, that is pretty near right. . . ."

Judge Healy then placed several letters in evidence. The first was written by Mr. Sheridan to Mr. Colton, the editor of *Aera*, on June 14, 1927, at the very time the Sheridan plan for buying up editors, placing advertising in newspapers where it would buy editorial support, and pinning the red label on those who were on the side of the public, was being universally employed. Mr. Sheridan had heard that Mr. Colton had made a protest "against a certain proposed plan to offset certain political movements affecting private ownership of public utilities," and had been moved by it. He wrote:

> May I modestly claim blood brotherhood with a little hammer-down Yankee who has the intestines, the intelligence and the native honesty to make the protest as related to me?
>
> You are a man, John Colton, and I am glad that there is one like you left; feller,—"What profiteth it for a man to gain the whole world if he loses his own soul?"
>
> From your action, as reported to me, I take renewed courage and renewed faith that the "Government of the people, by the people, and for the people shall not perish from the earth."

In business hours Mr. Sheridan did his best to establish government by big business; he was no longer a free man. If his faith in the utilities and his own redbaiting scheme was shaken he did not show it—in the office. Privately he was heartened by Mr. Colton's amazing reply:

> My dear J. B.: . . . If people ask me for my opinion, and I believe that it is worth while to give an opinion, I mean to give an honest one. A hypocrite is one of the poorest works of the Almighty; it isn't fair to the Almighty to ascribe to Him the creation of a hypocrite. Perhaps fear makes more hypocrites than any other cause. If that is so, pray God there will be an

The Wages of Redbaiting

improvement in the process of evolution.

Just at present I feel very much disillusioned. I am one of those simple-minded creatures who believe all men to be honest and sincere until I find them otherwise, and even then I doubt the justice of my own conclusions. When I am forced to acknowledge that men whom I believed were honest and sincere are only cheap, lying politicians, I have a feeling of sadness that is depressing to me. I do not resent this condition as much as I deplore it.

You are absolutely right when you ask the question, as it was asked 2,000 years ago. "What profiteth it for a man to gain the whole world if he loses his own soul? . . ."

Within a few days Sheridan replied, and his letter has now become Exhibit 2723 in the Federal Trade Commission's seventy-three volumes of testimony:

June 24, 1927.

Mr. John W. Colton,
American Electric Railway Association,
New York City, N. Y.

Dear Mr. Colton: A brave man is never foolish. If a man has not courage what has he?

Yea-up men are a little breed. Possession of property breeds liars and cowards. The man who invented private ownership was a mortal enemy of the human race.

Hot dog! Boy, I am strong for you. For 30 years I spoke as I felt. For 5 years I held my tongue. Now I mean to resume the greatest of human rights—that of free speech.

Damn it all, John, they never can make hypocrites and cowards of all the people. T'ell mit 'em.
Sincerely your friend,

J. B. Sheridan.

One more letter was offered in evidence, and it had become Mr. Colton's turn to tell the truth.

> The thing about the utility industry that disgusts me is the lying, trimming, faking and downright evasion of trust, or violation of trust that marks the progress toward enormous wealth of some of the so-called big men in the industry. When I see one of these fellows waving the flag, I am filled with not only disgust but rage, for they are anything but patriots. . . . I would thoroughly enjoy fighting some of these faking patriots through the editorial page of an influential newspaper. . . .

There is, of course, an honest utility industry, but Mr. Colton estimates it at only 10 percent. "I would enjoy being linked up with even so small a minority. . . ."

Whatever other letters were exchanged by these two employees of big business who hated big business is not known. The federal investigators had seized only four, and these were published—in the reports, but not in the press.

In April 1930, Mr. J. B. Sheridan, the originator of the redbaiting formula for the utilities propaganda campaign, committed suicide. The profits of redbaiting had been enormous, but the wages was death.

CHAPTER 7
Two Children and a Witch Trial

The profits in redbaiting, as has been said, are not all grist for the certified public accountant's mill. Some of them are payable in dividends of egotism and others can be recognized only by Freudian practitioners; and there are rewards in humor and tragedy, headlines, fame, and notoriety.

One of the strangest stories of redbaiting, a story never reported fairly or fully in the newspapers because it included a religious issue (religious controversy being Anathema No. 1 in the press of our country) presents the amazing spectacle of a husband redbaiting his wife for the purpose of blackening her reputation and getting possession of their two children. The story appeared briefly under the headings, "Woman's Red Creed Costs Her Children," or "Red Mother Loses Her Tots," and then disappeared from the news. But it was such a fundamental case of the violation of personal freedom that the American Civil Liberties Union and the Freethinkers of America fought the issue involved through the courts.

Mabel Eaton—Mrs. Warren P. Eaton—of Montclair, New Jersey, was the heroine, and victim, in this case. She was accused of being an atheist although she testified: "I believe in God as I know him." She was also accused of being a radical; and the judge, taking her children from her, gave as one of his reasons Mrs. Eaton's adherence to an economic doctrine not generally followed by the majority of people in the United States.

Mrs. Eaton's crime consisted of going to lectures at the Rand School in New York City. Now the Rand School is not Communist, as everyone with the exception of a certain

Mrs. Dilling, author of *The Red Network*, seems to know. Mrs. Dilling, who has never been able to advance beyond the discredited Lusk Report of the Great Red Scare of the 1920's, unearthed that document as a reason for smearing the institution. She was also stirred by the fact that Marie Stopes' book, *Love and Marriage,* was sold to students at the school; and she further disclosed the awful facts that among its lecturers were John Dewey, the dramatist Marc Connolly, the psychologist John B. Watson, and the writers Hendrik W. Van Loon and George Soule; that among those who attended a meeting to pledge support to the continuance of the school were Congressman (later Mayor) LaGuardia and Dr. John Haynes Holmes, New York's leading liberal minister; and that the signatories to a letter for the same purpose included Upton Sinclair, Paul Douglas, Gilbert Seldes, Dr. William H. Kilpatrick, Stuart Chase, Oswald Garrison Villard, Charles A. Beard, Heywood Broun, Helen Keller, Fannie Hurst, Jerome Davis, Broadus Mitchell, Elmer Rice, and Michael Strange.

Warren Eaton's attorney opened his case by trying to draw a red herring across the school.

"You know that the Rand School is a radical school of Socialism, Communism, and I.W.W.," he shouted at the defendant.

"No, it is not," replied Mrs. Eaton.

"What difference does it make?" broke in Advisory Master A. M. Grosman of the Chancery Court.

The attorney for the complainant, J. Raymond Tiffany, insisted on pressing the point.

> MR. TIFFANY: Do you believe in the principles of the I.W.W.?
> MRS. EATON: I don't know anything at all about it.
> MASTER: Answer yes or no.
> MRS. EATON: I don't know what it is about....
> MR. TIFFANY: Your answer is no.
> MRS. EATON: No.

Two Children and a Witch Trial

A large part of the testimony concerned religion, marriage, and Karl Marx. What was Mrs. Eaton's belief? She replied: "Belief in general? Well, being religion is part of an individual, I will put it in as few words as I possibly can; my duty towards myself, my fellowman and my duty towards God; that covers everything."

"Isn't that the Marxian definition?" asked the attorney.

"I don't know anything about religion in regard to Marx because he is an economist and not a religionist," was the reply.

What about the home? Witness believed it was necessary. What about the institution of marriage? "Well, I am married, like anybody else."

"Do you believe in the marriage institution as we have today or the Marxian theory of marriage?"

"I believe in our marriage institution, no matter what form it may be."

"Do you believe in the Marx theory of marriage?"

"I don't know what the Marx idea is."

"You don't know?"

"No."

"Don't you read and study him?"

"Yes."

"Yet you do not know what he stands for?"

"I don't know anything about marriage ceremonies and Marxian practices. Marx wrote a book of 3000 pages."

> MR. TIFFANY: Do you believe in the right of private property?
>
> MRS. EATON: Yes, I do.

(This certainly was making out a good case against Mrs. Eaton!)

"What is the difference between Marxism and capitalism?"

"You are telling me the difference. I am not preaching it, I am studying it."

Redirect examination by Bertram C. Duncan, Mrs. Eaton's attorney:

> QUESTION: Do you now, or did you ever belong to any so-called "red" organization of any kind or description?
> ANSWER: Never.
> QUESTION: Have you ever taken part in any way in any subversive movement?
> ANSWER: Never.
> QUESTION: Or in any street meetings?
> ANSWER: No.

Then there are reams of questions devoted to the actuality of God. Mrs. Eaton testified she believed in the Bible, in the sanctity of the Old Testament ("by the way I study that"), but not in Christ, yet in Christ's teachings. In explanation: "I believe in him as another man. I do not support the Christian church, for one, financially, and I do not believe that I have to have as my advisor, or intermediator between God and myself, Jesus Christ. If that charge makes me not a Christian. . . ."

Here the attorney interrupted by asking if she believed in evolution, and she said she did. In the immaculate conception? "I do not." She believed in Darwin. (There was a joke about making this a monkey trial.) More wrangling. Then, as if in finality, Mr. Tiffany asked for the last time: "Do you believe in God as we know Him?" And Mrs. Eaton replied: "I believe in God as I know Him."

Where in the world, then, could the court get the idea that Mrs. Eaton was an atheist, a Communist, a Wobbly, a woman unfit to be the mother of two future Republican (or Democratic) voters? Could it have been Darwin and evolution? Or Karl Marx and the Rand School of Social Science? Or perhaps the fact that Mrs. Eaton, who had a free and inquiring mind, told her smug conservative husband that *his* god was gold. The weekly *New Yorker*, which read the testimony, thought the judge apparently chose the type of mind to which the children should be exposed instead of weighing the evidence in the case.

The plea for custody of the children was made on the ground of cruelty. Mrs. Eaton had also sued her husband for divorce on the same ground. In finding for the father, the Master wrote in his decision:

> There is no question, to my mind, that the petitioner had permitted herself to become thoroughly imbued with communistic, atheistic and I.W.W. doctrines, even though she does not hold formal membership in those organizations.
>
> It is common knowledge that the principles of communism are the antithesis of those generally held by most Americans. They scoff at the belief in the Supreme Being, in the brotherhood of man, in the virtue of women, the marriage institution, as well as the personal relation between parent and child.
>
> The petitioner, of course, is the "mistress of her own soul." She may do with herself as she will, but she is not privileged to instil into the minds of these young children, against the will of their father, these doctrines, which she, herself, has embraced and which are looked upon with abhorrence by the vast majority of people living under the protection of our law.
>
> The children will remain in the custody of the father, subject to the right of visitation by the mother, which will continue only as long as she refrains from attempting to instil her atheistic and communistic beliefs in their minds. . . .

This is probably the only case on record of a woman deprived of her little children solely on the ground of her religious and political views. The decision, the conservative New York *Times* said editorially, was "a dangerous precedent . . . not many steps from Nazi practices." One Newark newspaper asked Master Grosman his impression of Mrs. Eaton and quoted him as saying: "She had the look of a tiger cat"; but whether or not she had that look, whether or not she was an atheist, a Communist, an I.W.W., a red, a radical, a freethinker, a follower of Karl Marx, a believer in evolution, and a doubter of the immaculate conception, it seems clearly a violation of our written and moral codes to apply political and religious tests in divorce cases. If this sort of practice is carried a logical step forward, Catholic, Protestant, and Jewish judges will favor the parent of their particular religion in divorces where there is intermarriage, and Democratic Party judges will hand children to Democratic fathers if the mothers are members of the Republican Party.

"The government of the United States of America is not, in any sense, founded upon the Christian religion." Who was it who said these supposedly final words about the place of religion in our country, specifically declaring unofficial the Christian branch of the world's many religions? Not Tom Paine, but another of the founders of this country whose ideas either have not penetrated certain legal minds or are considered irrelevant, immaterial, and inconsequential—the God-fearing Christian gentleman who signed himself *Geo. Washington,* who knew how much cruelty, sadism, and murder has been committed in the name of religion, and who wanted that issue banned from our national life forever. (The student of history will find it in Article II of the Treaty of Peace and Friendship between the United States of America and the Bey and Subjects of Tripoli or Barbary. It was ratified by the Senate on June 10, 1797.)

The Founding Fathers were men of property and passed laws to safeguard possessions, but they did not establish an official economic system, capitalist or co-operative or other; in fact they permitted the spread of revolutionary or radical ideas which would be called socialistic or communistic today, but which may still be legally advocated under the Constitution.

CHAPTER 8
Just Around the Corner

If the Eaton case and other examples of redbaiting in the previous chapters have the air of unreality, if they arouse an it-can't-happen-here attitude, if they make the reader feel that they concern a subject far away from his own sphere of life, he might perhaps be interested in the following little episode which occurred just around the corner from my temporary residence in South Wilton, Connecticut.

South Wilton is less than fifty miles from New York City, on Route 7, between Danbury and Norwalk. It no longer has a railroad station, but it is still a bus stop. Both sides of Route 7 are pretty well built up along there with private homes although there are chicken farms and antique shops and a newly completed "art metal studio."

In Norwalk and South Norwalk, however, there are old, established factories. The leading citizens, the chambers of commerce, and the politicians are always inviting employers to come across the state line, because not only is there no Connecticut income tax, but in some towns there are no unions. But ever since the C.I.O. started unionizing, there has been a growing fear that this profit utopia will be spoiled. The election of a Socialist mayor in Bridgeport and his reforms have not alarmed the business men one-tenth as much as the increase in numbers and power of the labor unions. Connecticut is Yankee, ruggedly individualist, and boasts of its inheritance from colonial times, not in order to keep alive the American tradition of resistance to tyrants, but rather, perhaps, in order to intimidate the large foreign-born labor element.

It happens that I have made the acquaintance of all the

other writers within a circumference of ten or fifteen miles from my home, and among them was the author of several novels and many movie scenarios. She had built a home here with money earned in Hollywood, but had not "gone Hollywood," as the saying has it. She was really interested in the people round about, and especially in the women and girls working in the Norwalk factories. In response to their plea, she started a dramatic class which met on Sundays at her home.

Some time in December 1939, an organizer of the Amalgamated Clothing Workers of America arrived in Norwalk to see if he could unionize some of the workers. According to the Supreme Court of the United States this was a perfectly legal thing to do, but according to the factory bosses of Norwalk it was a heinous red threat to profits. If the union organizer succeeded, it meant higher wages, better conditions in the factory, shorter hours, and other reforms—and every item involved a cut in income.

On December 15, 1939, therefore, the Norwalk *Sentinal* had a seven-column scoop headline:

NORWALK RED RING IS PROBED

and underneath:

Russian Tie Is Revealed; FBI Agents Enter Case

Session of East's Most Prominent Red Leaders Being Held Here

Grand Jury Action Is Expected—Fear Students Are Being Influenced

and this, in turn, was followed by:

STACK LAUDS DRIVE TO PURGE CITY OF RED ACTIVITIES

Urges Speed by Probers; Report Stirs Population

> No Room for Communistic Ring, Mayor Says—
> Urges Americanism
> Young Men and Women Are Being Taught in Classes

The first story said, in sensational part:

> Norwalk is one of the East's "hottest" communistic centers, a survey by The Sentinel revealed today.
>
> Communistic activities have brought agents from the Federal Bureau of Investigation to this city. They are conducting an intensive investigation at the present time and it is expected that Federal indictments may follow in the near future.
>
> The Norwalk ring has direct connections with Soviet Russia and one of its leaders returned from Moscow recently. This leader is alleged to have held conferences with high Soviet officials, while in Russia, regarding activities in this country.
>
> It is known to Federal agents that Norwalk has been the meeting place of some of the nation's most prominent Red leaders. Earl R. Browder . . . is believed to have attended. . . .
>
> The Sentinel's investigation has revealed that a school for communists is being operated. . . . Factory girls and boys . . . have been brought under the influence of the communistic ring . . . .
>
> The names of the various members of the ring are known to the Federal agents. . . .
>
> City officials . . . were indignant over the activities of the group.
>
> The Sentinel has learned . . .
>
> The evidence gathered may be presented to a grand jury. . . .

In the follow-up story Frank T. Stack, the mayor, was quoted as saying that the Norwalk police would co-operate with Federal authorities. "I hope that . . . the entire ring will be put out of business. We have no place in Norwalk for such activities."

With such headlines, sensational stories, interviews with the mayor of the town, and editorials praising itself, the *Sentinel* spread the red scare. Naturally enough, when it was asked to retract everything and to publish statements calling its entire story a fake, it refused.

But it was nothing more than one of the tens of thousands of similar things occurring in hundreds of towns in the United States; this one was just around my corner, and that is why I investigated it.

Early in 1940 the fourth annual meeting of the Connecticut Conference on Social and Labor Legislation was held in the Sterling Law Buildings at Yale. Its sponsors ranged all the way from college professors to union leaders, including William Brown of the Red Caps, Professor Calhoun of Yale Divinity School, Reverend Merrill Clarke, Jerome Davis, Ruth McKenney, State Senator Rourke, Isobel Walker Soule of the Descendants of the American Revolution, and Representative Tomassetti. The conference dealt largely with civil liberties for minority racial and religious groups, and especially for labor. One of the cases it was asked to consider was the one in which the Norwalk business men and Editor Le Roy Downs of the *Sentinel* originated a red scare to smash an attempt by a legitimate union to get a handhold in that town.

> The articles appearing in the *Sentinel* [said a speaker] are completely false and ridiculous. In reality, they are a thinly veiled, attempt to frighten and cajole the people of Norwalk and to prevent them from organizing themselves for decent wages and better working conditions. The articles bear the stamp of the Norwalk Chamber of Commerce, which to this day works to attract runaway sweatshops to Norwalk in boasting about our city as "the most open-shop town in the East."
>
> Nowhere in the articles does the *Sentinel* make a single statement of fact; nor does it oder proof of any kind.

We are surprised that Mayor Stack has given his approval to this sort of redbaiting and witch hunting. The Mayer stated in his campaign that he was fighting for the advancement of the standard of living of the people of Norwalk. He received the support of the trade unions and Labor's Non-Partisan League because he stated he believed in unions. The *Sentinel* should be the last to speak about the welfare of the people; it has fought the efforts of its reporters and editorial staff to organize in the Newspaper Guild.

A committee called on Mayor Stack. Mayor Stack denied that there was a plot anywhere; that the police were investigating; that the F.B.I. men had ever been on the story; he denied not only every word the *Sentinel* published, but he denied giving that paper the interview it said it had had with him.

"The thing to do is to get the *Sentinel* to publish a denial," a member of the committee said to the mayor. Stack replied he could not very well ask the *Sentinel* to do so because that was the only paper that had supported him. He said he would ask the Norwalk *Hour* to deny the story in the Norwalk *Sentinel*, but the *Hour* said it was none of its concern, it had not printed the story, and therefore it was not interested in the denial.

For weeks Mayor Stack kept the committee dangling. He needed the *Sentinel*, he needed the Chamber of Commerce, and he also needed union labor. So, like all politicians, he straddled everything and hoped for the best. In private he said the story was a lie; but in public he said nothing.

Some time earlier, I also learned, the Norwalk police had entered a hat factory to interview a workingman named C. They told him that his auto had figured in a robbery; they did not accuse him of being the bandit, but implied the evidence against him was bad. C. said the car had never left his sight, that no one had used it.

The police then said they had looked into the car and

found red propaganda. "You better lay off," the police said.

C. protested he had done nothing illegal in his life.

Two days later he was fired.

The owner of the hat factory told a friend of this workman that the Chamber of Commerce of Norwalk had told him to fire C. for being a radical. By radical they meant a man who spoke in favor of unionization.

At that time Mayor Stack had said to a labor delegation that he himself knew that the Chamber of Commerce was not only anti-labor but was fighting to keep unions and union men out of Norwalk, to keep wages down, to attract runaway factories from New York. He also knew about an electric light plant on the Boston Post Road which had been paying eighteen to nineteen dollars weekly and had been asked by the Chamber of Commerce to lower wages lest it encourage other workers to ask for more.

These instances from just around the corner are instructive examples of how the chambers of commerce, working with the daily press, may find profit in redbaiting. The *Sentinel* did its part in the fight against labor by publishing redbaiting fakes and by not publishing letters of protest to the editor. The profits in such episodes may not be large, but they provide a living for small politicians, commercial patriots, and prostitute sections of the press.

CHAPTER 9
Small-Town Fascism

No better example of co-operation between the "better citizens," leading business men, editors, publishers, and other "respectable" leaders of a small town, and thugs, murderers, and Ku Kluxers, can be found today than in the lumber districts of the State of Washington when labor troubles break out.

For decades murder was committed in Bloody Harlan County, Kentucky, for profit. Murder, kidnaping, flogging were used against the Joads of the California fruit and vegetable valleys for profits. The Ku Klux Klan, second version, killed and tortured in Florida for the profits of the tobacco and citrus interests. And in the demand addressed to Attorney-General Robert Jackson to have the Department of Justice investigate the murder of Laura Law of Grays Harbor County, Washington, 200,000 citizens, members of the Washington Commonwealth Federation, say that a conspiracy exists in that state "which uses murder and violence to subvert the Constitution for the sake of profit."

It is a conspiracy of the gentlemen of the press, the gentlemen of the banks, of big business (notably the lumber business), the gentlemen of law and order, who are linked with Klansmen and the Silver Shirts—all of them alien-baiters, labor-fighters, and redbaiters. It is a conspiracy directed chiefly against the Congress of Industrial Organizations. And behind all the controversy, all the yelling of *red*, all the disputes between union and non-union men, all the intrigue of the leaders of commerce and public opinion, there stands the real issue: the C.I.O. has won wage increases of $7,000,000 for the lumbermen. The big business interests have to pay the $7,000,000. Result: redbaiting and murder.

In a big city the same cause and effect may be present, but there are always many complications—and hypocrisies—whereas in the small towns of Washington, it is openly that terror walks the streets, that the fiery crosses of the Klan burn outside the homes of labor leaders, and that the gentlemen-owners of the free press write redbaiting editorials instigating bloodshed.

Dick Law, an organizer of the militant C.I.O. Woodworkers' union, is known as "the Harry Bridges of Grays Harbor." Laura Law was his wife and fellow-worker. She helped to organize, she made speeches, and on one occasion she led a march of hungry unemployed to the City Hall and asked the mayor to do something for them. But in Grays Harbor County (as Richard O. Boyer wrote in *Friday*[1]) it is un-American to ask for a raise in wages and "if you organize for wage increases there, you are 'a dirty Communist,'" so naturally the Laws were called reds—although Mrs. Luoma, Laura's Finnish mother, said Laura wasn't a red, "she was a Baptist."

Ever since 1937, when the Laws helped 50,000 lumbermen get their $7,000,000 raise, the fight against the C.I.O. by business interests, and by the press and political organizations they control, has been raging. The Ku Klux Klan has, of course, played its part, and so have other "patriotic" organizations, but if anyone is particularly to blame for the atmosphere of terrorism it is the chief agency of public opinion—the press.

There was a division of minds in Aberdeen, Washington, over the Russo-Finnish conflict, and when a dance was announced in one of the Finnish halls for December 2, 1939, the press and radio called for pickets—and trouble. The Aberdeen *World,* for example, put it this way:

---
[1] "Who Killed Laura Law?" *Friday,* March 22, 1940.

Small-Town Fascism

ANTI-COMMUNIST PICKETING PLANNED

> Those planning to picket the Workers Hall will gather in front of the Oregon-Washington district AFL sawmill union hall . . . the march will begin with the American flag at the head. . . .

The frequent announcements, taken with the fact that the police were not there, and were, in fact, very late in arriving after being summoned, bears out the suspicion that they were part of the conspiracy to wreck the building and injure the dancers. The festivities, however, had been called off. Nevertheless, the attack was made. The Associated Press reported that "a mob of 400 to 500 persons . . . rushed a group of some 30 dancing Communists . . . wrecking the interior of the structure and burning pictures of Joseph Stalin and Earl Browder in the street. . . ."

As usual, the Associated Press got its news from the papers it serves, and since the local papers were part of the vigilante movement, it is not surprising that its report is incorrect. There were no "30 dancing Communists," because the hall was empty. Among the pictures burned was one of President Roosevelt. And the A.P. did not state that the press of the town inspired the riot.

Suit for $30,000 against city and county officials, alleging that "said conspirators did unlawfully conspire together during the ten days immediately preceding December 2 to organize and direct a riot against the said hall for the purpose of wrecking and demolishing the same," names Richard J. Utlican, commissioner; Daniel McGillicuddy of the American Legion; and Ward Penning, former safety inspector. A second suit, charging knowledge of the conspiracy and failure to prevent the riot, names Mayor Horrocks, Police Chief George S. Dean, and Assistant Chief Robert Schmidt.

Dick Law believed that the leading business men and editors of the town had something to do with the riot; he also believed that the police were in the conspiracy; and he and his wife knew that the lumber corporations were back of all these men and elements. Dick Law therefore took it upon himself to produce the evidence.

On the night of January 5, 1940, he went out to make three union visits. He took Laura's father and mother to a movie and went on to address a meeting. The Luomas came back from the theater and found their daughter had been stabbed and hacked to death and the house ransacked. Apparently the murderer or murderers, searching for the evidence Dick Law had collected, had been opposed by Mrs. Law and they killed her.

Mrs. Luoma called the police and told them of the murder. The police refused to come for an hour. When they arrived they took the body, which lay on a couch, placed it on the floor, lifted the dress to expose the limbs, and placed a bottle near by. They then took photographs suggesting drunkenness and a sex crime.

Dick Law was found still speaking at the second meeting. He had just said that "there is a conspiracy to break the C.I.O. in Grays Harbor" when he was told of trouble at home. He rushed to the street, forgot his own car, took a taxi—and when he arrived at his house to find his wife dead, he was interrogated by the police in a manner implying they suspected him of murder. Law asked the police chief to round up men whom he named. The chief said: "I'm too tired, I'm going to bed." Law then appealed to the governor, but the governor refused to act.

Press reports of the time say that at the inquest Law was asked about his past, his relations with other women, and his union activities. He got tired of these questions and insisted that Deputy Prosecutor Manley question ten persons who he (Law) thought might have knowledge of the crime, several of them prominent citizens. The inquest was recessed and it has never been continued since.

Of the ten persons named by Dick Law six were makers of public opinion: four editors and two radio station men. More recently, Dick Law has asked the F.B.I. to have these ten sworn as witnesses in an inquest into the murder of his wife. The four editors and publishers Law named are:

> Russell V. Mack, publisher of Grays Harbor *Washingtonian;* chairman of Better Business Builders. (Besides running inciting editorials Mr. Mack also made a speech in which he said, "The Dick Laws must go.")
> Jack Clark, editor of the Grays Harbor *Post*, another executive member of the Better Business Builders and anti-union writer.
> C. C. Crow, publisher of *Crow's Pacific Coast Lumber Digest*, author of editorials favoring vigilante violence.
> W. A. Rupp, editor of the Aberdeen *Daily World;* member of executive committee, Better Business Builders.

The two radio men are Eddie Alexander of KXRO, organizer for the Better Business Builders, and Harry Spence, manager of the same station (which has not only consistently attacked labor but actually used programs which the C.I.O. says encouraged violence against it).

The other four leading citizens named by Law are:

> Joseph Schneider, former county chairman, Republican Central Committee member, leading union-fighter of the county; member of the Better Business Builders.
> E. I. Mosier, member of Grays Harbor Industrial Council and leader of the Order of Better Americans.
> W. Tucker, president, National Bank of Commerce, said to be one of the Weyerhaeuser banks.
> Dan McGillicuddy, lumber interests representative, organizer of the Better Business Builders.

Although C. C. Crow, editor of *Crow's Pacific Coast Lumber Digest*, is not a local man, his publication has been the chief instigator of vigilante action. For example, here is his editorial of November 15, two weeks before the raid on the Finnish Hall and some six weeks before the murder of Laura Law. It is headed: "What Are We Waiting For?" and says in part:

> The Pacific Coast has waited long enough and it is now time to take action independent of the federal government, which has made clear in more ways than one that it is in sympathy with Bridges and his cohorts and has no intention of enforcing the law. . . . Check the federal government off as a total loss so far as it is a protector of the rights of American citizens and American businessmen on the Pacific Coast. . . .
>
> There should be an interstate vigilante society formed with a closely knitted body that could act as a man from the Canadian border to the Mexico line. This should be made up of American citizens only. . . .
>
> The time has come for action, militant action. . . . The time has come for the people to form a vigilante group so representative and strong that they may go to their regular constituted regional law-enforcing officers and not only ask for protection against this foreign invasion but demand it. . . .
>
> *What are we waiting for?*

Crow also attacks President Roosevelt and the New Deal. He once charged that "a handful of federal-backed Reds are bulldozing the 8,195,000 people of the Pacific Coast into bankruptcy." The local press is just as violent. Here are two small samples:

> Grays Harbor *Post:* From now on the citizens of Grays Harbor are fighting mad and intend to stay that way until the causes for the "red label" are removed. A quarter of a century ago red-blooded Americans of Grays Harbor took drastic action to clean out the IWW's who had kept up continual disturbances. . . .
>
> Hoquiam *Shopper:* The Law isn't drastic enough! The Communist is far more dangerous than a murderer. A murderer in a fit of temper kills, or through vicious brooding, kills one. The Communist spends his life

trying to bring about a revolution that will slaughter millions. . . .

The press is considered the first and worst of the six elements responsible for the terrorism which led to the murder of Laura Law. The other elements are: the law and order forces, notably the deputies; the patriotic organizations; the radio; the scabs, thugs, and strikebreakers used on occasions; and the vigilante groups formed by the "better" citizens.

The Ku Klux Klan, which in its second revival has changed its policy from anti-Semitism and anti-Catholicism to anti-communism and anti-trade-unionism, apparently sprang to life in Grays Harbor County, Washington, in 1912, for at that time a young labor attorney named Homer T. Bone (now United States senator) arrived to defend some woodworkers and was greeted with a fiery cross. The K.K.K. was strong in its heyday, from 1920 to 1926, but almost disappeared after the great exposes of that time. However, its revival coincided with the depression year of 1937, when it changed to an anti-labor policy, and by 1940 the K.K.K. was again an important and violent factor in community life.

For several years the woodworkers, union men and union sympathizers, have been terrorized by a vigilante movement which over the signature *KKK* sent threatening letters and posted threatening notices, in a campaign directed chiefly against the C.I.O. and Harry Bridges. The Klan burned fiery crosses on such occasions as the vigilante mob's destruction of the Finnish Hall and the murder of Laura Law.

The Order of Better Americans keeps its membership secret, but the publishers of the two local newspapers and several county officials who have opposed the C.I.O. are known to belong. This is one of the thousands of organizations supposedly preaching "Americanism" and attacking all other "isms" and red-branding all forces, notably labor, which would lessen the profits of profit-makers. Thus the International Woodworkers of America is called alien and un-American by the Better Americans, who own the press and whose profits come from their businesses, not from their readers. The press intimidates I.W.A. members editorially; Better Americans intimidate labor leaders on the streets of Aberdeen.

The Better Americans and the Better Business Builders have about the same membership and directional set-up. The latter organization is more openly for profit and the suppression of a progressive labor movement. It also seeks to extend its activities throughout industry. Among its notable achievements are: radio programs glorifying the vigilante activities of 1912 and 1919 (when murder and lynching occurred); support of its own candidates for union offices; mass meetings attacking union ofiicials, notably Dick Law; interference with collective bargaining; and "fact-finding" always in favor of the employers.

Pelley's Silver Shirts began their activities in 1936 but decreased them when the Better Business Builders became active in 1938. Their programs are the same regarding labor; there is the same redbaiting, the same attacks on the I.W.A. and the C.I.O.; but the Silver Shirts add anti-Semitism and are more violent attackers of the Roosevelt New Deal than the Better Business Builders.

Two other organizations devoted almost entirely to calling the unions "communist" or "communist-inspired" are the Committee for Industrial Stabilization and the Grays Harbor Citizens Committee, whose memberships are not disclosed. The Grays Harbor Industrial Council, however, is not anonymous. It consists of the major lumber operators and the representatives of other businesses, and its main activity has been to bring pressure on the governor to use the National Guard in Grays Harbor during the 1935 strike, and to employ strike-breakers.

In addition to the activities of these and other bodies in fighting labor, there is a tremendous campaign which calls for violence and bloodshed, but the authors of leaflets and oral illegalities cannot be traced. Their work, however, goes only a logical step beyond that signed, or subscribed to, by the Kluxers, the Silver Shirts, and the Better Business men.

Joseph Schneider, head of the Better Business Builders and representative of employers in their conflict with employees, has publicly announced that he did not kill Laura Law. His bodyguard also denies knowledge of the crime. Joe Cartell, a deputy sheriff, has told all who would listen to him where he was on the night of the murder. Other leading citizens have made similar unasked-for statements.

It is most probable that Laura Law was killed by hoodlums. But apparently there is fear that the actual murderers might tell who hired them, for certain officials have done their best not to solve the crime. The only hope is for federal agents to defy the terrorism which the better citizens, the press, and the radio have created in the county.

Richard Mellon once said: "You can't run a coal mine without machine-guns." Apparently you can't cut lumber in Washington without violence. In 1912 and in 1915 there were riots and deportations of foreign workers; in 1916 there was the Everett massacre; in 1919, the Centralia lynching, in which American Legionnaires played the bloodiest role. In 1937 there was a violent strike, but the Laws helped win that one.

Now they say that Dick Law is a red, that his wife was a red, and that therefore the murder need not be investigated. John Caughlan, deputy prosecuting attorney of Washington, who tried to keep the case going, has been dismissed. "A smokescreen of 'redbaiting' has been raised in an effort to hide the real issues," concludes the National Grays Harbor Committee report.[2]

---

2 This report may be obtained by writing to: National Grays Harbor Committee, 112 East 19th Street, New York City.

Part III

Sample Redbaitors

CHAPTER 10
Easley: America's No. 1 Redbaiter

Who has been the leading redbaiter of America? Hearst? Coughlin? Congressman Dies? Westbrook Pegler? Or Ralph M. Easley?

Most of the great redbaiters simply call themselves patriots. Even Christian Fronters deny that they ever bait anyone. But at least one well-known citizen has declared himself frankly as a redbaiter; Ralph Easley always maintained that he was No. 1 of what Mr. Pegler would call "that ilk."

He was important for two reasons: because for almost forty years he ran the National Civic Federation, which is regarded as one of the most powerful superpatriotic anti-labor organizations of the United States, and because in his career and activities Ralph M. Easley illustrated strikingly the characteristic union of big business, commercial patriotism, obscurantism, and redbaiting. When the Liberty League was formed, Heywood Broun said he approved of one thing about it: that it united every enemy of the American people into one organization and therefore made the attack easier; but the League never had one-tenth the activities and ramifications of the older and equally reactionary National Civic Federation.

Ralph Easley began his career as a newspaperman; in his youth he founded the *Daily News* of Hutchinson, Kansas, whence he moved on to Chicago to write for the *Inter-Ocean* on politics and economics, subjects on which he was an authority, if having violent prejudices makes one an authority. In Chicago he became a "reformer"—at least, so the press informs us—founding the Chicago Civic Federation. Later he transferred to New York and in 1904;

became chairman of a new organization, the National Civic Federation. From 1904 on he devoted himself to attacking labor, and he always boasted that he used the red label against labor long before the red flag was hoisted over the Winter Palace in St. Petersburg.

In the hysteria which followed the World War, Easley joined forces with a group of White Russians, wining and dining titled Tsarist émigrés, keeping them in funds, publishing their plans to restore the Tsar, and circulating their forgeries.

> Soviet Russia [wrote Norman Hapgood] is of course Mr. Easley's chief abomination. He has freely sponsored the cause of the Tsarists, with Mr. Boris Brasol as his chief adviser. Mr. Brasol, one of the heads of the old Russian Black Hundreds [terrorists] came to the United States as a refugee from the revolution, to enlist support for the restoration of the Tsar.[1]

Sidney Howard, the dramatist, wrote at this same time that the professional patriots were co-operating with William J. Burns, who "when he hadn't evidence to convict these 'so-called liberals' and worse," turned the patriots loose

> in his treasure house of rumors and portentous subversive documents. There was meat for them and precious little danger of libel suits, too, with such authority behind them. Dwight Braman sat in the offices of the Allied Patriotic Societies, Inc., and boasted that he was "in almost daily communication with the Department of Justice." Ralph Easley printed the Burns assistance right out in his prospectus of the National Civic Federation's forthcoming "Survey of Progress." A survey of progress, by the National Civic Federation, by the way, is not without certain elements of humor. But

---
1 *Professional Patriots*, edited by Norman Hapgood; material assembled by Sidney Howard and John Hearly (A. & C. Boni, 1927), p. 47.

they had "the co-operation of governmental agencies at Washington . . . !"

In 1926 Easley, who had had his first taste of strike-breaking in 1902 (anthracite) and another in 1916 (steel), entered his Civic Federation into the fight against the textile workers of Passaic, during a strike in which Noel Sargeant of the National Association of Manufacturers was also active. Easley at this time expressed himself in favor of Mussolini, who was then known as the greatest strike-breaker in history. Mussolini, Easley wrote to Ivy Lee, press agent for the Rockefellers, would have made "short work" of Professor Scott Nearing, Dr. Harry F. Ward of Union Theological Seminary, and "all the other reds and pink organizers who are either conducting or aiding and abetting the lesson in Revolution in Passaic. . . ." Two others whom Easley smeared were Professor Jerome Davis of Yale Divinity School and President MacCracken of Vassar.

By 1930 the wiser economists and cleverer business men were becoming aware that the theories of Marx, Engels, and their followers were worth more than a footnote in college text-books: the Russian Five Year Plan had begun to look like a real menace to dollars and profits. Mr. Easley sought to capitalize on the spirit of the moment. In 1931 his Civic Federation brought out a "Plan for an International Movement to Combat the Red Menace." Although Easley tacked on the usual ethical and patriotic trimmings, this plan was frankly commercial. The Civic Federation began its campaign, appropriately, at the Bankers' Club, with His Excellency M. Georges Theunis, former prime minister of Belgium and president of the International Chamber of Commerce, as honor guest and keynote sounder. But while the idealistic Mr. Easley limited himself to noble albeit hysterical generalities, the realistic M. Theunis came out openly for the seizure of Russia's resources.

The first speaker to combat the red menace was the Honorable James W. Gerard, chairman of the Industrial Inquiry Commission of the Federation. Mr. Gerard also spoke frankly:

> We are faced by competition from Russia more serious than mere dumping of goods. It is economic war. . . . Only a change in the Sherman [anti-trust] law will permit us to compete and then on equal terms because we cannot put our workmen on the living scale of Russia.

Matthew Woll, then acting president of the Civic Federation and vice-president of the American Federation of Labor, spoke of Russia as "this Red Monster—this Madman." M. Theunis, after announcing that "business men have a moral responsibility from which they cannot escape," got down to his Russian muttons, or rather, Russian oil for France, Russian lumber for Belgium and England, Russian flax, and Russian agricultural products. If the Five Year Plan succeeded—and M. Theunis quoted figures showing its success by 1931—"the intensified production must find its outlets outside of Russia, on the foreign markets." And there you had the whole story of why Russia was a menace—to the National Civic Federation.

The N.C.F. devoted itself largely to social and political matters, which in Easley's interpretation became strike-breaking, anti-labor propaganda, and redbaiting, but apparently Easley felt the need for a special organization to handle the third of these activities, for he became chairman of the executive committee of a new society—the American Section of the International Committee to Combat the World Menace of Communism. Many of its officers were also Civic Federation officers; others were professional redbaiters, including one (Jung) who was almost immediately exposed as a disseminator of the forgeries known as the *Protocols of Zion*. The first advisory

Easley: America's No. 1 Redbaiter 119

committee of the A.S.I.C.C.W.M.C. consisted of:

> Walter C. Cole, chairman, Council of National Defense, Detroit Board of Commerce
> Brigadier-General John Rose Delafield, commander-in-chief, Military Order of the World War
> Ralph M. Easley, politico-economic writer
> Hamilton Fish, Jr.
> Elon Huntington Hooker, chairman, American Defense Society
> F. O. Johnson, president, Better America Federation
> Lieutenant-Colonel Orvel Johnson, R.O.T.C. Association of the United States
> Harry A. Jung, American Vigilant Intelligence Federation
> Samuel McRoberts, banker
> C. G. Norman, chairman, Building Trades Employers' Association
> Ellis Searles, editor, *The United Mine Worker*
> Walter S. Steele, *National Repubic*

Mr. Easley's next venture was in anti-Semitism, mixed with redbaiting, and a deal with Nazi Germany. He proposed to Morris Waldman, secretary of the American Jewish Committee, that the lies of Hitler against the Jews be answered in a pamphlet. This looked good to the Waldman group. But simultaneously with his conferences with the conservative Jewish leaders, Easley was in touch with George Sylvester Viereck, spokesman for Nazi Germany, to whom he made this proposal: that, immediately after the American Jewish Committee published its statement, Matthew Woll and General Delafield of the Civic Federation should refer the matter to "our German-American members, Messrs. Herman A. Metz, Bernard and Victor Ridder, and George Sylvester Viereck," and ". . . the answer to the American Jewish Committee's pamphlet will open the way for the National Socialist Party of Germany to give its whole case"—after which Easley might propose that the Jews of America drop their boycott of Germany, and the Germans ease restrictions on the Jews.

Easley next proposed that several conservative Jews, notably Judge Joseph Proskauer, endorse a Nazi book, *Communism in Germany,* which was the usual double-barrelled attack on Jews and communism. The judge refused. He wrote two letters explaining his position. In one, addressed to General Delafield, he says: "I need hardly say to you that I am no communist, but that the National Civic Federation should be misled into giving the stamp of its approval on this particular work is to me incredible. . . . I very earnestly trust that the National Civic Federation, in which I have a deep interest, will not make any such misstep." To Mr. Easley, Judge Proskauer wrote: "Any book which directly and by innuendo identifies Jews and Communists is an anti-Semitic book. This is the essence of the situation. The rest is embroidery. . . . I sincerely hope that this project will be abandoned."

When Hearst needed a special list of big-money redbaiters, he went to Easley; when Easley wanted to publicize one of his particularly unsavory ventures, he had only to send his writings to Hearst to get them disseminated throughout the nation. Naturally, it was therefore a *faux pas* to ask Mr. Easley to participate in a demonstration "against the outstanding peddler of jaundiced journalism" (Mr. Hearst), but Mr. Easley was asked and his reply is worth noting:

> I do not endorse all the things Mr. Hearst has said and done during the last twenty years. When during the World War he was supporting the German cause, I wanted to shoot him.
>
> But what he has been doing the past two years to clean the Reds out of this country has been so wonderful and fine that all my feeling against him has disappeared. Today he has more patriotism in his little finger than is to be found in the whole bunch of Reds in the American League Against War and Fascism.

Easley: America's No. 1 Redbaiter

> If l were going to do any shooting now, I should pick out some members of the "Peoples Committee Against Hearst."

This confession of the killer-instinct in our leading patriot aroused the well-known columnist, Ernest L. Meyer, who pointed out that Easley's associates in the National Civic Federation were: Archibald E. Stevenson, counsel, "chief witch sniffer during the anti-Red drives of the past 15 years . . . bankers, pastors, big industrialists, Senator Royal S. Copeland of New York, a member of the ranks of the Hearstlings, and Dr. Frederick B. Robinson, president of the College of the City of New York, who once used an umbrella to disperse campus radicals and therefore cannot be accused of advocating shooting but merely bumbershooting." He added:

> The purposes of the National Civic Federation as outlined in its literature are "to organize the best brains of the nation in an educational movement . . . to aid thus in crystallization of the most enlightened public opinion. . . ."
>
> If I read Mr. Easley's letter correctly, he would aid in organizing the best brains of the country by blowing them out with a shotgun.

When the La Follette committee was going after the violators of the Bill of Rights, the labor-baiters, the employers of spies and thugs, the users of poison gas against workmen, it was planned to call the directors of the following organizations to determine what part, if any, they have played in thwarting "the right of labor to organize and bargain collectively":

1. National Association of Manufacturers
2. National Civic Federation
3. Constitutional Educational League (Connecticut)
4. League for Industrial Rights

5. New York State Economic Council
6. Johnstown, Pennsylvania, Chamber of Commerce[2]

John O'Donnell and Doris Eleeson reported that it was planned to call Easley to make him testify under oath "with respect to the truth of 'Red scare charges' alleged to be circulated to needle up cash contributions" for his organization. Easley, the Washington correspondents continued, "blossomed forth as a self-appointed strategist in the Jeremiah Mahoney staff headquarters," from where he conducted his redbaiting campaign. The committee also intended to question Matthew Woll and ex-Ambassador James W. Gerard. Mayor LaGuardia, the correspondents concluded, was laughing up his sleeve at the impending expose of Easley and his National Civic Federation, because

> . . . One of the last chores that La Guardia polished off as a member of Congress was to puncture the "Communist Plot" scare which Easley, Congressman Ham Fish, and the then Police Cornmissioner of New York, Grover Whalen, suddenly flashed on a jittery Congress eight years ago with solemn warnings that Red spies were about to take over New York and the nation.
>
> At that time, in a manner never yet made clear, Easley, Whalen and Fish got possession of identical copies of supposedly Communist revolutionary plans of Moscow origin. After the trio placed them before Congress, LaGuardia traced the "Moscow papers" to an East Side printing press where an ambitious gentleman with a rough knowledge of Russian had dictated a few documents for sale to what was later described as "the sucker trade."

(There is one slight error in this report: the discoverer of the plot to smear the reds and the exposer of the forgery was a New York reporter named John L. Spivak, ace

---

[2] New York *Daily News*, November 11, 1937, p. 16.

investigator-journalist of America.)

In a long life devoted almost exclusively to fighting labor, liberals, radicals, and reds, Easley served big business and the *status quo* with great devotion. In turn he attacked the American Federation of Labor, the Industrial Workers of the World, and the Congress of Industrial Organizations. (At other times he embraced the A.F. of L., co-operated with Samuel Gompers, and later with Matthew Woll, and tried his best to split the labor movement, when he was not actually helping discredit it.)

In 1930 Easley got Elihu Root, honorary president of the Civic Federation, to sign a letter urging the "creation of a federal spy force . . . to hound and harry radical workers."

On October 7, 1938, Easley announced the formation of a Committee of One Hundred on American Civil and Property Rights in Mexico, to protect American-owned mining, oil, timber, fruit and farm lands, factories, and other properties; to co-operate with a million stockholders who had interests in and drew dividends from Mexico. Its purpose was to put more pressure on the State Department (which already was under the pressure of Standard Oil of New Jersey and other big American businesses) to defeat the great social experiment in Mexico which aims to wipe out poverty at the expense of big property. The usual cry of "Red Mexico" was raised.

It is interesting to note that baiters—whether red-, labor-, Jew-, Catholic-, or alien-baiters—generally oppose all progress in laws, education, and social welfare. Thus we find the National Civic Federation on record:

> Opposed to minimum wages for women
> Opposed to social insurance
> Favoring a Mussolini in American affairs (Easley)
> Publishing a pamphlet, "Free Speech a Nuisance"
> Opposing old-age legislation
> Opposing labor's right to organize
> Opposing the closed shop
> Attacking the recognition of the Soviets

Opposing the youth movement

This is the history of the self-announced No. 1 redbaiter in America. If ever there was an open-and-shut case of redbaiting for profit, this was it; but Easley was a hero to the American press, the favorite spokesman for Hearst, and rarely in almost forty years was his financial motivation ever mentioned.

Chapter 11
George E. Sokolsky

The New York *Herald Tribune* not only refused to publish factual advertisements for *Lords of the Press* but it suppressed a review of this book at the time it was published. Recently, however, a vicious attack on the book and upon myself as its author appeared in the column written by George E. Sokolsky, on the editorial page of this great Republican Party newspaper.

The publication of this smear creates a delicate problem for me, so I have decided not to say anything about Mr. Sokolsky, but to let the record speak for itself. The rest of this chapter consists of quotations from government and other documents and from the press. This is the raw material from which articles are written, and the reader will have to piece it together and draw his own conclusions without editorial assistance.

Document No. 1 is from the Nye-Vandenberg senatorial investigations of the munitions industry—the "merchants of death" story:

> SENATOR CLARK: Along further in that letter [from a munitions maker], in the second paragraph on the second page, you say:
>
> "So you would know what we are doing, we gave you in confidence the name of George Sokolsky, who is now in New York, and, according to our information, although he does not say so himself, Mr. Sokolsky represents the Soong interests. You know Mr. T. V. Soong is the Chinese finance minister, and his sister is the wife of President Chiang Kai-shek. At our request Mr. Sokolsky about two weeks ago sent a cable in his

private code to Mr. T. V. Soong, asking if he was interested in obtaining supplies of 7.9 cartridges, but so far no response has come in."

So you identify Mr. Sokolsky, whom you had send cables over to China for you.

MR. MONAGHAN: I do not recall how I met Mr. Sokolsky. I did meet him in New York at that time.

SENATOR CLARK: During that time he was a foreign correspondent for the New York *Times*, wasn't he?

MR. MONAGHAN: I recall reading articles of his in the New York *Times* that impressed me greatly.

SENATOR CLARK: That was his ostensible business, was it not, being correspondent for the New York *Times?*

MR. MONAGHAN: I do not know.

SENATOR CLARK: Mr. Sokolsky, so I am informed, is now touring the United States lecturing in the interests of the necessity for heavy armaments.

Agnes Smedley, the author, writing of the "Corrupt Press in China," said:

> The Japanese are by no means niggardly in dealing with the press in China. An outstanding example of their methods is the *Far Eastern Review,* an American-owned and registered engineering monthly which is openly financed by the Japanese. The owner and editor is George Bronson Rea, who perambulated around Washington as "adiviser" to the Japanese puppet state of Manchoukuo—at a fat salary. When Mr. Rea was away from China on his sacred mission of aiding Japanese imperialism his position on the *Review* was taken for a time by another American, George Sokolsky. Mr. Sokolsky, however, seemed a bit more broad-minded than Mr. Rea, for he traveled back and forth between the *Review* office and the office of the Ministry of Finance of the Nanking government, with occasional side trips to the British consulate.[1]

The *Nation* book review of Sokolsky's book, *Labor*

---
1 *The Nation*, July 3, 1935.

Fights for Power (an anti-labor book) said: "If Mr. Sokolsky's book has not yet been subsidized by the National Association of Manufacturers, it should have been."

In his *Herald Tribune* column of April 20, 1936, Sokolsky chided his fellow-columnist, Dorothy Thompson, for denouncing those who employ the 200 detective agencies' thugs and strike-breakers in industry. Sokolsky wrote: "Who hired these agencies? Why not give the names of the agencies?" (Almost immediately the La Follette committee did so, naming also writers employed by the same business corporations, including Mr. Sokolsky.)

In his August 1936 article in the *Atlantic Monthly*, Sokolsky wrote:

> I speak as a conservative. In my youth I ran the gamut of revolutionary movements. Anarchist, pacifist, I.W.W. sympathizer, I have sought a better, a more commodious life, not only for myself, but for all men. . . . Let no man think of me as a tory . . . a heartless marauder in a predatory world. For I have nothing to defend. I have nothing of the goods of this world but what I earn and consume today.

Reviewing reactionary and other columnists, the *Nation* wrote in its October 24, 1936, issue:

> The liberal reader may feel that Walter Lippmann has gone over to the enemy with altogether too much gusto, or that Dorothy Thompson's sympathies lie too far to the right to be consistent with her experience in Hitler's Germany. As for Mark Sullivan, he is almost an appealing figure as he stands roundly in the ranks of the redbaitors much more vicious than himself, still striking out at Tugwell with his trusty cutlass. Even a "Red" would scarcely accuse these writers of being worse than conservative or reactionary. There is, however, one burned-out star in the *Herald Tribune's* galaxy which should be replaced before it shortcircuits the whole

string. We refer to George E. Sokolsky. On October 19th Mr. Sokolsky wrote an article on the American Labor Party. Maintaining his old pretense of being an "expert" on labor and radicalism (some of his best friends are radicals!) he cooked up a mess of misrepresentation, labor-, Jew-, and alien-baiting which Sokolsky himself has seldom surpassed. We feel that the *Herald Tribune,* aside from soiling its pages, is keeping apart two minds that run as one. Isn't it possible that Mr. Sokolsky could be auctioned off to William Randolph Hearst? He long ago reached the stage of journalistic ripeness which usually precedes that fall.

In December 1937 word got around that the La Follette civil liberties committee was about to expose the newspapers, newspaper columnists, magazine writers, advertising agencies, and others who had worked for the Little Steel corporations and helped break the strike. On December 20, 1937, Sokolsky devoted his column to an explanation of his double job as columnist in the supposedly free and decent newspapers and employee of the National Association of Manufacturers, who were breaking a strike. He wrote:

> Well, it was not long before I became a sort of consultant for the National Association of Manufacturers. What they wanted of me was my point of view, and then they seemed to go their own middle course. . . .
>
> Subsequently I came into the same relationship with the American Iron and Steel Institute, and there I found some congenial spirits, but others who regard me as a queer duck. . . .
>
> There is tremendous value in this relationship—particularly since I have been writing these pieces. Journalism is supposed to be objective, but objectivity has the defect of always seeing things altogether from the outside. This relationship has given me an opportunity to see things from the inside. . . .

> But through it all there has been this magnificent possibility, that I might be doing something of value for a country which I happen to love, because I was hammering on a fundamental philosophy of life. . . . And my conservatism made me a Republican. . . .

Throughout 1936 and 1937, Mr. Sokolsky wrote dozens of attacks on the C.I.O. He referred to "communist influence" in the C.I.O. and quoted Ben Stolberg, a writer of similar anti-labor pieces for the *World-Telegram.* He also wrote:

> Let it never be forgotten that the Bolsheviks were once in a united front with Kerensky. . . . We are living through the most critical period in American history since the Civil War—a period of evolution in which the Government united with the revolutionists to change the form of government . . . a revolution by an administration against the people. Instead of resorting to seizures of private property, strikes, inquisitions and destructive legislation are the tools of the revolutionists. . . .

Mr. Sokolsky also wrote: "A communist parade looks Jewish"; and "Jews who believe that they must be 'liberals' and 'progressives' as a protest against Hitler are risking the welfare of all the Jews of the United States."

Now let us see what a really liberal, independent, and honest journalist, Kenneth Crawford, later president of the Newspaper Guild, has to say:

> Girdler was able to break the Little Steel strike under the protective armor not only of company guards, police and National Guardsmen, but of sympathetic public opinion as well.
> Girdler's Republic Steel spent $1,950,000 to break the strike. It hired a large force of company gorillas, equipped them with quantities of tear gas, rifles, pistols and slugs. Its police officers hired spies. . . .

> The La Follette Civil Liberties Committee got around to its investigation of the Little Steel strike a year after the event. . . . It stripped away the curtain of pretense and told the real story. Girdler's pious statements prove to be flimsy tissues. But the newspapers were not interested. Truth was too slow to catch up with untruth. . . .
>
> During the C.I.O. steel organization campaign, Hill & Knowlton, which had connections with the N.A.M. and the Iron & Steel Institute as well as Republic Steel, devised various ingenious schemes for turning public opinion against the union. . . . Besides financing the newspaper advertisements, the N.A.M., through Hill & Knowlton, pawned off George Sokolsky, New York *Herald Tribune* columnist, as an impartial speaker at meetings sponsored by the local associations. Sokolsky was on the Hill & Knowlton payroll at $1000 a month, but his salary was paid to the publicity firm by the N.A.M. In fact, the N.A.M. not only paid Sokolsky well for "consultation" but also gave the local organizations a fee of $50 to finance the meetings he addressed.

The Steel City Industrial Union (Pittsburgh) passed the following resolution:

> Whereas the Pittsburgh *Post-Gazette* in its report of the La Follette findings deleted from the Associated Press news stories all references to the fact that George Sokolsky was thus exposed. . . .
>
> Resolved, that we condemn such editorial conduct on the part of the Pittsburgh *Post-Gazette* as being designed to mislead and deceive the public.

The *Post-Gazette* replied:

> . . . The story we ran was in exact accordance with the story we received from the Associated Press. . . . We sent to the AP and asked them for a copy of the story that was sent to us and I am enclosing it and you will find that it is exactly in accordance with what we ran in our

paper. In fact, we would have no right to change a story sent by any news service. . . .

So far as Mr. George Sokolsky is concerned, after what I have now heard and read, I think we will cut him out of our paper, because interesting and capable as his writing may be, we do not want any propagandist to write for our paper and, from the information you have sent in, it looks very much as if he could come under the head of a propagandist.

I am not claiming that he is such. I know nothing about it. . . .

[Signed] PAUL BLOCK

But David J. McDonald, Secretary of the Steel City Independent Union Council, was not satisfied. He wrote:

I am forced to take exception to your explanation of the fact that the Pittsburgh *Post-Gazette* did not publish one word about the fact that George Sokolsky was on the payroll of the National Manufacturers Association, and other information about him revealed by the La Follette Civil Liberties Committee.

. . . Your letter conveys the impression that the Associated Press denied to its morning paper clients all knowledge of the Sokolsky exposé. I wonder are you aware that within an hour or two after the "Night Lead Civil Liberties" story cleared on the Associated Press wires, the same news agency carried several hundred additional words dealing with the Sokolsky angle? We had knowledge of these facts. . . .

The New York *Post* and the *World-Telegram* played the story of the exposure of George Sokolsky on the front page, using his name in the headline. The *Herald Tribune* got around to the name in the second part of the headline. The *Times* did not use the name in the headline at all, and suppressed most of the news about the columnist, in fact suppressed much more of the La Follette evidence than the

Herald Tribune suppressed. The *Herald Tribune,* however, wrote an editorial in which it did not mention the scandal but merely said that there were all kinds of pressures being used on newspapers.

Heywood Broun accused the New York *Sun* of totally suppressing the story of Sokolsky and the *Herald Tribune.* He also accused the *Post, World-Telegram, Times, Herald Tribune*, and especially the Associated Press, which sent the item to its 1200 papers, of suppressing the name of the *Herald Tribune* and Sokolsky's connection with it. Broun suggested that a congressional investigation of the newspapers of America take up "l'affaire Sokolsky," that "the American Newspaper Publishers Association would have been wise years ago to have created a group within its own ranks to police the ethics of the craft and discourage questionable practices. . . ." Broun also suggested that if Sokolsky's column should no longer appear in the Herald Tribune "it might be possible to procure an equally impartial commentator on the subject of the rights of labor. There's always Gerald K. Smith."

In conclusion Heywood Broun wrote: "Mr. Sokolsky should choose whether to remain as vox populi or vox Republic. In either case he will not suffer, for the time seems just about ripe for him to write a book entitled 'From Reds to Riches.'"

In mid-summer 1940, Sokolsky quit the *Herald Tribune* to join the New York *Sun,* thus reaching the nadir in commercial journalism.

CHAPTER 12
Matthews: Convert to Redbaiting

A follower of Karl Marx and believer in socialism as a scientific, economic, and philosophic system for the betterment of the world, J. B. Matthews made his contribution by exposing commercial corruption. With the collaboration of Miss Ruth Shallcross, formerly of the New York State Labor Department, he wrote a book designed to help the reader detect dishonest trade practices in America. Speaking of the situation in general, he wrote: "Business is a . . . series of frauds, utilizing methods, both in its production and distribution, which are indistinguishable in spirit and effects from the practices of gangsterism."

But that is not all. "In business, plunder is of the essence. The spirit of thought as well as the sources of physical life for the masses are poisoned when poisoning is profitable, adulterated when adulteration is profitable, and otherwise exploited in ways that blight and despoil."

And what is the ultimate end of our big business system, our national practice of fraud? Mr. Matthews and his associate come to the conclusion that there will be "an out-and-out Fascist regime . . . in the intensification of the normal and accepted practices of conventional business, and in the sanctification of those practices by charlatans and more sober officials in government service." Unless stopped, business will enter "into the excesses of black reaction. . . ." America faces a fascist rule dominated by men of the Du Pont-Morgan tribe, the group which Lundberg later called the "Sixty Families."

In 1935 the employees of Consumers Research, of which Matthews was a director, went out on strike. They were striking against a wage of $13.13 a week, and they wanted to join the American Federation of Labor. The National Labor Relations Board not only decided in their favor but insisted that Consumers Research pay the strikers a thousand dollars.

One of the managers of the organization who stood by the workers was Arthur Kallet, co-author with F. J. Schlink (head of Consumers Research) of the book, 100,000,000 *Guinea Pigs*. Kallet, with the sympathy and co-operation of scores of leading citizens throughout the country, announced the formation of Consumers Union, a testing and reporting laboratory similar to Consumers Research, but a non-profit-making venture and a union shop in which all employees would receive the best wages possible, depending on membership subscriptions. Within a short time its membership outstripped that of its rival, and C.U. became so important that the New York *Times*, with its big-money advertisers in mind, refused to accept the little money which C.U. could spend on its campaign to enlighten the American consumer about his purchases.

How important the various non-profit-making pro-consumer movements had become throughout the nation was soon realized by the advertising fraternity, which controls the expenditure of between one billion and one and a half billion dollars a year (of which $500,000,000 is for making fraudulent claims, according to W. E. Humphreys, Federal Trade Commissioner). According to *Time*, big business for ten years has been debating whether to treat consumer education as a flea in its ear or a bulldog at its throat; it estimated the number of persons who were receiving some sort of consumer enlightenment at twenty-nine million, and viewed with alarm the increased activity of the government in this field under the New Deal, with the A.A.A. Consumers' Counsel Division, the Home Economics Bureau, the Extension Service of the Department of Agriculture, the Office of Education. Naturally enough, the most powerful leader against this form of public education and for the protection of those who advertise and sell was William Randolph Hearst. (One of the institutions criticized and exposed by C.U. was Hearst's *Good Housekeeping* together with its seals of approval, its institute, and its other obscure services to the advertising world.)

In the late thirties big business launched an advertising campaign against the co-operatives and consumer groups. It is, however, difficult to find weapons to fight a movement which has nothing but humanitarian, philanthropic aims and which seeks to further the general welfare of the people rather than the pocketbooks of a few individuals. Evidently the defenders of the profit-seekers knew this very well, for they could find no better line of attack than to pin the old red flag on the consumer and co-operative movements.

In 1937, Director Matthews of Consumers Research, who had been among the first to point out the relationship between reactionary big business and advertising and the ultimate working arrangement between the two to the detriment of the people's welfare, now devoted his writing to attacking labor organizations and Communists and praising "private competitive enterprise" as the "best available servant of consumers' interests." In 1938 the efforts of Consumers Research to smear those with whom it had been closely associated in the past led even *Newsweek*, itself dependent upon advertising, to say that "although Schlink was once considered a pro-labor liberal, the C.R. strike shifted him and his organization (which he, his wife and two others control) far to the Right. His . . . *Consumers Digest* now frightens its 40,000 readers with Red scares in the best 1920 manner."

Matthews and Schlink, indeed, tried to out-Palmer Mitchell Palmer, and naturally enough among those they redbaited was the rival which was gaining members at a greater pace than their own organization. In February 1938 these two bitter men published in their magazine two articles, one "A Consumers' Program" and the other entitled "A New Way for Making Suckers," in which violent language, hysterics, smearing propaganda, and redbaiting are mixed in about equal proportions. They alleged that "the entire philosophy of the New Deal has made depression one of its social ideals"; all the liberal reform laws were denounced and their repeal demanded; the Wagner Act was called "the greatest piece of legislative chicane"; the Social Security Act was called "the most dishonest piece of legislation ever devised," and the new farm law "fascistic intervention." Finally, eleven pages were devoted to alleging that all consumer-advice organizations except their own, but notably their rival, are really the Communist Party in disguise. Said the *New Republic:* "We hope few, if any, alert consumers will be taken in by *Consumers Digest's* malicious false branding in the field of political commentary."

J. B. Matthews had been what is sneeringly known as a "fellow-traveler," meaning that he was on the side of labor, of progressive movements, for democracy, against fascism, and willing to co-operate in any popular or united front of the people—including even Republicans, and not excluding Communists, Socialists, and others generally labeled reds. In fact, Mr. Matthews had been so devout a worker for human rights and the general welfare that he reached high positions and played a considerable role in these fields. All this came to an end when he was caught on the employers' side of the strike against a wage of thirteen dollars a week.

Naturally enough the whole liberal-labor movement was incensed by the actions of Matthews, Schlink, and company in fighting their employees and labeling the strikers reds; and when the Labor Board ruled in favor of the working men and women, the liberal press poured vitriolic irony over Consumers Research. As for the commercial press, it had an Olympian field day. Here was a chance for double revenge: against Matthews, Schlink, *et al* personally and, more important, against a consumer organization which had boasted it was serving the people and was found to be underpaying its help.

The *Herald Tribune*, for example, sneered at the "sterling purity of purpose, the sea green incorruptibility and stern, unbending devotion to the common man of Consumers Research, Inc." (The strike, of course, had nothing to do with the integrity of the goods-testing of CR; moreover, the *Herald Tribune* had suppressed the news of the strike at the National Biscuit Company, in which the Tribune owner had six millions of dollars' worth of stock.) After reporting "dissension in that righteous heaven," the editorial writer concluded that "the calling of a strike against Consumers Research is confirmation of the doubts as to whether there has been, except in the fleeting moments of outrage over some particularly flagrant gyp, such a thing as The Consumer." It was all very good-natured irony, different from the uncouth language in the liberal-labor press, showing that the *Herald Tribune* is so superior it can afford "tolerance."

But four years later, when Matthews had plodded the long road from fellow-traveler of the reds to agent of the Dies committee, the Herald Tribune was no longer supercilious about him. It now made him a five-and-one-half column hero; it was the only paper that spread over the front page and over onto the inside pages, complete to the last syllable, his redbaiting, his personal revenge on past associates, his renegade blasts at all his old friends, and his general smear of liberal institutions.

One can, however, marvel at the crude effrontery of the newly created Dies agent: the first man he smeared was his former colleague, Arthur Kallet, now director of Consumers Union; and the first woman smeared was Susan Jenkins, who had not liked the thirteen-dollar-a-week wage Matthews' Consumers Research was paying, who had picketed the place, and who had enlisted the sympathy of many organizations, including the League of Women Shoppers.

The complete list of consumer organizations smeared in the Matthews report to the Dies committee as being "under

Communist influence" are:

> New York Consumers' Council
> Greenwich Village High Cost of Living Conference
> City Action Committee against High Cost of Living
> Consumers' National Federation
> United Conference against High Cost of Living
> League of Women Shoppers
> Consumers Union
> Committee for Boycott against Japanese Aggression
> Milk Consumers Protective Committee
> Consumers-Farmer Milk Co-operative
> Central Action Committee against High Cost of Living (Detroit)
> Central Action Committee against High Cost of Living (Bronx)
> United Conference against High Cost of Living (Los Angeles)

From the very titles of the organizations it is obvious that they have such objectives as the protection of the people against manufacturers or middlemen who would cheat them, co-operation, or the dissemination of American policies such as the boycott of Japan and a square deal for labor. But it is also obvious that the majority of these organizations are merely there for show, like "filler" in a cheap pie; the objectives of the big smear were Consumers Union and the League of Women Shoppers, the two institutions against which Matthews had a personal grudge, and whose harm would be to Matthews's profit.

Consumers Union does the same kind of analysis as the Matthews-Schlink Consumers Research, but in addition it tells its subscribers about the labor policy of manufacturers, endorsing the good, exposing the bad, and perhaps more important still, it is not a profit-making business. The rival is. As for the League of Women Shoppers, it is an organization whose membership includes socially prominent, wealthy, and conservative women and whose purpose is to make impartial investigations of labor troubles. It uses its buying power for economic justice, and that is the policy which Matthews once wholeheartedly endorsed but now opposed.

The entire report is based on *association*. Miss Jenkins worked for the League of Women Shoppers, Miss Jenkins was once a telephone operator at the *Daily Worker*, the *Daily Worker* is the newspaper of the Communist Party; therefore, the League of Women Shoppers is Communist. But Stuart Chase immediately applied the same reasoning to Dies, Matthews, Pegler, and the National Association of Manufacturers. Mr. Dies hired Matthews; Matthews was once a fellow-traveler; fellow-travelers, according to the redbaiters, are Communists. "Follow your own logic," concludes Mr. Chase. "Once a Communist always a Communist. . . . You are now being run by a Communist. . . . You associate night and day with a Communist. Therefore, without any ifs, ands or buts, Mr. Dies, *you are a Communist!*"[1] (In the same way: Communists are members of the Newspaper Guild; Pegler is a member of the Guild; therefore, Pegler is a Communist.) Similarly, Matthews alleges that "all those who criticize advertising are attempting to destroy capitalism, and so are part of the Red legions. The advertising agencies have long maintained Better Business Bureaus, whose function is to uncover, attack and destroy fraudulent and misleading advertising. Consumers similarly attack fraudulent and misleading advertising." Therefore, the Matthews claim that consumers' organizations subscribe to the philosophy of Lenin in doing this work applies equally to the advertisers.

The Matthews report as a defense of advertising takes on added interest when compared with his writing of only a few years back:

> Advertising, in its spirit and purpose, is germinal fascism. Hitler was the first European politician who

---
1 *New Republic*, January 29, 1940.

saw the significance of the technique of commercial advertising for politics. In *Mein Kampf* he used the distinctly commercial word *"Reklame"*—advertising—to describe his political method. Advertising is more than sales ballyhoo: it is a form of social organization which utilizes the most mechanical contrivances for a regimentation that is both commercial and political.

By one of those coincidences which sometimes enlighten the world, both the New York *Times* and *Herald Tribune* carried on their front pages, along with the Matthews attack on consumer groups, the story of how the Federal Trade Commission had declared fraudulent the advertising of the leading automobile corporations of America. General Motors and Ford had been ordered to cease and desist from advertising their instalment plan as adding only 6 percent to the price. Millions of Americans had been fooled by this advertising for years, but although Consumers Union had exposed its fallacy, the newspapers still took the auto ads and refused to take those of CU. If ever there was a vindication for the liberal and radical weeklies, the labor press, and consumer organizations, it was this government action; if ever there was an indictment of the corruption of our self-styled free press, it was this same government action; for the former had published the news for years, the latter had suppressed it for years.

The commercial press, however, did not pay any attention to this ironical and revealing coincidence; on the contrary, it let loose all its largest redbaiting headlines. The New York *Sun* had, for example, a two-column head reading: "Another Red 'Trojan Horse.' Dies Committee Investigator Relates How Communists Rule Consumer Groups." And a one-column head; "Report Shows Red Onslaught on Advertising." To the answers of three organizations that the report was slanderous, libelous, and false, the *Sun* gave exactly three paragraphs at the bottom of the one-column story. The only newspaper which carried the story in an ethical manner was the New York *Post,* which gave equal space to the attacks and the replies. Some of the papers carried the replies in full, some in part, some suppressed them. Consumers Union issued a statement which offered to produce "sworn statements by Mr. Matthews himself which contradict testimony given by him later before the Dies committee and which open the motivations of his present charge to serious question. In this connection Consumers Union's counsel, Mr. A. J. Isserman, officially presented to the Dies committee some time ago evidence of perjury by Mr. Matthews in his testimony before the committee. The committee has failed to take any cognizance of this."

Every organization named branded the report a lie. Every organization knew that inasmuch as Matthews had issued his report through a congressman, there could be no suit for libel. The redbaiting damage had been done. And no one could expect that the press, whose lifeblood is advertising, would give the smeared organizations a square deal. In no New York newspaper except the *Daily Worker* can I find the following answer to Dies by Secretary of the Interior Ickes, who said in an address at Town Hall, Newark:

> When we reach the point where consumer services are damned as communistic in official releases of a Congressional committee simply because they dare to warn housewives against claims of fake advertising, it is time for us to begin to wonder whether a body supposedly functioning to protect the public from subversive influence isn't really being perverted to protect subversive influences from the public.

Among the few newspapers which editorially discredited Matthews and his work was the St. Louis *Post-Dispatch,* which said:

> Consumer organizations are performing a vital work. . . . Can an unbiased observer find any taint of Moscow

in such efforts to protect the public from injury and fraud? There are Communists among the members of these groups, to be sure, but there are also Democrats, Republicans and Socialists. The new attitude of Mr. Matthews, ex-champion of consumer interests, is a sorry attempt to injure an increasingly helpful work.

Within a few days came another reply—and it too was suppressed by most of our "free and independent" newspapers. It concerned a piece of secret maneuvering behind the scenes by Hearst's biggest money-making publication, some of the manufacturers of nostrums which have been exposed by both Consumers Research and Consumers Union, and by George E. Sokolsky.

The Federal Trade Commission had taken action. Its press release said:

> Hearst Magazines, Inc., 57th Street and 8th Avenue, New York, of which *Good Housekeeping* is a wholly owned subsidiary, is charged in a complaint issued by the Federal Trade Commission with misleading and deceptive acts and practices in the issuance of Guarantees, Seals of Approval, and the publication in its advertising pages of grossly exaggerated and false claims for products advertised therein.

This was a tremendous thing, a brave thing even for a government body, for the F.T.C. was challenging the Lord of San Simeon, something no administration, Republican or Democratic, liberal or reactionary, had ever done. Not even the administrations which Hearst had smeared for a half-century had ever attacked his profits, so fearful is everyone of the power of the press, and especially of Hearst's yellow, redbaiting press. *Advertising Age* thought the action "the most significant news of the year," and *Business Week* said the entire advertising trade felt the "concussion" of the government's "bomb."

Ever since 1902, *Good Housekeeping* has guaranteed its

advertising pages, and for a long time it has been handing out seals which manufacturers could put on their products. *Good Housekeeping* claims these seals are given regardless of advertising, though that claim was disputed by at least one advertiser at the government hearings. But one thing not disputed is that many products advertised in *Good Housekeeping* from 1902 on have from time to time been found fraudulent, or in violation of food and drug laws, and their manufacturers compelled to change their formulas and advertising by the federal government. Moreover, scores of articles which get the *Good Housekeeping* Seal of Approval, get the Consumers Union bronx cheer. For example, C.U. disapproved of all dentrifices containing sodium perborate, which burns the mouth and which should be used only on dentists' orders; this was in accordance with the findings of the American Dental Association, but *Good Housekeeping* gave its seal to several dentrifices reported to contain this possibly harmful substance.

Good Housekeeping has brought Mr. Hearst about two million dollars' profit a year. It is one of the biggest advertising mediums in America, but Consumers Union found that frequently "products bearing one or another of the *Good Housekeeping* seals were inferior, or potentially harmful, or overpriced, or otherwise poor buys."

One of *Good Housekeeping's* biggest advertisers is The Lambert Pharmacal Co., which ran a page advertisement for Listerine with these headlines: "The New, Easy, Scientific Way
to GET RID OF DANDRUFF." The Federal Trade Commission investigated Listerine, and later announced that the Lambert company had agreed to cease and desist from representing that Listerine either cures or permanently relieves dandruff, that it "kills the dandruff germ," "attacks the cause of dandruff," or "gets at the cause"; that it has "marked curative properties," etc., when such are not the facts.

More embarrassing still were the cases of

Fleischmann's Yeast and Welch's Grape Juice. They had advertised in *Good Housekeeping; Good Housekeeping* had guaranteed their ads and given them Seals of Approval; and later Fleischmann and Welch confessed to the F.T.C. that their claims were "false and misleading." Even worse than that, *Advertising Age* quotes F.T.C. officials as saying that "about 80 prominent national advertisers whose copy appears regularly in *Good Housekeeping* have entered into stipulations with the Commission to cease and desist from certain advertising practices since the Wheeler-Lea Act went into effect. . . ." They admitted their advertising fraudulent. CU said it would take a very clever lawyer indeed to extricate *Good Housekeeping* from this dilemma.

Richard E. Berlin, executive vice-president of Hearst Magazines, Inc., answered the governments triple charge—that (1) many buyers were confused and misled; (2) the guarantees were open to misunderstanding; (3) the advertisements contained "grossly exaggerated and false claims"—with three thousand telegrams to advertisers and publishers in which he charged that it was all a deep-dyed red plot and promised publicly to expose the "subversive" consumer movement.

"Certain subversive elements, pretending to serve the consuming public but actually motivated by Communistic theories," repeated Mr. Berlin, during the hearings, "have persistently been attacking the institution of advertising and *Good Housekeeping* as a leading medium in the field. We believe that this subversive movement must be publicly exposed."

Mr. Berlin bought full-page advertisements in the magazines and in the newspapers. Perhaps it was a coincidence that the news of the four months' hearings were generally suppressed. Frank Jellinek wrote in the *New Republic:*

> When the hearings opened on October 31 there was no news about them in the New York dailies so far as I

can discover. There was, however, an extremely prominent report of the speech by Martin Dies at the annual luncheon of the Associated Grocery Manufacturers of America at the Waldorf Astoria. In this speech he threatened to investigate "Communistic influences" in consumer groups and called for "business leadership" to drive out "demagogues and racketeers who are able to sway the emotions of an uninformed people and teach them the damnable doctrines of socialism and communism? That same day, no doubt by coincidence, the New York *Times* carried a full-page advertisement for *Good Housekeeping.* The New York *Herald Tribune* of November 6 had a sharp attack by George Sokolsky, the columnist whose connection with the NAM is a matter of public record, in which he struck out at a book by George Seldes, *Lords of the Press*. As *New Republic* readers know, it is the thesis of this book that large financial interests, through their control of advertising, often exert powerful pressure on the policies of periodicals. The *Good Housekeeping* full page appeared in the same issue of the *Herald Tribune* as the Sokolsky tirade. Large space was also bought in many other papers, including the weeklies *Time* and *Newsweek,* neither of which, so far as I can find, printed a word about the F.T.C. proceedings before Matthews himself broke the story.

And finally the profiteers of redbaiting were completely exposed by Drew Pearson and Robert S. Allen (co-authors of *Washington Merry-Go-Round*) and by David Munro, publisher of *Space & Time*. Mr. Pearson has permitted me to use their report in full, and here it is. He and Allen wrote on Christmas morning, 1939:

> Congressman Dies may not realize it yet, but he has just made the greatest mistake of his entire un-American Activities career. He has ignored the oldest adage of smart politicians, lawyers, newspaper editors and others who have to get along with folks—namely, never to attack a woman.

Dies has ignored that rule to the point of attacking thousands of women. Through a chief investigator, J. B. Matthews, he issued a report tying the tag of "COMMUNIST" upon the League of Women Shoppers and various other ladies' consumer organizations.

They are so irate that they plan to turn the tables on Dies and have his committee investigated at the next session of Congress. And, judging from some of their inside sleuthing, it looks as if they might succeed.

Most startling thing the ladies claim to have discovered is that at about the time J. B. Matthews issued his report calling consumers' organizations communistic, he attended a dinner in New York at which various bigshot manufacturers advised with him on his strategy.

The dinner was given at the home of George Sokolsky, who has been closely identified with the National Association of Manufacturers and others unsympathetic with consumer attempts to report on the quality of manufactured goods.

Sokolsky, now a writer for the New York *Herald Tribune,* once was paid $6000 by the National Association of Manufacturers as a lecturer and pamphleteer. He was also paid $14,000 by Tom Girdler, chairman of Republic Steel, to serve as "writer, lecturer and publicity man." Also, he was employed to write speeches for Steelman Ernest Weir.

Present at the Sokolsky dinner was Robert Lund of St. Louis, former president of the Manufacturers Association and head of the Lambert Pharmacal Company, together with several other big manufacturers of household and consumers' goods. The National Association of Manufacturers, however, did not know of, or have anything to do with, the meeting.

The irate lady shoppers have information that at this dinner the strategy of calling them "Communists" was approved and applauded; so now they propose having the dinner guests called before a congressional committee.

The ladies also have unearthed the fact that another

guest at the Sokolsky dinner was F. J. Schlink. It so happens that Schlink is Matthews' partner in conducting Consumers Research. This organization was NOT attacked by the Dies Committee.

Consumers Research publishes *Consumers Digest*, of which Matthews has been vice-president and managing editor. His wife is one of the four largest stockholders in this organization. Consumers Research is the direct competitor of Consumers Union, to which Matthews pinned the tag of communism.

So the lady consumers and the lady shoppers are ready to deluge Congress with accusations that the Dies Committee was favoring one consumers' group against the others.

Mr. Munro has also given me permission to reprint his confidential newsletter report from which I quote:

Berlin Was Serious

When Hearst's Richard E. Berlin saw red last August 17, on being cited by F.T.C. for guaranteeing, through *Good Housekeeping*, false and fraudulent advertising, the saner advertising element was inclined to give him the laugh. . . . But almost every one (in the advertising fraternity) wanted to see something done to scotch the growing consumer movement, or to "send the damned reds back where they came from." They were scared. And mad. They went along with Berlin. They began to operate behind the scenes.

. . . No U.S. Tories have ever been able to collect and connive to put down a popular movement without someone smelling gunpowder. . . . Here are details known to date of this "fascist grand council" which was formed to put the U.S. consumer back in his place.

. . . The organizing meeting, which gave the whole play away, took place . . . in the home of Mr. George Sokolsky, a clever writer whose connection, as paid apologist, with the National Association of Manufacturers has been brought out in open court, The N.A.M. was further tied in, inferentially, by the presence of a representative of Young & Rubicam's Raymond Rubicam, who is the public relations expert for the Manufacturers. But no direct connection with Hearst has yet been revealed.

Other members present were Henry F. Bristol, president of Bristol-Myers Pharmacal Co., J. B. Matthews of the Dies Committee and his old boss F. J. Schlink, president of Consumers Research. There were a dozen or so others, all men controlling vast advertising expenditures.

The Food & Drug Putsch

When the meeting got under way, the idea was obvious. J. B. Matthews declaimed his call-the-consumer-a-red "report of the Dies Committee." George Sokolsky outlined general purposes. Obviously the boys were all set to take over all the heights on the publicity front—by withdrawing advertising from recalcitrant publications. Within three days the Dies Committee held its famous meeting of one member, and released the report that had been O-Kayed by the grand council.

Meanwhile Trial Ends

. . . Highlight of the closing days of the testimony was the evidence that Warren G. Akers, publisher of *Good Housekeeping,* had admitted that certain of the advertisements in the magazine were "misleading." . . .

We now have the perfect picture. Here is everything: American big business, the nostrum dealers, the Hearst enterprises, the suppressing press, a former progressive whose pocketbook was harmed by his former friends, and the advertising fraternity—in fact, everyone who stands to lose money through the dissemination of intelligent and honest information—uniting in a vast redbaiting campaign, a campaign which enlisted the leading newspapers of the country, which smeared many of our best citizens, which brought a small revenge to the tortured soul of J. B. Matthews, radical turned redbaiter.

CHAPTER 13
From Capone to Coughlin

ALPHONSE CAPONE

In his own modest way Scarface Al Capone is just as convinced a redbaiter as Messrs. Matthews, Sokolsky, and Easley, though it is not as apparent how he derives any profit from this faith. What could have been the interests this most notorious gangster in America was protecting when, in his pre-prison prime, he wrote this credo for a popular magazine?

> Bolshevism is knocking at our gates. We can't afford to let it in. We have got to organize ourselves against it, and put our shoulders together and hold fast.
>
> We must keep America whole and safe and unspoiled. We must keep the worker away from red literature and red ruses; we must see that his mind remains healthy.

CHARLES M. SCHWAB

A racketeer in a totally different class, a pillar of society and the church, one of the founders of the Navy League of America, and one of the greatest professional patriots and redbaiters of his time was Charles M. Schwab. History records the violence and bloodshed caused by the steel company owners in their fight to prevent the unionization of workmen. As late as 1910, when l was a cub reporter on the Pittsburgh *Leader,* the steel companies were still circulating, illegally to be sure, a blacklist of steel workers, and after every name appeared one of these three terms: *labor leader, agitator, socialist*. Mr. Schwab's Bethlehem Steel Company was just as guilty of this practice as the Carnegie Steel, Jones & Laughlin, and the U.S. Steel

Corporation, and it was indeed a pleasure for me to so inform the Stanley steel trust investigating committee, although I was immediately howled down by noted attorneys and my story was either suppressed or derided by my own colleagues and their newspapers.

But who was this man Schwab, this leader of the American people according to the commercial press, this enemy of labor and redbaiter according to the liberal viewpoint? In the records of Congress and its investigating committees will be found most interesting testimony.

It appears that blowholes were found in the armor of the best vessels of the American fleet, and imperfections in guns, which sometimes exploded and killed our sailors and marines. The Carnegie Steel Company was accused of swindling the United States Government. William E. Corey, president of Midvale Steel & Ordnance and director of International Nickel, was called to testify:

> Q.: Did anybody above you—did a superior officer —know that you were doing this thing?
> A.: Yes, sir.
> Q.: Who was it?
> A.: Mr. Schwab knew about it in a general way.
> Q.: Did anybody else?
> A.: No, sir.[1]

"This thing" was sending out faulty armor for our ships, including Admiral Dewey's flagship at Manila Bay.

Mr. Schwab could not deny the charge. He admitted that he had given the order that blowholes should not mean rejection of the plates; he said it was "likely" that his company "did really conceal the fact of blowholes in the plates." The government found it was more than likely; it fined Mr. Schwab's company, and the fine was paid.

Mr. Schwab lived to become an admirer of Mussolini;

---

[1] House of Representatives, Report No. 1468, Fifty-third Congress, and Session (Washington, D. C.: Government Printing Office, 1894), p. 559.

he even said kind words about Adolf Hitler in one of his boat interviews on landing in New York; he continued to give money to the superpatriotic societies and fight labor till he died; and he was an old reliable user of the red label in his political and social career. *De mortuis nil nisi bonum!*

CHARLES R. WALGREEN

Walgreen, "founder of a drugstore empire" worth $50,000,000, was one of the three or four men, including Liggett, who made drugstores out of pharmacies, and cut-rate department stores out of drugstores. A heavy advertiser, in 1935 Walgreen made the front page of the press with his own personal affairs: he accused the University of Chicago of "indoctrinating [its students with] Communism and other un-American beliefs," said his niece was in danger of losing her (reactionary) peace of mind, and called for a legislative investigation.

It was held. President Hutchins was cleared and Walgreen and Mrs. Dilling and their queer friends given the good old American horse-laugh. But what the press did not print at the time was the following rather interesting little item sent to the newspapers by the United States Department of Agriculture. It reads:

> Adulteration of Elixir Iron, Quinine, and Strychnine, and adulteration and misbranding of Milk of Bismuth.
> U.S. vs. Walgreen Co.
> Plea of Guilty. Fine $100.
> Food & Drug No. 30319
> Sample Nos. 4339A-4345A
>
> that the Elixir Iron, Quinine, and Strychnine was adulterated in that it was sold under a name recognized in the National Formulary, and differed from the standard of strength, quality, and purity as determined by the tests laid down in the National Formulary official at the time of investigation.
>
> Adulteration of the Milk of Bismuth was alleged for

the reason that its strength and purity fell below the professed standard and quality under which it was sold.

Misbranding of the Milk of Bismuth was alleged for the reason that the statement "stronger than the N.F. Product."

On May 17, 1934, a plea of guilty was entered on behalf of the defendant company, and the court imposed a fine of $100.[2]

The patent-medicine interests, in their fight against the Tugwell pure food and drug bill, were labeling every critic of their products and their advertising, and every hacker of a law to safeguard the public, "reds" and "un-American." It is not a coincidence that Mr. Walgreen the redbaiter should also be Mr. Walgreen the adulterator, and that to his mind any college course that discusses criticisms of the business system he represents is subversive.

Mrs. Dilling's Network

So full of misstatement and so preposterous is The *Red Network,* the chef d'œuvre of Elizabeth (Mrs. Albert W.) Dilling, that it has been customary to dismiss her and her work as belonging to the lunatic fringe, the crackpots, the hysterical cuckoos of our time. But readers of a preceding chapter, which shows how poison-gas corporations raise the red scarce against labor through the wholesale distribution of this preposterous volume, will realize how much harm to individuals and liberal institutions can be caused by the hysteria of the rattle-brained.

William Randolph Hearst is no crackpot, no hysterical old man playing with his hobby, but shrewd exploiter intent on saving a financial empire valued at $220,000,000, which includes, in addition to newspaper properties, great lands in California and Mexico and one of the biggest mines in the world; Colonel Robert Rutherford McCormick is no crackpot; nor is Harry A. Jung of the American Vigilant

---

[2] *United States Dept. of Agriculture Bulletin,* Feb. 25, 1935; Case 22585; p. 287.

Intelligence Federation; yet all three of them not only endorse the Dilling masterpiece, but also make use of it in their own redbaiting activities.

On December 29, 1934, before the Special Committee on Un-American Activities, one Walter S. Steele gave some testimony on how "red networks" are built up for the use of the professional-patriotic and redbaiting world, which is itself also a "network" with many ramifications.

The question of permitting John Strachey, the British author, to continue his speaking tour in America, or of deporting him as an undesirable alien, was to the fore at the time. Leading citizens, interested in preserving the constitutional right of free speech, insisted that Strachey remain to speak. And that was enough for the network brigade. Not only Strachey himself (who denied he was a member of the Communist Party) but also every person who was reported as saying that Strachey had the right to speak was smeared as a red; then all the men who associated with those who had endorsed Strachey were in turn called reds, until very shortly almost every intelligent person in America became eligible for listing in the Dilling Who's Who. (In fact, I know many writers who, having seen the names of Theodore Dreiser, Sinclair Lewis, Upton Sinclair, and other leading intellectuals, including practically all the younger writers, in the Dilling Network, felt it a slight to their *amour propre* to have been omitted, and one at least wrote a request to be included in a new edition.)

The hearings revealed that the professional patriots, such as the Sentinels, Crusaders, Patriotic Coalitions, etc., quote Mrs. Dilling, and Mrs. Dilling, in turn, quotes the Sentinels, Crusaders, and Coalitions. Or they both quote privileged documents which are only libel-proof because some congressman has read them into the records in the House or Senate, or some rattlebrain has made a statement before a government commission. Thus the discredited Lusk report does duty every day among the redbaiters, and every sacred word of the Honorable Fish is repeated and re-repeated by one patriotic group to another. For science, they go to Madison Grant and Lathrop Stoddard and all the authors of racial nonsense; for truth, they go to such fraudulent and forged writings as the *Protocols of Zion* and the Zinoviev letter (which a crooked British publisher invented as an election maneuver); for authority in general, they go to crackpot congressmen; for patriotism, they go to Hearst.

Mrs. Dilling, for example, gives as her first authority for *The Red Network* the letterheads of liberal or radical organizations. These are never reliable; and the chances are that the majority of persons who let their names appear as endorsers or sponsors are not thoroughly acquainted with the work, and certainly not with any change of political policy which may take place in the course of time. Secondly, Mrs. Dilling uses the *American Labor Year Book* and the *American Labor Who's Who,* since in her view appearance in a labor book apparently is automatically subversive. Then follow the Lusk reports; then the Honorable Fish; then "literature and data sheets of Mr. Fred Marvin, national secretary of the American Coalition," who is about as trustworthy in this respect as Mrs. Dilling; then "reports by Mr. Francis Ralston Welsh of Philadelphia, attorney, long a patriotic research authority on subversive activities"; then "documentary files of the Advisory Associates, Chicago"; and finally "data furnished by the Better America Federation of California; and from other reliable sources."

The Dilling smear is rather cleverly applied—even if it does defeat itself in the end by being too universal. Mrs. Dilling announces a list of 1300 names of "persons who are or have been members of Communist, Anarchist, Socialist, I.W.W. Or pacifist controlled organizations, and who through these memberships, knowingly or unknowingly, have contributed in some measures to one or more phases of the Red movement in the United States." By adding "pacifists" she can name anyone in what is evidently a blacklist—it was so used by the D.A.R. And other professional patriots in choosing lecturers.

The fact is that Mrs. Dilling merely calls people red; she has no proof, but none seems to be needed, since this sort of attack is libel-proof. Let us pick out a few names merely by glancing through her first alphabetical categories:

Persons under "A"
Jane Addams, Judge Amidon, Congressman Amlie, Sherwood Anderson, Norman Angell.

Institutions under "A"
Abraham Lincoln Center, Chicago
Amalgamated Banks
Amalgamated Clothing Workers of America
American Anti-Bible Society, Inc.
American Association for Advancement of Atheism
American Birth Control League
American Civil Liberties Union
American Federation of Labor
American Friends Service Committee
American Newspaper Guild

Persons under "B"
Newton D. Baker, Emily Greene Balch, Harry Elmer Barnes, Carleton Beals, Dr. Charles A. Beard, William Rose Benet, Alfred Bingham, Paul Blanchard, Harriet Blatch, Bruce Bliven, Prof. Franz Boas, Arthur Bodansky, Margaret Bondfield, Senator Borah, Mrs. Louis D. Brandeis, Sophonisba P. Breckenridge, Fenner Brockway, Senator Brookhart, Heywood Broun, Howard Brubaker, Ambassador William Bullitt.

Among the notable people in *The Red Network* is William Allen White. When Mr. White was chosen to nominate Landon for president, readers of *The Red Network* wrote in confusion to the weekly, *Time*, one saying he had heard this was a "sinister communist plot." *Time* replied (in "Letters," June 22, 1936):

> William Allen White is listed . . . along with Mrs. Roosevelt, the late Jane Addams, Newton D. Baker, Stuart Chase, Dr. Albert Einstein, Dr. Harry Emerson Fosdick, Harriet Monroe, Margaret Sanger, Fannie Hurst, Dr. John Haynes Holmes, Justice Louis Brandeis, Senator Borah, Secretary Ickes and many other persons whom no unbiased judgment could list as Reds. Mrs. Dilling's Who's Who of Radicals, which former Police Commissioner O'Ryan of New York is said to have added to the Police Department files, also lists as radical New York's Mayor Fiorello La Guardia. Other Radicals include Edna St. Vincent Millar, Judge Ben B. Lindsey, Dr. S. Parkes Cadman, Harry Elmer Barnes, Mahatma Gandhi and Eamon de Valera.

The same stupid hysteria is also evident in other Dilling publications, notably in *Borah: "Borer from Within"* and *The Roosevelt Red Record and Its Background*, and in the Dilling lectures. Mrs. Dilling supplied the press with dramatic as well as ludicrous columns during the hearings of Drugman Walgreen's charges against the University of Chicago. Five senators were present. Mrs. Dilling, a group of the Daughters of the American Revolution, the Paul Reveres, Harry Jung, and Walgreen appeared against President Robert Hutchins of the University and his stall. It was a field day for redbaiting. Mrs. Dilling, breathless, excited, hysterical, raised the red scare, threw pamphlets at senators, flung about with her arms, rolled her eyes wildly, and shouted:

"Yes, they are all affiliated with the Communists. Professor Robert Morss Lovett, Professor Schuman, Dean Gilkey. The whole University is filled with them. Jane Addams was on many of their committees. So is Mary Macowell. . . ."

"I notice," interrupted Senator Barbour with a cynical

laugh, "that you have Justice Brandeis of the United States Supreme Court in your book. Is he a Communist?"

"Yes," shouted Mrs. Dilling. "He is. Judge Brandeis is one of the biggest contributors to that filthy, lousy little communist college down in Arkansas."

From the D.A.R. section a bubble of applause; from the radical bloc a loud laugh. A voice was heard saying: "They ought to kill every Communist."

Mrs. Dilling then turned on the American Civil Liberties Union. Several leading University of Chicago professors were members; the Union had sent out lawyers to defend the constitutional right of free speech; among the men and women defended were Communists; ergo, the Union was "communistic"; ergo, the professors were "communistic."

"And Mr. Harold Swift?" asked the laughing senator.

"Oh, yes, there's a cream-puff type for you," replied Mrs. Dilling. "He's just the kind who will permit Communists to talk at the University and they'll cut his throat and take his money away. Some rich men play with chorus girls, some with booze and others with communism. Mr. Swift wouldn't have a nickel left—he wouldn't have that pretty suit he wore at the last session—if the ideas he was playing with had their way."

Harry Jung, looking like a Goering crossed with a Mussolini, testified proudly:

"I've been accused of being a petty racketeer. I've been accused of being an anti-Semite. . . . I've been accused of being a redbaiter and a strike-breaker. . . .

"As for being a redbaiter and a strike-breaker, yes, I'm proud to say I am both. Yes, I'm proud that I believe in the ideals of America. . . ."

The ladies of the D.A.R. could not restrain themselves at this point.

"Is that Mrs. Dillinger?" asked a little bespectacled man, pointing at Mrs. Dilling.

The man next to him, big in gray flannels, turned

around in a mad rage and smashed the questioner in the face, yelling: "You dirty little Jew." The big man, according to newspaper reports, was Mr. Dilling.

To a reporter of the Philadelphia *Evening Ledger* the high priestess of redbaiting uttered delphic statements, such as these:

> Communism from the national boards of the Young Men's and Young Women's Christian Association is seeping down through all its branches; the American Student Union also meets in their buildings.
>
> Christ isn't mentioned once in the Communist songs.
> . . .
> The Anti-Lynching Bill is only designed to enable the national government to take control of police throughout the country for Communist aid. . . .
>
> Philadelphia is a city ridden with Communism. Beware of anything dripping "sweetness and light." That is the Communist method of boring from within.

Even more hilarious than the foregoing is the attack Mrs. Dilling once made on George Sokolsky. As Upton Sinclair recounts the episode, Sokolsky told Mrs. Dilling that he had "reformed," that he was no longer an anarchist or radical.

> But that did not help him in the least with Mrs. Dilling; because, you see, it is her basic tenet that the "Red" disease is incurable, and that anybody who has ever had it is just trying to fool her by posing as a conservative. Sokolsky told me how he assured her solemnly that he no longer sympathized with the "Reds"; but a few minutes later he made a dreadful blunder, employing some phrase of economic science, such as "materialistic interpretation"—whereupon Mrs. Dilling burst out in a fury, saying that he was a cheat and a part of the "red" camouflage. Afterwards, she wrote about him such falsehoods that he was seriously thinking of suing her and putting her on the witness stand.

Mrs. Dilling's motives, Sinclair explains, are simple: the most fundamental of all American institutions are the private ownership of property and the conduct of business for private profit; the Constitution was written for their protection and the Christian religion founded for the same purpose; and any criticism of the profit system is, according to Mrs. Dilling, treason and blasphemy, and should be made a crime by law.

Jung's Vigilantes

In the dedication to *The Red Network*, Mrs. Dilling gives credit to Harry A. Jung, who "kindly loaned the author some documents." Mr. Jung is one of the peddlers of the notorious forgeries called *The Protocols of Zion*. But whereas Mrs. Dilling acts like a crackpot, Harry Jung is one of the most astute of the hate-mongers of our time. In fact he is so clever that he obtained money from members of the Sears Roebuck and Florsheim Shoe companies, two Jewish businesses, while doing a wholesale business in anti-Semitic literature.

Harry Augustus Jung was first exposed many years ago by Norman Hapgood in *Professional Patriots.* In 1926 Jung was an agent for the National Clay Products Industries Association which conducted a labor spy service.[3] He lectured on the evils of labor unions and co-operated with such anti-union champions as Fred Marvin of the National Republic and Noel Sargeant of the National Association of Manufacturers.

On December 1, 1933, Jung wrote to Harry F. Sieber of the Silver Legion offering the *Protocols* at sixty cents "in quantity lots"; also, at fifteen cents, an anti-Semitic pamphlet written by a Nazi agent who has since fled to Germany.

John L. Spivak, in *Plotting America's Pogroms,* has charged that Jung is one of the protégés of Colonel

---

3 Cf. George Seldes, *You Can't Do That* (Modern Age, 1938), pp. 156-159.

McCormick of the Chicago *Tribune* and "supplies the colonel with a great deal of his 'inside' information about Communists and Jews."

In 1935 the McCormack-Dickstein committee completely exposed Jung. Here is what its report says:

> Another of these organizations is the American Vigilante (*sic*) Intelligence Federation, of which Harry A. Jung, Chicago, is the founder, promoter, and honorary general manager.
>
> Testimony of Jung's secretary, Miss Rose Peterson, taken at Chicago, stated "we have never gotten around to getting up bylaws or electing officers." Her testimony and corroborating records showed that a solicitor had been paid 40 percent of all money he collected as his fee and that many nationally-known organizations and individuals had contributed. The committee finds the contributors had no knowledge of the purpose for which the money was used.
>
> Miss Peterson's testimony showed that Harry A. Jung and the A.V.I.F. had published and circulated great masses of literature tending to incite racial and religious intolerance.
>
> Because this committee has seen the true purpose behind these various groups, it will lump them together and characterize them as un-American, as unworthy of support and created and operated for the financial welfare of those who guide them and who do not hesitate to stoop to racial and religious intolerance in order to achieve their selfish purposes.
>
> This activity your committee believes to be distinctly and dangerously un-American and we denounce, without qualification, any attempt, from any source, to stir up hatreds and prejudices against any one or more groups of our people because of either race, color or creed. . . .[4]

---

4 *Investigation of Nazi and Certain Other Propaganda Activities: Hearings Before the Special Committee on Un-American Activities*, United States House of Representatives, Seventy-fourth Congress, 1st Session (Washington, D. C.: Government Printing Office, 1935),

The La Follette civil liberties investigation went still further. It said:

> National Labor Relations Board Report:
> Patriotic Associations as Undercover Agents
>
> Spy and strikebreaking agencies not infrequently assume the masks of patriotism, ultra Americanism, or some form of public service. They sometimes set up affiliates under patriotic camouflage or sponsor citizens' committees for an alleged public purpose.
>
> Conversely organizations actually or originally patriotic have been known to engage in industrial espionage and strikebreaking.
>
> The most insidious and reprehensible form of activities in this mixed field is that represented by certain "associations" whose purpose is private gain, and whose methods include making business by spreading scares or actually fomenting disturbances. The most frequent guise for these associations is some form of "Red Hunting." The sustenance of such associations is usually from industry and finance, and its "services" may include strikebreaking.
>
> A typical concern of this sort is A.V.I.F., the American Vigilant Intelligence Federation with offices in the Chicago Tribune Tower Building, Chicago, which is the expression of its "honorary manager," one Harry Augustus Jung. Exposed frequently in the past dozen years by the Chicago Federation of Labor, its record was written into the investigation of the congressional committee on Nazi and other propaganda, whose report, issued February 15, 1935, stated concerning certain allegedly patriotic associations, "many are in reality the breeding places of racial and religious intolerance and their financial statements show them to be petty rackets." The report names American Vigilant Intelligence Federation as one such.
>
> Jung and his colleague, Nelson E. Hewitt, were associated with Mrs. Albert W. Dilling in compiling a book called *The Red Network*.

Report 153, p. 12.

> Testimony before the congressional committee included a letter from Henry T. Rainey, former Speaker of the House, dated November 23, 1931, denouncing Jung for fomenting strikes, racketeering, and doing "the slimy, stool-pigeon work necessary for the purpose of destroying organized labor."
>
> As recently as midsummer of 1935, American Vigilant Intelligence Federation . . . were distributing provocative spy reports. . . .
>
> The congressional committee forced him to reveal his supporting subscribers from industry and finance.
>
> The list shows that he collected $5,075 alone from Mrs. Finley J. Sheppard. . . .[5]

The chief contributors to Jung's vigilantism were Chicago banks, notably the First National, Dawes's Northern Central Trust, Continental Illinois; also International Harvester, Corn Products, Bendix, Sears Roebuck, General American Tank Car, Stewart Warner, Florsheim Shoe, William Wrigley, A. B. Dick, and H. B. Joy, the Detroit banker.

The profits in this sort of redbaiting have been named by the congressional committee.

MCCORMICK'S CHICAGO "TRIBUNE"

Mrs. Dilling, Harry Jung, and Colonel McCormick make up a trinity of Chicago's best-known redbaiters.

Jung supplies "documents" to Mrs. Dilling; he is known as a "protégé" of McCormick; and McCormick in turn endorses Dilling.

In connection with the offer of a rival paper to forfeit a thousand dollars if one of the Chicago *Tribune's* redbaiting stories could be proved anything but a lie, it is interesting to compare the numerous misstatements in *The Red Network* and those in a copy of the Chicago *Tribune* when it deals

---

5 *Violations of Free Speech and Rights of Labor; Subcommittee of the Committee on Education and Labor;* U. S. Senate, Seventy-fourth Congress, 2nd Session: Pursuant to Senate Resolution 266.

with Russia, the New Deal, or liberalism. *The Red Network* has the complete endorsement of the publisher of the *Tribune.* "I am glad to have it for reference," said the editor and publisher of what he calls "the world's greatest paper," "and trust that the book will have a large sale so that Americans will know who are the enemies of society within our gate. You are to be commended highly for the patriotism and devotion to the welfare of our country that enabled you to publish this book."

For ten years Colonel McCormick was my employer, but he had not then adopted his present policies. During that time he was chiefly concerned with taxation, and when the Roosevelt regime came in and began spending billions to help the farmers and the ten million unemployed, the colonel grew angrier and angrier and shouted: "Turn the rascals out." True, he redbaited the New Deal, but every Republican paper was doing the same. Besides, the colonel is a multi-millionaire, heads corporations worth fifty or a hundred million dollars, and naturally devotes himself to the preservation of big money. So far as I know, however, the colonel had not heretofore indulged in such actions as endorsing crackpots or associating with peddlers of forgeries.

Merwin K. Hart

Scratch a redbaiter and you will find . . .

In the case of Merwin K. Hart you will find a spokesman for the *Caudillo* or the Spanish Fuehrer, General Franco.

You will find the man who proposed the disfranchisement of the ten million American citizens who have been forced to go on relief.

You will find a man who proposes the outlawing of strikes and the denial to labor of all the rights and privileges which it has gained since it began its fight against industrial serfdom.

You will find a man who would cut state aid for

education.

Naturally, the man will preside at meetings sponsoring the Dies committee, meetings at which Fritz Kuhn, the Hitler leader in America, and Father Coughlin are cheered and the President of the United States is booed and called a red.

But that is not all.

If the reader will name any man, idea, movement, plan, bill in Congress or in his state legislature that favors the general welfare of the American people, he can with certainty place among the opposition the name of Merwin K. Hart. If, on the other hand, the reader will list men, organizations, and ideas in America which closely approximate the Black and Brown reaction of Europe, he can with certainty place the name of Hart and his associates as in favor. (And these are the men who call themselves the "better Americans," the men who are the chief alien-baiters and fighters of "foreign ideologies" of our decade.)

"We oppose any form of compulsory health or sickness insurance." This is point No. 8 in the platform of the New York State Economic Council of which Mr. Hart is president, pooh-bah, and propagandist; a similar plank is No. 4: "We oppose any plan which seeks to bring about compulsory unemployment insurance." But the best of the fifteen, the one which suggests the mind of a Franco or Hitler, is No. 7, which provides for the disfranchisement of the unemployed.

The New York State Economic Council, which claims it has 50,000 members, contented itself for many years with two objectives: attacking labor and protecting real-estate owners from increased taxation. When the fascists rebelled in Spain, Hart leaped into that fight on their side, and since then his office has become a meeting-place for Francoists.

In 1938, when Martin Dies, self-styled demagogue, was generally being hailed as a clown—before the reactionaries rallied around him—Hart gave the Texan publicity-hound a big luncheon in New York City. Among the guests, were

Major General Harbord of the Radio Corporation of America, Thomas McInnerney of National Dairy Products, William C. Dickerman of American Locomotive, Louis K. Comstock, head of the Merchants Association, Captain John B. Trevor of the American Coalition of Patriotic Societies, Archibald E. Stevenson, associate of Easley, and Fritz Kuhn.

Mr. Hart's next public appearance was as chairman of a pro-Franco rally in the Seventh Regiment Armory in New York City. The heroes who got the big applause were, in addition to Franco, the dictators Hitler and Mussolini, but the high moment of the evening was the arrival of a Christian Front delegation with a picture of Father Coughlin. Among the speakers were Dr. Alexander Hamilton Rice; the Reverend Dr. Joseph F. Thorning, S.J., professor of sociology and social history at Mount St. Mary's College and author of a statement apologizing for the Francoist aviator-murderers of women and children; and Ogden H. Hammond, former ambassador to Spain. When the editorial board of *The Nation* protested that the use of the armory was a violation of the state law which forbids use of such buildings for religious or political purposes, Colonel Ralph C. Tobin, commanding officer, reminded the editors of the libel law but refused them permission to quote his letter.

When Hart presided at the "big Dies rally" in Madison Square Garden shortly afterwards, a guard of honor of the Seventh Regiment was present in dress uniform. The speakers were George U. Harvey, borough president of Queens, Joseph P. Ryan of the International Longshoremen's Association, Jeremiah Cross, past state commander of the American Legion,
Laurens Hamilton (son-in-law of J. P. Morgan) of the Sons of the American Revolution, and Jean Mathias, New York State commander of the Jewish War Veterans.

The sponsors and their affiliations tell an interesting story. Almost all persons were connected with banks, industrial corporations, and pro-fascist and anti-Semitic organizations. James Wheeler-Hill, secretary of the Nazi Bund, who had been present at the Hart-Dies luncheon (and who later went to the penitentiary for perjury), appeared on the printed list. So did John B. Trevor, Jr., son of the patrioteer of the same name. Miss Vail Andress was listed, as an official of the Chase National Bank. W. E. McKell, president of the New York Board of Trade, which had sponsored a meeting for General Van Horn Moseley at which a massacre of radicals was advocated, was on the Dies sponsoring committee. And others were: Robert Appleton of the American Defense Society; Robert H. Harris of the New York Cotton Exchange; Philip Liebmann of Liebmann Breweries; Messmore Kendall, president of the Sons of the American Revolution; George H. Timone of the Knights of Columbus. Grouped around Mr. Hart in seats of honor were State Senator McNaboe, leading redbaiter of the New York State Legislature; Mrs. Ralph Easley; and Ralph Appleton, who had once provided free office space for the Christian Mobilizers.

Mr. Hart spoke for Franco. He introduced speakers who attacked the C.I.O., foreign agents, class consciousness, Mayor LaGuardia, Miss Frances Perkins, and "Marxists masquerading as Liberals." The presence of the Jewish war veterans did not intimidate the Christian Fronters or cause them to cease their anti-Semitic shouting.

And to round out the picture of Mr. Hart: on his return from Spain he was given a front-page pro-Franco interview in the *Herald Tribune;* he has written for the New York *Sun;* he has tried to pin a red tag on President Roosevelt; he has denounced the Spanish Republicans for being "hypnotized by the ideas of the French and American revolutions," causing Vincent Sheean to ask if the principles of the American Revolution have become un-American; he has circulated Senator Burke's speech entitled "We Must Amend the Wagner Act"; he boasts that it was he who called the child labor amendment the "youth control amendrnent," and thereby helped kill it; he has consistently fought the New Deal in America and upheld the old deal, the fascism-plus-murder deal of Franco in Spain.

Mr. Hart is also, therefore, a perfect specimen of redbaiter for profit.

Heavenly Redbaiter

America's leading anti-Semite is also one of our leading redbaiters. Of Father Coughlin, spiritual head of a Michigan parish, and of the Christian Front, the following seven statements will suffice:

(1) Father Coughlin has broken at least one of the Ten Commandments. He is a bearer of false witness, and among those who have said so publicly is Alfred E. Smith, the leading Catholic layman of America.

(2) Father Coughlin is an enemy of labor. His church buildings were erected by scab workmen whom he paid about 40 percent less than the union wage scale. He has his printing done in a non-union shop. (The International Typographical Union and the Cleveland Federation of Labor appointed a committee to try to persuade Coughlin to use union printing at a fair price, but Coughlin refused to receive the committee.) He has denounced John L. Lewis of the C.I.O., calling him "a stooge of the Communist party" and in the same address denounced Monsignor John A. Ryan, the leading Catholic liberal priest in America, saying he was "promoting the policies of the Communist Party in the Catholic Church."

(3) Father Coughlin violates canon law—something which *should* concern his superiors, who have hitherto been able to silence priests who spoke or worked for liberal causes, but who seemingly can do nothing about reactionaries and fascists. (Consult the Reverend Father Edward V. Dargin, J.C.D., on canon law.[6])

(4) Father Coughlin has lied. This is a harsh word, but

---
6 *Ecclesiastical Review*, July 1935.

to justify it there is no less an authority than Monsignor Ryan, who has thoroughly exposed a whole series of Coughlin falsifications in an article in *The Commonweal,* leading Catholic weekly (December 30, 1938). When Coughlin could not reply to the documentation, he yelled red at Monsignor Ryan.

(5) Father Coughlin fathered the Christian Front. Following the F.B.I. arrest of a group of its members in New York, he immediately denied he had anything to do with them, but then, no doubt realizing that the radio sermons in which he had proposed and fostered the Front had been printed by himself, he turned about the next day and took his stand by it. The reader may look up Coughlin's volume of radio addresses of November 6, 1938, to January 1, 1939, and find this statement on page 14: "It is necessary for us to solidify and strengthen a virile, closely woven Christian Front . . ." and on page 15: "Today you can choose your sides. Today you can be powerful enough to overcome communism by moral force. Tomorrow it may be necessary to use physical force."

(6) Coughlin has preached civil war in America. Said *The Commonweal* (October 9, 1936) of one of Coughlin's incitements to violence:

> The radio priest has said . . . that if ballots failed to put down communistic tendencies bullets would be in order. In Detroit, Bishop Gallagher thought, according to the Associated Press, that the use of bullets against a hypothetical "upstart dictator" of communist persuasions was perfectly legitimate. He therefore gave the impression that he did not consider Coughlin "morally in error." . . . The bishops are the custodians of Catholic moral teachings.

(7) Coughlin is a fascist demagogue. The fact that he has co-operated and was friendly with Huey Long, once America's potential Fuehrer, was approvingly announced by Father Joseph Thorning, S. J., in *America,* Jesuit organ

(April 13, 1935). Evidence of Father Coughlin's leanings toward Hitlerism (in addition to his verbatim use of Hitler propaganda without as much as a thank-you credit) has appeared in his *Social Justice* writings over a period of years. These writings were largely redbaiting, pro-Fascist, pro-Nazi propaganda. When the United States began to move for preparedness and possible war with Germany, Coughlin dropped his pro-Nazi writings. He also stopped his radio anti-Semitism. But he never gave up his redbaiting. That, in fact, became more common as the war hysteria mounted.

CHAPTER 14
In Congress and Out

NEWTON D. BAKER AND JAMES M. BECK

Newton D. Baker in his heyday was a great liberal. For two-score years Baker was a notable figure in all the progressive libertarian movements in America—and then he got the job of lawyer for big business.

James M. Beck was once a member of the House of Representatives and a great expounder of the Constitution.

But in 1935 these two joined with other lawyers of the Edison Electric Institute to appoint themselves a super-Supreme Court of the United States and to declare unconstitutional:

(1) the Tennessee Valley Authority;

(2) the Electric Home and Farm Authority;

(3) loans to municipalities for construction of municipal power systems;

(4) government construction of dams for power;

(5) allocation of funds to build generating plants and lines for a national "grid" system.

This series of "decisions" was made on one ground: the "danger of laying a framework for communism by the government." The administration's power plan—which is today beginning to reclaim vast areas—was called red by the lawyers representing the Edison Electric Institute.

"If," said the self-appointed law-makers, "the government engage in one business merely because it is interstate business . . . then it may engage in all; and if it may engage in them to any degree it can make them government monopolies. By such an interpretation the Constitution would become a fundamental framework for the creation of a communistic state."

What followed this judicial utterance was a tremendous campaign of redbaiting from all the spokesmen of the monopoly interests, and all the patriotic societies financed by them.

The Edison Electric Institute is the successor to the National Electric Light Association, the notorious N.E.L.A. which maintained an annual fund of about $25,000,000 for corrupting the press and other means of making public opinion. It was the N.E.L.A. which, the reader will recall, put into practice the policy of pinning the red label on all movements seeking public ownership of public utilities.

SENATOR TYDINGS

A man named Tydings was having a more difficult time than he had expected in his campaign for re-election to the Senate. It was good politics to attack the Roosevelt administration as red, and to link the big and growing labor movement under the direction of John L. Lewis with the reds, and a little misrepresentation goes a long way. So the following advertisement was placed by the Tydings campaign committee in eighty Maryland weeklies during the 1933 campaign:

> CITIZENS OF MARYLAND
> DEFEND YOUR STATE
> AGAINST FEDERAL
> INVASION:
>
> YOUR DECLARATION OF ADOPTED BY YOUR FOREFATHERS IN 1776—THE FOUNDATION AND BULWARK OF YOUR CONSTITUTION—DECLARES:
>
> Art. 4. That the people of this State have the sole and exclusive right of regulating the internal government . . . as a free, sovereign and independent State.
>
> Art. 7. Elections ought to be free. . . .
>
> Art. 8. That the legislative, executive and judicial powers of government ought to be forever separate and distinct from each other: AND NO PERSON EXERCISING

In Congress and Out

THE FUNCTION OF ONE OF SAID DEPARTMENS SHALL ASSUME OR DISCHARGE THE DUTIES OF ANY OTHER.

YOUR CONSTITUTIONAL RIGHTS ARE THREATENED BY THE FEDERAL ADMINISTRATION SUPPORTED BY

THE C.I.O
JOHN L. LEWIS
AND
THE COMMUNISTS

Preserve your civil and religious liberties guaranteed to you under your Bill of Rights and State Constitution.

Vote for
MILLARD E. TYDINGS
for
United States Senator.
Primary day, Sept. 12, falls this year on historic defenders' day. Defend your rights on defenders' day
and
KEEP THE FREE STATE FREE
(Published by Authority of Fred A. Delfield, treasurer, Tydings' campaign committee.)

SENATOR EDWARD R. BURKE

There is no rule which says that a redbaiter must be a lover of Adolf Hitler and a spokesman for big business in America, but in Senator Burke of Nebraska these characteristics are inseparably mingled.

The very day Neville Chamberlain made the shameful Munich peace with Hitler, Senator Burke arrived in New York by ship. He "praised without stint the accomplishments of the Nazi regime in Germany. He saw Adolf Hitler as even 'a greater man than Bismarck' and declared that the annexation of the Sudeten territory by the Reich was justified. . . . Beaming enthusiasm for conditions as he found them in Germany . . . Senator Burke would not compare working conditions for general laborers in

Germany with those of the United States, explaining that trade unions had been abolished in the Reich."

Burke since then has become the leader of the attack upon the Wagner Act in Congress. "He is regarded as the spokesman for the National Association of Manufacturers," charged Kenneth Crawford, Washington correspondent, then president of the Newspaper Guild. In March 1939, Crawford accused the senator, also known as "Throttlebottom Burke," with "circularizing employers and their associations with N.A.M. propaganda for amendment of the Wagner labor disputes act" and using his franking privilege to send the literature postage-free.

In 1934, while running for Congress, Burke made a notable defense of the New Deal: its ethics were Christian; it was as new as the Declaration of Independence and the Constitution; its motives were the same; "it voices the deathless cry of good men and good women for the opportunity to live and work in freedom . . . protect themselves against the ruthless and the cunning"; "it recognizes that man is indeed his brother's keeper, insists that the laborer is worthy of his hire, demands . . . justice. . . .

He was elected. And no sooner was he in office than he attacked the court reform plan, the reorganization bill, voted against the Wages and Hours Act, against the 1937 farm bill, against every measure of the New Deal which he had praised, and finally wound up as spokesman for the reactionary employers.

When Chairman Madden of the N.L.R.B. challenged Senator Burke to produce some evidence to back up his redbaiting charges against the Board, Madden waited six months, but Burke, who had shouted over the radio that he was getting a hundred and fifty to two hundred complaints a day against the Board, failed to produce one. Mr. Madden then concluded that Senator Burke's statements were "often unfounded in fact."

What does it profit a liberal to turn reactionary? Burke

was a corporation lawyer before he decided to use pro-New Deal demagogy to get into Congress. "His services to organized employers," concludes Crawford, "probably won't hurt his business when, after leaving the Senate, he goes back to Omaha to dust off his shingle. In fact his firm has done nicely in corporate practice during his absence."

SENATOR ROBERT RICE REYNOLDS

Up to September 1939, when war broke out in Europe, after which it became political suicide for an American politician to defend Hitler, Senator Robert Rice Reynolds of North Carolina was the greatest exponent of Hitlerism (and Italian Fascism) in Congress.

"Our Bob," as this demagogue styles himself, is a would-be Fuehrer, according to the Washington correspondents Frank Rhylick and Allan Michie; his voice carries "the tune of Fascism," he is "all the Coughlins, Hagues and Winrods of America rolled into one and bound in the *Congressional Record.*"

*Wh*en he first came to the Senate in 1932, Reynolds was considered a clown. He got himself photographed kissing Jean Harlow, he endorsed a cigarette for $1000 and had his picture used in advertisements, and he ranted against aliens.

A trip to Europe gave him the Fuehrer-complex. He arrived home full of misinformation and half-lies, such as: "Hitler has solved the unemployment problem. There is no unemployment in Italy." (Hitler then had already begun to conscript labor, to employ hundreds of thousands without pay, to build an army of millions, and to impose a modern serfdom differing very little from medieval slavery—and Mussolini had devised a means of lowering the standard of living to its lowest point since the war and dividing semi-starvation among all the working people.)

To further his ambition as a Fuehrer, Reynolds organized the American Vindicators, Inc., a superpatriotic organization "to protect American prosperity by stopping all immigration for ten years . . . to register and fingerprint all aliens . . . to promote the national defense. . . ." To sell this product the senator added the flag and redbaiting. "The American people," he said, "have for the time being neglected their fight against communism, the most deadly, poisonous, destructive, murderous, and anti-religious ism of them all."

Ever since his visit to San Simeon in 1935, Reynolds has also spread the Hearst doctrines. "Mr. William Randolph Hearst," he said on emerging from the castle, "deserves the credit of all patriotic people. . . . I believe his attacks on the Red Menace are warranted by the facts."

Campaigning against Cam Morrison, a wealthy opponent, Reynolds pulled a jar of caviar from his pocket and yelled: "Friends, it pains me to tell you that Cam Morrison eats fish eggs. This here jar ain't a jar of squirrel shot; it's fish eggs, and Red Russian fish eggs at that, and they cost two dollars. . . ." There are no ludicrous depths to which Reynolds will hesitate to carry his redbaiting.

Two years before he went over to Hearst he had visited Russia and on returning expressed his astonishment at the "tremendous activity" there: the "people seemed content. All were working . . . with enthusiasm and not as workers frequently do to a task which they regard as drudgery." But that line did not pay; in fact, it threatened to ruin him in national politics and so he changed to the redbaiting tunes written by Father Coughlin, Hitler, and the other professional international redbaiters. "Reynolds is a pushover for any cause, as long as the push given him is a profitable one," conclude Rhylick and Michie.

George Deatherage of the Knights of the White Camellia, promoter of the American Nationalist Confederation (who said he hoped to make his organization "*the* Fascist party of America"), was cross-examined by the Dies committee concerning his mailing out of a thousand copies of a Reynolds speech bearing the Reynolds postal frank and presumably furnished by the senator. The Dies committee, however, hastened to cover up Reynolds's connection with Deatherage.

Reynolds has appeared as a speaker before the American Defense Society. Among the prominent participants on the occasion were Fritz Kuhn, then head of the German-American Bund; nine of the Bund's directors; Bainbridge Colby, former secretary of state; Rear-Admiral Belknap; and Major-General Byrne. Kuhn and the Nazis applauded Reynolds; Reynolds said he was "tickled to death" to have Kuhn present. Reynolds's oration was directed chiefly against the suggestion made by Senator Wagner that America permit 20,000 refugee German children to come to America; the rest was a tirade against aliens, democracy, Stalin, and the W.P.A.

As is typical of all baiters, Reynolds has a way of disregarding facts and drawing fallacious conclusions. Recently he attacked the "7,000,000 aliens in America," taking his figure from Congressman Dies. This figure is refuted by the United States Census and the Department of Immigration and Labor. Reynolds, demanding deportation of "alien criminals and undesirable aliens," states that the jails are full of them, whereas the Wickersham report has proven that there is a relatively lower percentage of alien criminals than native.

For all his baiting activities Senator Reynolds has earned the support of the Christian Front and rated a full-page encomium in Father Coughlin's *Social Justice.*

REPRESENTATIVE JACOB THORKELSON

When Proust wrote that we see in others our own characteristics and faults, he must have had someone like Representative Jacob Thorkelson of Montana in mind. This congressman recently spoke contemptuously of his rivals saying:

> I have often wondered, when listening to certain political candidates, what sort of a kink they have in their mental machinery. . . . These men offer nothing

constructive but wear themselves out fighting imaginary foes. They set up bogies and then work themselves into a lather knocking them down. I can only pity such warped mentalities. . . . From beginning to end you cannot find one constructive thought . . . a hodge-podge of attacks, accusations and insinuations bristling with misstatements and untruths.

In his double capacity of Jew-baiter and redbaiter, Thorkelson, on June 22, 1939, made one of his typical speeches, consisting of "a hodge-podge of attacks, accusations and insinuations bristling with misstatements and untruths." He urged Congress to direct an investigation of "communistic activities that exist in every public place, colleges and Federal departments," and added darkly: "The leaders in Congress are well known, but the chairmen of the committees often remain in obscurity," after which he listed the names of Representatives Dickstein, Bloom, Sirovich, and Celler, all New York Democrats who head House committees. It happens that Dickstein led a redbaiting investigation before Dies, that Bloom was a booster of Mussolini, that Sirovich was a straight organization Democrat, and that Celler is a liberal; there is not a pink or mauve trace in any of them. But they are all four Jews and this is the Hitler-Thorkelson method of smearing. Representative Bruce Barton, Republican, protested against the slur.

Thorkelson came to New York to address a meeting of the Christian Mobilizers, "a split-off group of Father Coughlin's Christian Front, which has recently veered to the Nazi Bund. The Fuehrer of this outfit is Ku Kluxer Joseph McWilliams. The police records of leading Mobilizers show that they include as precious a pack of cutthroats, rapists, and pickpockets as ever graced a rogues' gallery."[1] The audience consisted entirely of Nazis, Coughlinites, Fascists and reactionary Catholics, all united

---
1 *Equality*, April 1940.

by redbaiting and Jew-baiting. The "literature" sold consisted of the *Deutscher Weckruf und Beobachter*, the Bund's official organ; the *Tablet*, official organ of the Roman Catholic diocese of Brooklyn; *Liberation*, published by Pelley of the Silver Shirts; other of Pelley's publications, including one entitled *Roosevelt's Jewish Ancestry;* Coughlin's *Social Justice;* and anti-Semitic pamphlets by Thorkelson.

The only literature distributed free was a sheet with the words "Buy Christian" on it.

Some of the Mobilizers are after the small profits which that slogan would bring them in their little shops. Thorkelson is out for publicity. He wants something to show the voters in Montana. Since defeating Jerry O'Connell, the progressive liberal Catholic who had the courage to speak for Loyalist Spain and to defy the copper trust, Thorkelson has engaged in redbaiting as a daily exercise. The *Montana Standard* and other papers, almost all of them under Anaconda Copper influence, have said little or nothing about Thorkelson's association with the Mobilizers, Coughlinites, and other promoters of civil strife; but they have played up his redbaiting speeches. On the other hand the miners' papers are against the demagogue.

Those who had profits to protect had a staunch representative in Mr. Thorkelson. He was defeated in 1940.

More Honorable Gentlemen

Representative Clare E. Hoffman of Michigan takes full advantage of his congressional immunity. The C.I.O., he said in one of his speeches, "is controlled by Communists or by those who are criminals or have been engaged in criminal activities." He cannot be sued for libel; he is privileged.

Among those who profit by such slanderous charges are the manufacturers who do not want to pay higher wages or raise standards in their shops. The Muskin Shoe Company of Maryland reprinted the Hoffman statements and distributed them in an effort to misrepresent a union which sought to win over its employees. Likewise the Constitutional Educational League of New Haven, Connecticut, got Representative Hoffman to speak to the employees of the Remington-Rand factories against the Wagner Labor Act, John L. Lewis, and the C.I.O. organizers ("a bunch of hoodlums"). Hoffman concluded by telling the workmen that the real purpose of Lewis and the C.I.O. is "to destroy our American form of government."

Representative J. Parnell Thomas, né Feeney, is one of the most notorious redbaiters on the Dies redbaiting committee. He was formerly head of the bond department of Paine, Webber and Company, of Wall Street, and is known as a Wall Street spokesman in Congress. Mayor Louis A. Keidel, of Allentown, New Jersey, a vice-president of the Bankers Trust Company, accused Thomas of being the town's "Hooligan No. 1."

Senator Sam McReynolds said that the demand for the lifting of the embargo on Loyalist Spain was "inspired by Communists." He thus pinned the red label on such persons as Bishop Paddock, former Secretary of State Stimson, Helen Keller, Dorothy Thompson, Carrie Chapman Catt, Dr. William Allan Neilson, Bishop Tucker, and scores of the most prominent liberals of America.

The author of the Hobbs concentration camp bill, *Representative Samuel Francis Hobbs* of Alabama., proposes that the United States follow the Hitler system of Dachau and the Daladier plan in the Pyrenees, where the 150,000 Spanish Loyalist refugees were imprisoned. (Concentration camps already exist in certain fascist districts in rural California, but not for aliens: they are stockades for migrant workers, who get about the same treatment from the vigilantes as Jews get in Hitler's camps.)

Another notorious redbaiter, and one who made that practice his main activity in Washington, was *Tom Blanton* of Texas. As chairman of the subcommittee on appropriations for the District of Columbia, he tacked on the "red rider" to the appropriations bill which forced the capital's teachers to eliminate mention of Soviet Union in history and geography. "Blah Blah" Blanton, in fact, made so much of a fool of himself that his constituency refused to return him in autumn 1936. However, in a time of war hysteria Blanton would be riding high and roughshod over the Bill of Rights, and would again be the darling of the Hearst press. His timing was wrong.

Governor Earle

Governor Earle of Pennsylvania was another, like Frank Murphy, who suddenly found himself needing clean skirts when a high federal post became his ambition. In order to become an ambassador, he had to live down a strongly pro-labor, liberal past, during which he had addressed an American Legion convention in Wilkes-Barre, on August 22, 1935, as follows:

> I warn you that our civilization is in danger if we heed the deceptive cries of special privilege, if we permit our men of great wealth to send us on a wild goose chase after so-called radicals while they continue to plunder the people. . . . We are constantly told of the evils of Socialism and Communism. The label is applied to every man, woman, and child who dares to say a word which does not have the approval of Wall Street.

But on the Fourth of July, 1937, when the labor-fighting forces in Johnstown, Pennsylvania, were calling the C.I.O. "Moscow-directed," Governor Earle appeared before the commercial patriots of the town and shouted: "Stamp those goddamn Communists out of the labor movement."

George U. Harvey

The New Deal, according to Borough President George U. Harvey of Queens, New York, is communistic; and so is the Home Relief Bureau; and all anti-war college students are reds, as are members of anti-fascist societies; and Maine and Vermont are the only real American states left. "In other words," concluded an editorial in the New York *Post* (January 14, 1938):

> Anybody who doesn't agree with His Royal Highness . . . is a "Communist" and, ipso facto, ought to be strung up on a telegraph pole. Let Harvey get away with his attack on Communists as a group and the next step will be the use of veterans' organizations to fight all liberals, labor unions, the New Deal and even conservatives of an anti-Harvey persuasion.

Rarely do liberal and conservative papers take the same line, but in the case of New York's chief political office-holding redbaiter, George Harvey, the New York *Times* expressed itself in similar vein. Commenting on Harvey's orders rescinding the constitutional right of free speech to candidates of the Communist Party (and in one instance, the Socialist Party), the *Times* said:

> It serves to give color to one of their favorite contentions, that there is no "real" liberty in a democratic, capitalist State . . . the folly and harmfulness of this sort of action are much broader. . . . Once we suppress the right of free speech and assembly for any group, however small or obnoxious, we violate the basic principle of liberal democracy. We establish a precedent that ends in the suppression of all groups except the increasingly narrow group that finally rules by force.

But Harvey's fame is not based merely on the suppression of the United States Constitution. Harvey is noted for three other things: (1) the proposal to arm all the police with rubber hose to bludgeon radicals; (2) the proposal to lynch said radicals; and (3) the proposal of a new patriotic organization which while fighting reds would incidentally provide jobs for all its patriotic members.

The first of these proposals was made at a meeting sponsored by the American Association against Communism, Inc., one of the two organizations run by Father Edward Lodge Curran of Brooklyn (the other being named the International Truth Society, Inc.—believe it or not). The *Post* said it did not know "whether the association has any connection with Hitler's World League against Communism in Berlin, but it certainly seems to be similar in philosophy and outlook." Nevertheless, "on the platform with President Harvey were Alfred E. Smith, Matthew Woll and Raoul E. Desvernine of the American Liberty League." (Mr. Desvernine, former head of the lawyers' committee of the Liberty League and also president of the Crucible Steel Company, has recently written me saying his presence in this company had no significance. However, it was not the Liberty League but Mayor LaGuardia who protested against the Harvey plan of bludgeoning dissenters.)

The lynching idea came in an address before the Kings County American Legion convention (reported in the *Post*, July 13, 1937) and was received with applause. It is interesting to learn that at this meeting the Legion decided that strikebreaking and other anti-labor activities by its members in the future would not be done in uniform. The practice of scabbing, spying, strike-breaking, was not discouraged; it was merely divorced from the uniform which goes on patriotic parades. The American Legion, according to Major General Smedley Butler, had been the biggest strike-breaking organization in the country.

In 1938 Harvey tried to capitalize on all his prejudices and red phobias by founding "We Americans," which was to organize the entire United States by election districts. "The secret of success," said his General Order No. 1, "will be to give every member a job." However, one American

Legion branch immediately spotted Colonel Harvey's idea as a counterpart of Colonel de la Rocque's Croix de Feu and denounced it, saying: "This is plainly an attempt to use the American Legion, the Veterans of Foreign Wars and other major veterans' organizations to foist Fascism on this country." The Council of Veterans, which includes such notables as General Graves, General Glassford, and Colonel Maurice Simmons, issued this statement:

> To combat what he calls "un-American influences," George U. Harvey has fashioned the most un-American organization yet known among veterans in this country. He has contrived to drape the Black Legion idea with the robes of the Legion of Valor. . . . He has created a setup along the lines of the Fascist Croix de Feu. . . . In this matter of Americanism everybody is out of step but the Colonel. . . . It is G. U. Harvey who is un-American. He has shown it before in his threats to use the rubber hose and hanging from telephone poles, to silence those with whom he disagrees and whom he calls reds and radicals.

In 1939 Harvey proposed that he and his sheriff organize a force of 25,000 spy-, alien-, and red-hunters. He also denounced Mayor LaGuardia for participating in a "Stop Hitler" parade, and in an address to the Catholic Social Workers Guild proposed exile for aliens and concentration camps for Americans, some of whom he said "go around preaching sedition and yet they are rewarded by being invited to the White House for afternoon tea." In 1940, hearing of the arrest of seventeen Christian Fronters by the F.B.I., he screamed indignantly; "They're Americans."

And so is Mr. Harvey.

HAGUE MACHINE PROFITS

Even enemies of Mayor Hague believe that he is sincere in thinking himself "one of the last bulwarks of old-fashioned Americanism against the tide of red 'naturalism.'" However, Hague and the Hague machine, rallying the political payroll, American Legion mercenaries, the Chamber of Commerce of Jersey City, nearly all the Holy Name Societies, the majority of Catholic organizations, the local press, the Hearst press in New York, and the half-hearted New York *Sun,* engaged in a redbaiting campaign directed chiefly against the C.I.O. which resulted in actions the Supreme Court of the United States found illegal.

A typical Hague redbaiting blast was given a great display by the Hearst *Journal and American* under the headline:

HAGUE SEES PLOT BY REDS IN CIO
Overthrow of Courts, Schools, Press Sought, He Tells Chamber

Said the mayor:

Can't you see that Communists are penetrating our educational system by planting agents in every university?

Can't you see that by organizing the lawyers they are planning to overthrow the courts?

Can't you see that by organizing the Newspaper Guild, which belongs to the C.I.O., they are threatening the freedom of the press?

The progress they have made in labor is dangerous. It is the duty not only of Mayor Hague but of every public official in the country to protect the interests of this government and protect the American flag.

All that I hear is a lot of talk about constitutional rights, free speech, free press. Every time I hear remarks of that kind I say, "That's a Communist." . . .

If I had yielded to the Communist invasion as officials in other cities did, millions of dollars would have been lost in wages and Jersey City industries would have been destroyed.

The rest of the speech more openly attacks the C.I.O., the majority of whose membership is affiliated with the Roman Catholic Church, of which Mayor Hague is a moral and financial pillar. The Hague machine fought the C.I.O. by smearing it as red; but the motives of the fight were purely financial: the C.I.O. wants to organize labor in New Jersey, whereas the Hague machine wants to keep New Jersey an open-shop state where rugged individualism can exist among manufacturers and poverty among employees.

The Hearst press, the New York *Sun*, the reactionary press of America, and the scared press of Jersey City have never told the truth about the Hague machine's profiteering in redbaiting. However, a courageous reporter named David G. Wittels, employed on the New York *Post* during the editorship of J. David Stern, did expose the fascist muck in New Jersey. One of his stories was appropriately headlined:

RED $CARE IN N. J. I$ $MOKE $CREEN FOR $50,000,000 "BU$$INE$$"

Mr. Wittels charged that:

> The true motive behind Mayor Frank Hague's red scare and reign of terror is . . . $ $ $ $. For the Hague organization is a $50,000,000 a year "business," set up like an underworld empire; and the Hague crowd fights to protect it just as any other gang battles for its racket: viciously, violently, terroristically. . . .
>
> Fifty million dollars is a staggering lot of money, Hague, a backward pupil at school, who still can't speak or write English correctly, without a profession, business or trade, became a very rich man. . . .
>
> Mayor Hague is no crackpot. He is a shrewd, hardheaded, practical politician, one of the slickest alive. He knows that neither the C.I.O. nor the American Civil Liberties Union, from which he is so violently "saving" Jersey City, is communistic.
>
> He knows that Congressman Jerry O'Connell, whom his henchmen beat up the other night, is no Red, but a

In Congress and Out

better Democrat than he is. He knows that John L. Lewis is really hated by the Reds, and that Norman Thomas, whom he had "deported" . . . is no Communist, but a Socialist who hates Communists so much he wouldn't even march in a recent May Day parade because Communists were in it. . . .

Yet Hague continues to "defend" Jersey City against a "Red Invasion." He has his city all steamed up with one of the biggest Red scares in history. . . . Why does Hague do it? . . .

You can't build an organization like his without there being some things in it you daren't allow the public to know about. You can't build a $50,000,000 a year machine without somebody, somewhere, getting a terrible lot of graft. You can't operate it without sharing, permitting, or at least shutting your eyes to things for which the law provides jail sentences. Every politician, every political observer knows that. It is axiomatic.

The Hague machine is even more corrupt than most other notorious ones. It is built to a greater extent on graft and payroll padding than probably any other in American history. . . . His machine is in danger. So badly has it looted Jersey City that the city is, except by grace of trick bookkeeping, in bankruptcy. Taxpayers have become desperate. . . . Industries fled the excessive taxation and are still fleeing.

The machine was tottering badly. The whole $50,000,000 a year empire threatened to topple on Hague and his henchmen. . . . The situation was desperate. . . . An issue, an all-inclusive issue, a vague issue appealing to emotion and fear, was needed. A dirty name was needed, a charge that could be plastered indiscriminately against almost anyone who tried to attack the Hague $50,000,000 a year racket.

Another politician might have racked his brains for something subtle, something clever. But Hague is smarter than that. He knows that in dealing with a mass of people you needn't worry much about being too obvious. He knew you needn't bother about the fact that intelligent people, people enough removed from the scene to be objective, would see through you as a fraud. Besides, he was desperate.

So he trotted out the same old Red Scare he saw Attorney General A. Mitchell Palmer use so effectively in the railroad strike of 1920; the same old Red Scare that had licked Hague when he was trying to help the strikers then. How he sold that bill of goods to Jersey City is a masterpiece of showmanship, ballyhoo and engineering.

It was another machine politician, Matt Quay of Pennsylvania, who said that when you had a weak candidate, wrap him in the stars and stripes. Hague has found that the first part of the tricolor is enough to wrap around an enemy.

The racket in Jersey City continues. The C.I.O. is making progress, it is true, and labor may some day come into its own there; but despite the Supreme Court ruling against Hague, the machine, with its graft and corruption, continues to flourish. At present both parties, Republican and Democratic, are sharers of the loot, the $50,000,000 a year, hidden behind the red scare.

It has been the same in New Orleans, in Kansas City, and wherever political machines, Republican and Democratic alike, have plundered the treasury and the public. The red scare is just as much a weapon for an American racketeering politician as it was for Hitler and Mussolini.

Part IV

Big Business as Usual

CHAPTER 15
Business Patriotism

By and large the little merchant is more concerned over his weekly take than in preserving the constitutional rights of free speech, free press, and free assembly. This becomes at once apparent whenever in any city people Want to speak, to print and distribute handbills, to meet in protest, to march in the streets, to attend free open meetings on public affairs, and these things happen to interfere five dollars, worth with little business.

Thus the Journal Square Merchants Association of Jersey City, in the dispute between Mayor Hague on the one hand and, on the other, Socialist presidential candidate Norman Thomas, the Civil Liberties Union, the C.I.O., and other labor unions, refused to consider it as a question concerned with the Bill of Rights; all it pretended to know was that such public disputes hurt business because the sidewalks became full of people, and cops had to break a few heads, and there were riot calls and police wagons—and how are you going to sell a customer something with all this nonsensical excitement about free speech and the rights of American citizens going on?

"The total losses were estimated at thousands of dollars," one merchant sadly told a newspaper reporter—and the result was the headline:

JERSEY CITY MERCHANTS ASK BAN ON ALL
RALLIES THAT HALT BUSINESS

This was the case which was so important that it went directly to the Supreme Court, which gave a notable decision making the right to speak on public streets a part of the free speech of America, and which affirmed the right of C.I.O. organizers to invade the fascist stronghold which Mayor Hague (vice-chairman of the Democratic Party) rules for the financial benefit of himself and his clique.

The Fifth Avenue merchants' association in New York City comes out with a blast every year when the labor unions ask permission to march on that street on May Day. But in this case the same merchants do not get excited when professional patriotic (and redbaiting) organizations ask for permits.

The West Central Park Association wants the New York City administration to ban public meetings in Columbus Circle, America's Hyde Park corner. It does not say that it objects to what is being preached there, as red, radical, subversive, or un-American; it merely says that all oratory is bad for business. "At night," said Russell B. Corey, president, to a gathering of property owners and their agents, merchants, and bankers, "every soapbox orator north of Forty-second Street is in the Circle talking to crowds and when these people are gone the place is left littered and untidy."

The Twenty-third Street Association is even more bitter about the use of Madison Square for what the New York *Times* calls "motley gatherings" of soapbox orators and sponsors of open-air forums. The day of the New England town meeting has, of course, passed, and with it, it seems, the rights for which the Founding Fathers fought.

THE CONSTITUTIONAL EDUCATIONAL LEAGUE

In its investigation of the forces that interfere with the rights of labor—notably the gunmen, munitions-makers, thugs, spies, and strike-breakers—the La Follette civil liberties committee included a number of self-styled patriotic organizations which proved to be nothing but organized redbaiters of labor for the benefit of business, big and little. These tight all labor, including the A.F. of L., but they concentrate on the newcomer, the C.I.O., and their

Business Patriotism

first line of attack is to brand it red.

The committee subpoenaed officials of the National Civic Federation, the Constitutional Educational League, the National Association of Manufacturers, the League for Industrial Rights, the New York State Economic Council, the Citizens Alliance and Associated Industries of Minneapolis, the Johnstown Chamber of Commerce, the Johnstown Citizens Committee, and similar groups.

Each differs from the other, but space will not permit mentioning even the highlights of the redbaiting and labor-baiting methods of all these patriotic groups. As a sample of nationally organized big business activity in this field I will give some facts about the Johnstown Citizens in a later chapter; the sample patriotic organization I have chosen here is the Constitutional Educational League.

It has offices in Connecticut and New York but functions chiefly in the former state. The reader will remember the fact that Connecticut (as well as Mayor Hague's part of New Jersey and many Southern states) appeals to manufacturers in New York and other unionized zones to escape paying decent wages by moving into a non-union, underpaid, and frequently terrorized area. Sometimes the attractiveness of the spot is enhanced by a well-functioning Ku Klux Klan organization; sometimes there are only the Hague police thugs; in Connecticut there are the chambers of commerce and the Constitutional Educational League.

The C.E.L. takes first prize for hypocrisy. After many years in which it boasted that its purpose was to uphold the Constitution, and to educate the public in its gospel, the C.E.L. had to admit that it knew nothing about the functions for which it was incorporated and which it claimed to fulfill, but that it is almost purely a labor-baiting outfit in masquerade, as the following testimony before the La Follette committee shows:

SENATOR THOMAS: Mr. Hanson, what is the meaning

of the Constitutional Educational League? . . .

Mr. Hanson: It is education pertaining to the Constitution, interpretation of the Constitution, and education, information pertaining to subversive movements in this country which are working against or for the destruction of the Constitution of the United States.

Senator Thomas asked how many articles and how many amendments there were to the Constitution. Mr. Hanson replied he did not know the number of articles. Asked about the preamble, he began with "We the people of the United States, in order to form a more perfect union," and then quit. "I could not recite the entire preamble," said Mr. Hanson.

Mr. Hanson then confounded the Constitution and Lincoln's Gettysburg Address as regards "the philosophy in the Constitution," which he testified consisted of the phrase "a government of, by, and for the people."

> Senator Thomas: What is in Article I of the Constitution?
> Mr. Hanson: I could not tell you, sir.
> Senator Thomas: What is in Article II?
> Mr. Hanson: I do not know.
> Senator Thomas: Article III?
> Mr. Hanson: I do not know.
> Senator Thomas: Article IV?
> Mr. Hanson: No. . . .
> Senator Thomas: Do you know what is in any single article of the Constitution?
> Mr. Hanson: You mean specifically, the specific wording?
> Senator Thomas: Yes.
> Mr. Hanson: I do not; no.

Senator Thomas asked Mr. Hanson where he got the term "Bill of Rights" for the first ten amendments. Mr. Hanson did not know. Was the tenth amendment a part? Mr.

Hanson did not know.

Senator Thomas then asked if he knew what the amendments were about. He gave them by number and Mr. Hanson said he did not know about most of them. The Thirteenth he said he believed to be something about slavery, likewise the Fourteenth, but he did not know the Fifteenth, Sixteenth, or Seventeenth. He spoke up brightly about the Eighteenth, the prohibition amendment, but did not know its sections and what each said.

Mr. Hanson admitted that he makes speeches, but not about the Constitution; he speaks about "communistic activities."

> SENATOR THOMAS: Just what is a communistic activity?
> MR. HANSON: It is an activity—communism is a philosophy of government based on—that teaches collective ownership and democratic management of all the means of production, distribution, and exchange.
> SENATOR THOMAS: Is our public-school system a communistic organization?
> MR. HANSON: I do not think that is a fair question, sir.
> SENATOR THOMAS: You do not think that is a fair question?
> MR. HANSON: It is in a measure. It is a government—it is a socialized institution; it is a government-owned institution.

Asked to name a communist government or communistic experiments, Mr. Hanson said Russia and the Brook Farm experiment. Asked if there was anything in the Brook Farm experiment "antagonistic to American government principles," he replied: "No."

Senator Thomas wanted to know what the "educational" meant in the organization's name. Mr. Hanson replied that Mr. Kamp, the president of the C.E.L., lectured. Asked to explain Mr. Kamp's training in the subject of the Constitution, Mr. Hanson replied: "Our activity is not so much pro-Constitution as anti-Communist."

The C.E.L. was also fighting socialism and Norman Thomas. Asked why he was fighting Thomas, Hanson replied: "Because he wants to do away with the Constitution." Asked to give one specific instance of a statement by Norman Thomas proving this, Mr. Hanson said he could not, but that there were "numerous occasions, in his writing, in his speeches." (From now on, no doubt, redbaiters will be able to say that on page 7256 of Part 16 of the La Follette hearings, a privileged government document, it was testified that Norman Thomas advocated the destruction of the Constitution of the United States.)

Finally, Senator Thomas took the patriotic witness to task about his organization. "I can judge quite correctly from what you say then," he concluded, "that the word 'constitutional' does not have any meaning in your Constitutional Educational League." Mr. Hanson assented. "And the word 'educational' has no meaning," added the senator. . . . Now, then, what is 'league'? We have gotten rid of 'constitution,' gotten rid of 'education.' Now let us see if we can get rid of 'league.'" Mr. Hanson insisted that there were "several thousand members," but could give no other information.

As for President Joseph Kamp, who rode away in his car with the subpoenaed records of the C.E.L., he is listed as one of the editors of the *Awakener,* an openly pro-fascist weekly. Kamp also publishes news sheets, pamphlets, broadsides, leaflets, a tremendous amount of propaganda material—all devoted to just one subject: smearing the C.I.O. as red, and incidentally smearing labor and everything liberal and progressive. Wherever there is any labor-baiting to be done, wherever an employer has labor troubles and wants to keep the C.I.O. and other unions out, he uses the Kamp "literature." Here are some of the titles:

The Faked Contract, with a picture of a C.I.O. dues collector, looking very much like Lewis, gouging a workingman.

The Worker's Road to Independence, by the Hon. Clare E. Hoffman of Michigan.

Battalions of Death, by the same Honorable. A skull and crossbones with the C.I.O. initials on the cover.

Vote for John L. Lewis and Communism, by Richard W. O'Neill, chairman of the C.E.L. Veterans Committee. The same type of propaganda as the chief Lewis booklet.

Communism's Iron Grip on the CIO, another Hoffman oration.

Warning! This Is the Red Christian Front, a folder accusing the United Christian Council for Democracy, an organization of Episcopalian, Methodist, Baptist, Unitarian, Presbyterian, Quaker, Congregationalist, Evangelical and Disciples preachers and professors, of being a "smokescreen" for Communism. Evidence: the Hearst New York *Journal and American.*

Revolution, by George E. Sokolsky. Reprinted from the New York Herald Tribune by the Constitutional Democracy Association.

Headlines. "All the facts that should be printed. For speakers, writers and students." A very well-printed eight-page magazine supplementing the anti-C.I.O. pamphlets—and just about as reliable.

In Volume 1, No. 1, of the last-named publication, Editor Kamp writes and editorial, "Who Is a Red?" in which he says:

> The term "Red" has been bandied back and forth so much in recent years that on hearing it the ordinary American finds himself in a quandary—or it leaves him altogether "cold." It must be admitted that the term has been loosely used—and, on the other hand, deliberately abused. To be perfectly frank, in the latter category, real Reds have been successful, through facetious repetition, in having the term thoroughly ridiculous. It has become a joke. Everybody's "Red." . . .

On the same editorial page is this statement:

> Why *Headlines?* 1. Because there is a vital need to acquaint the public with the *true facts* behind the many stories in the news these days which have Communist implications [The italics and grammar are Mr. Kamp's.] . . . The TRUTH in *Headlines* is certified; every item may be used with confidence. . . .

Here are some headlines from *Headlines* (space considerations forbid details):

> [W.P.A.] PROJECT WRITER TAUGHT TO SHOOT AMERICAN TROOPS
> RELIEF FUNS HELP REDS IN SPAIN
> ALIEN RED LEADERS THANK ALLIANCE [Re: Bridges and Pritchett]
> NEW YORK WPA THEATER PROJECT FULLY STAFFED WITH COMMUNISTS
> G.O.P. AND DEMOCRATS HELP BUILD RED FRONT
> A.L.P. [American Labor Party] STRATEGY PLANNED BY BROWDER
> O'CONNOR BRANDED HARRY HOPKINS AS SOCIALIST VOTER
> A.L.P. JOINS WITH RED RAND SCHOOL TO TRAIN LEADERS
> COHEN AND CORCORAN TRIED TO STIFLE DIES QUIZ. ICKES, PERKINS AND LA FOLLETTE SPIES PLAY PARTS IN PLOT . . . "RED TRAIL TO WHITE HOUSE"
> F.D.R. REBUKE [to Dies] PLANNED WITH RED
> TAXPAYERS PAY FOR RED PROPAGANDA AND FILTH [Re: W.P.A.]
> W.P.A, "WRITERS" HELP ORGANIZE NEW JERSEY REVOLT.
> COMMUNISTS KIDNAP DIES WITNESS WHO TESTIFIED ABOUT RED WRITERS
> RED W.P.A. "WRITERS" EXPOSE THEMSELVES
> ANARCHIST ALSBERG W.P.A. WRITERS HEAD INSPIRED SITDOWN

Refused to join Communist Party they are fired!

Red spies "check up" on Dies agents

There may be some wholly accurate and truthful news items in the Constitutional Educational League's magazine, *Headlines,* but there is not one which is free of bias or propaganda. And all of it is called TRUTH and "all the facts that should be printed."

One distinguishing feature of the Kamp output is this challenge: "$1,000 reward will be paid to anyone who can prove that a single charge made in this booklet is untrue. A similar reward is offered if it can be shown that any of the published quotations are not strictly accurate."

So far as regards the chief Kamp opus, entitled *Join the C.I.O. and Help Build a Soviet America,* it may be said that the entire booklet is made up of many half-truths that are worse than lies; it is all bias and distortion; it is full of quotations torn from context and of misinterpretation; in short it is anything but the TRUTH. But more than that, it is claimed by the Labor Research Association, of which Robert Dunn is director, that there are twenty outright lies in the pamphlet, and Mr. Kamp refuses to permit neutrals to judge the charge and he refuses to pay the thousand dollars or make corrections. In claiming the reward the L.R.A. says that the whole thesis of the pamphlet (that the C.I.O. is Communist) is completely false. The C.I.O. is not Communist; the executive officers are not Communists; the membership is not Communist, nor is a majority or even an important fraction thereof Communist. (Since this statement, which nullifies the Kamp pamphlet, was made, Congressman Dies, who had also made the red charge against the C.I.O., has withdrawn it. There is now, therefore, no reason for the thousand dollars not to be paid over.)

In the Kamp booklet there is a red network department. One item reads: "Frank L. Palmer, onetime I.W.W. agitator, former head of the Communist news wire service, the Federated Press, and now the editor of a Communist tabloid."

The L.R.A. says that every statement in this sentence is false. Frank Palmer was never an I.W.W. agitator, but was once connected with Grace Church in Denver. Federated Press, of which he was eastern bureau manager, has never had any connection whatever with the Communist Party. It serves labor and liberal publications, mostly labor. *People's Press*, of which Palmer is now editor, is not a Communist tabloid; it has no connection whatsoever with the Communist Party.

Mr. Kamp repeats the old lie about Detroit being renamed Lewistown on a Moscow map. The L.R.A. declares no such map has been placed in the Moscow Revolutionary Museum, that the story is a figment of some redbaiter's imagination. There is a Lewiston in Michigan, eleven of them in the United States.

On page 6, Kamp publishes what he calls the "Communist Honor Roll for 1937," with the Soviet hammer and sickle, which Kamp claims he reprints from the *Western Worker* of January 7, 1937. The L.R.A. points out that this is another fraud: that the *Western Worker* published the same list of names as "Labor's Honor Roll," that there was no hammer and sickle, no mention of Communist, and that Kamp also altered the line after the name of Largo Caballero. (In the original it read "head of People's Front Government in Spain"; in Kamp's version the word "Government" is omitted, giving it an entirely different complexion.)

The Labor Research Association tried to get its thousand-dollar reward by entering suit, but did not press the matter when it learned that the most prominent reactionary citizens of Connecticut are listed as being on the advisory board of the League, among them: Colonel Anthony Sunderland, commissioner of police of Hartford; Judge John L. Gilson of the New Haven Probate Court;

Charles D. Lockwood, a law partner of former Attorney-General Homer Cummings.

In the Southern (Seventh) Edition of the anti-C.I.O. Pamphlet, the Constitutional Educational League still maintains that it is "an educational organization with a patriotic objective." Taking cognizance of the fact that "red critics, within and without the C.I.O.," accuse it of being "a strike-breaking agency, a manufacturers outfit, an anti-union racket," it declares that "since 1919 the League has been engaged in combating the Red elements through the medium of the printed and spoken word. In this endeavor it has enjoyed the co-operation of loyal American labor. High officials of the A. F. of L. have written for its publications and have spoken from its rostrums."

When, however, Mr. Kamp disappeared with the records, the La Follette committee was unable to find out who really backs the C.E.L. and whose money pays for the flood of propaganda.

It is interesting to note that by October 1937 the C.I.O. was able to announce that "the American standard of living has been raised to a sizeable extent through the activities of the C.I.O. in winning wage increases for millions of previously unorganized workers. . . . Approximately $1,000,000,000 a year has been added to the pay envelope of workers benefiting from the union agreements won by the C.I.O."

But in a report on anti-labor organizations in the United States made by the economists of the National Labor Relations Board (David J. Saposs, assisted by Elizabeth T. Bliss), one of the organizations exposed is the Constitutional Educational League. The report says:

> Its technique in fighting the C.I.O, follows the well-established pattern employed by all anti-labor organizations. Through its educational and publicity departments it is seeking:
> 1. To label the C.I.O. as a "communistic" organization.

2. To attribute such violence as has occurred during the present labor disputes to the C.I.O.

3. To picture John L. Lewis as a fabulously wealthy power-mad individual, intent upon exploiting the workers in the C.I.O. for the sake of personal ambition. . . .

The anti-union employers are operating through a well-organized mass offensive in their fight against organized labor. Forbidden by law to interfere with their employees' right to organize, these employers and their allies have turned from open opposition to indirect anti-labor maneuvers and stratagems in order to fulfill their old objectives. In their attempts to confuse and intimidate their employees and to evade the National Labor Relations Act, they have recognized the importance of capturing the support of the "Third Party," the general public. Accordingly, they have concentrated their energies on creating public opinion hostile to organized labor. The increasing skill with which these employers crystallize public opinion through their manipulations of the "independents," back-to-work movements, citizens committees for "law and order," and the vigilante groups places in grave jeopardy their employees' right to organize and bargain collectively.

Merchant of Red Herrings

When a slaughter of workingmen takes place, such as the Chicago Memorial Day Massacre, the dead and the wounded are denounced at the coroner's inquest as agitators, aliens, reds, or the victims of radical leadership, and the police involved are found not guilty by a jury of American Legionnaires. The Republic Steel company is absolved. Tom Girdler, its head, is not arrested. On the contrary, he goes about addressing associations of manufacturers and chambers of commerce on the subject of real Americanism.

Those who look below the surface of newspaper reports know that it is actually the big business set-up of the nation which is responsible for both the massacre of workers in times of strike, and the redbaiting campaign against them at all times—a campaign which aims to keep them from organizing and therefore from getting higher wages. In other words, it is the universal devil of profits which is responsible, and not particularly a personal devil like Tom Girdler.

In the ensuing chapters the detailed story of the present-day endeavors of the following big business organizations will be told: the United States Chamber of Commerce; some local chambers of commerce; the National Association of Manufacturers; the Associated Farmers; the Liberty League; and the Johnstown Citizens Committee.

The activities of business men when they organize against progressive movements of the American people are rarely reported in the press. After all, it is the local banker and shopkeeper who pay the small-town editor's expenses, and big business which makes possible big newspapers. However, when there are congressional investigations into the methods and conspiracies of big business, the newspapers are forced to make some reports. It is most interesting to note, therefore, that as recently as 1939 and 1940 the press of the United States suppressed or buried in its back pages the sensational disclosures of the La Follette investigation of the Associated Farmers, while putting on its front pages the falsehoods, distortions, and hysterics of the Martin Dies outfit.

Three times in its history the La Follette committee found that secret forces were trying to kill it by lobbying in Congress against an extension of funds. Labor's Non-Partisan League on one of these occasions issued a statement accusing "Big Business sympathizers in the Senate" of "attempting to gag the La Follette Committee."

> Investigations by the La Follette Committee have not contributed to the peace and happiness of ruthless big businessmen. In its investigation of the Chicago massacre outside the steel plant, the committee proved

that unarmed workers parading peacefully were shot in the back by Chicago's police and armed thugs. In its inquiry into strikebreaking activities the committee disclosed before the nation that brutal and barbaric attack upon organized labor by organized business and its legions of the underworld. . . .

In one of its notable reports the La Follette committee exposes both the trickery and the violence with which big business fights the labor movement.

> The investigations reveal [that] the employer directs his spy forces against any kind of union activity . . . [and] cloaks his hostility under the pretext that he is defending himself and country against communism. . . . Employers' money is paid to corrupt their workers by bribery. . . . Espionage has become the habit of American management. Until it is stamped out, the rights of labor to organize, freedom of speech, freedom of assembly, will be meaningless phrases. . . . Only one side is armed. Workers do not buy either armaments or gas.[1]

One of the great myths sponsored and propagated by big business blames aliens, agitators, and radicals of all colors and stripes for much of the individual and mass violence which have marked the bloody course of our industrial and social-economic history. There is no doubt that public opinion has come to accept as a fact the charge that it is the aliens and radicals who are usually responsible for this violence and that they habitually advocate violence in the settling of labor disputes. The truth is just the opposite. The Civil Liberties Union writes:

> WHO IN FACT ADVOCATES VIOLENCE?
> In all our experience of the last fifteen years in handling free speech cases all over the country, we do not know of a single case of a specific incitement to

---

[1] *La Follette Reports*, Seventy-fifth Congress, 1st Session; Report No. 46, p.5.

violence by any radical. Nor in all the cases of I.W.W.'s, Communists and others which we have handled, was there any incitement to violence even in general terms. Not a single act of violence has ever been proved against a member of the I.W.W. or Communist Party in the last decade in connection with any of the activities of those organizations.

Acts of violence in strikes are common, chiefly by strikers against strike-breakers. But that has nothing to do with radical propaganda. Such acts of violence are common on the part of orthodox trade-unionists affiliated with the A. F. of L. Anyone familiar with strikes knows that the leaders always counsel against such violence. We know of no strike leader convicted for inciting even that form of violence, so common in strikes.

But we know of scores of convictions of radicals under state sedition and criminal syndicalism laws punishing mere advocacies of violence, in which nothing was proved but the expression of general radical views, or mere membership in an organization construed to favor political or industrial changes by violent means.

But when it comes to advocacy of violence by reactionaries, the story is different. Those who call for violence against radicals, strikers and Negroes go scot free. Not a conviction, not a prosecution in years! Lynching of Negroes in the south is commonly condoned or encouraged in private utterances. Excited employers or professional patriots often urge violence against reds and strikers. The Civil Liberties Union is opposed to prosecuting them, if by chance any prosecutor were rash enough to attempt it.

The declarations of various semi-Fascist "shirt" organizations which have sprung up in recent years advocate far more violence in seizing the government than can be found in Communist publications. Yet not a single leader has been prosecuted for such language, though prosecutors would be quick to move against Communists using it.

But the reactionaries not only incite violence; they

practice it. Witness the story of almost any strike. Look at the record of the attacks on the Communist Party, the I.W.W. Reflect on the brutal treatment of the Negro, our shameful lynchings. Take the Ku Klux Klan alone in its hey-day. Hundreds of Negroes, Catholics, aliens and others opposed by the Ku Klux Klan were mobbed, tarred and feathered and beaten. Over two thousand cases of mob violence were cited in an official investigation of Klan activities in the state of Oklahoma alone. And yet not a single person committing or inciting these violent acts against strikers, Negroes or radicals has ever been punished.

It is plain, therefore, that those who defend majority prejudice or property rights may not only advocate but practice violence against their enemies without fear of prosecution. But those who agitate revolutionary ideals of a workers' world or of practical resistance to capitalism on the job or in strikes are fought by every weapon in the arsenal of reaction. They are prosecuted for alleged advocacy of violence, when as a matter of plain fact no act of violence is involved. But prosecutors see future violence implied in a revolutionary goal. Many I.W.W.'s and Communists have gone to prison merely for joining an organization whose program is construed to champion future violence, if and when necessary for the workers to take power.

A confirmation to the foregoing Civil Liberties Union statement was written some time ago by J. B Matthews, who later became the chief tattletale of the Dies redbaiting committee. In his book, *Partners in Plunder,* it is stated that in the first two weeks of the 1934 textile strike fourteen workmen were killed by police and militiamen. Theodore Francis Green, governor of Rhode Island and heavy investor in textile mills,

> sent a message full of anti-communist hysteria to the legislature asking for an extraordinary session for the purpose of ousting every "red" from the state. Just how pink a man could be before being considered "red" was

not specified.

After five hours of heated debate the legislature concluded that the governor had exaggerated the "red" menace. However, the legislature voted $100,000 to hire more police. Government under business is a dictatorship of the owning class and that dictatorship is expressed more and more openly and violently as property interests require it.[2]

When business men foregather these days, they no longer conceal their hatred of labor, directed chiefly against the C.I.O., with whom they have not been able to make the deals that have hitherto sometimes been possible with unions.

At a meeting of the National Industrial Council, the C.I.O. was denounced as "communistic" and "racketeering"; it was alleged that it was in financial difficulties; and resistance to it was called "democratic." The Wagner Act was recommended for scrapping and the dissolution of the National Labor Relations Board was urged. Wages in 1937 were called "inflated" and the "right of a laborer to his job" was labeled a "vicious notion."[3] The authors of these phrases and holders of these reactionary ideas were C. M. White of Republic Steel; Lewis H. Haney, professor of economics at New York University and better known as writer on the Hearst papers; and Hartley W. Barclay, editor of the magazine, *Mill and Factory*.

Another glimpse of the views of organized big business is this compilation (from its own documents) of the program of the New York Board of Trade:

Business is against:
Thirty-hour week bill
Labor relations board bill
Child labor amendment

---

2 J. B. Matthews and R. E. Shallcross, *Partners in Plunder* (Covici-Friede, 1935).
3 New York *Times*, December 7, 1937.

Minimum wage laws
Closed shop
Higher taxes on the rich
Corporation surplus tax
Chain store tax
Relief spending
Municipal power plants
Municipal power authority
Increased pay for labor
Strong labor leaders
Government banking control
Restoration of pay cuts
Threats of sit-down strikes

Business is for:

Curbs on unions
Direct taxation, broader base
Pay-as-you-go relief
Prohibition of sympathy strikes
Incorporation of labor unions
Reduction up to 50 percent in number of cases carried and the cost of relief (New Jersey plan)
"Law and order" (vigilantism)
Balanced budget
Economy in public expenditures
Broadening income tax base
Safeguarding value of existing business investments
Profits

In *The Spirit and Structure of German Fascism,* Professor Robert A. Brady has compared the programs of American business organizations with those in Europe which have finally established fascism, or Business plus Bayonets. Professor Brady quotes a long series of fascist doctrines side by side with quotations from the "literature" of American big business which parallel the doctrines.[4]

Since big business favors fascism in America also, it

---

4 Robert A. Brady, *The Spirit and Structure of German Fascism* (Viking, 1937).

has adopted the fascist idea of redbaiting as its propaganda weapon. How this has been done by the largest business organizations is told in the following pages.

CHAPTER 16
The Chambers of Commerce

We have now seen redbaiting in action, some of its results, and a few of its practitioners. We come now to the organized forces behind it.

The most important of them are the Chamber of Commerce of the United States, the local chambers, and the other societies, institutes, and associations which represent big business. It is true that in listing the agencies of repression the Civil Liberties Union annually places the American Legion first and the chambers of commerce second (generally followed by the Hearst press and the Ku Klux Klan), but this listing is based on many physical actions by the Legion, such as raids, demonstrations, individual and organized violence, whereas the chambers of commerce as a rule do not indulge themselves in that manner. They are the powers behind the scene.

The profits in redbaiting for big business are the most obvious—and the largest in dollars and cents. Under the "American way" that it stands for there is not enough food, clothing, and shelter for everyone. When the President once said that one-third the population was dispossessed, he was only underestimating, for later official figures have shown that two-thirds of the families of the nation average about eight hundred dollars a year, an income that does not permit a civilized standard of decency. There are, of course, ways to remedy the situation, but every one of them would mean a decrease in profits—if not the abolition of private profits altogether—and therefore big business and its agencies, the Chamber of Commerce, the National Association of Manufacturers, the Associated Farmers, and the rest, are opposed to such changes in the *status quo.* Change itself is called radical, is branded red, is blamed on Moscow, and nationwide campaigns of baiting are encouraged.

The Easleys, Matthewses, Sokolskys, the professional-patriotic associations, the scores of writers, columnists and calumnists, propaganda agents, and plutogogues are the small fry of redbaiting compared to the great red-herring mongers of the Chamber of Commerce of the United States and its subsidiaries in every big and little town in the country. The Big Money, which subsidizes the Republican and Democratic Parties, which frequently succeeds in buying the Presidency,[1] which maintains the biggest and most powerful lobby in Washington, and which pretty well controls the lives of the majority of people in this country, is the same power which controls the Chamber of Commerce and which directs all its activities.

Examine the list of members of the United States Chamber of Commerce Committee on Combating Subversive Activities: it does not include the very biggest men, not one of the five who told Miss Dorothy Thompson that they dealt in Presidents and ran the United States, but it gives a fair sample of the wealth and power behind the campaign. The first name on the list is that of the chairman, Felix M. McWhirter of the Peoples State Bank of Indianapolis. . . .

In one of the few days in which the Dies committee was not devoting itself to redbaiting, it made a show of being impartial by attempting to expose some fascist plans and plottings. It took up the case of General Van Horn Moseley, who with his associates was accused of conspiring to bring off a beerhall *Putsch* "to save the country from the reds." Some $8000 had been provided, it was testified, by Dudley Pierrepont Gilbert; strategy was in the hands of George Deatherage, and propaganda was conducted by James E.

---

[1] The New York *World* on January 13, 1924, exposed one instance in which the leading bankers and business men of America bought themselves a President. See also: Seldes, *You Can't Do That, pp. 212-13.*

Campbell. Deatherage and Campbell discussed "military action" in their letters. All the Nazi bundists, the fascist organizations, the anti-Semites, and the anti-labor organizations in the country were being lined up behind the first person thought capable of uniting reaction into a marching force: General Van Horn Moseley.

In the course of the hearings it was testified that Banker McWhirter, who is also treasurer of the state committee of the Republican Party in Indiana, had corresponded with Campbell and interceded with him to get Moseley to address a special meeting of the Republican Party in Indianapolis at which "some 300 to 400 business men from all parts of Indiana, 72 newly elected mayors, 283 newspaper editors and publishers, and 67 legislators" were to be present.

McWhirter's colleagues in the Chamber of Commerce witch hunt are: James A. Farrell and William C. Teagle, representing two of the biggest corporations in the world; Lewis E. Pierson of the Irving Trust; Philip J. Fay of San Francisco; Adolf Schleicher of United States Rubber; and Silas Strawn.

These men, their corporations, and their interests parallel the group composed of Thyssen, Hugenberg, Stinnes, Vogel, and Flick, which financed Hitler, or the group of the Liga Industriale and the manufacturers association which financed Mussolini; and although their committee is supposed to discover, expose, and attack every subversive movement, no matter from which side it comes, it has devoted years to attacking labor, liberals, leftists, Socialists, and Communists, and it has never discovered, exposed, or attacked any Hitlerites, fascists, or reactionaries of any sort, as subversive.

The members of the Chamber of Commerce of the United States do a nice profitable business with Japan. Japan is a fascistic or dictatorial state and its world ambitions are regarded as inimical to ours. The members of the Chamber of Commerce of the United States, up to 1940 at least, did a nice business with Nazi Germany. The same business men and patriots do business with Italy, whose fascism is defined by its founder, Mussolini, as "illiberal, anti-liberal, anti-democratic, and reactionary."

Throughout the years 1935 to 1940 when this committee against subversive activities was in action, it went on record month by month against communism in America and in Russia, against aliens, against radicals, against the unions, and against everything liberal and progressive in American life. It took actions, published resolutions, condemned, recommended, cheered, raised the flag, denounced. . . .

But it never even mentioned fascism. It never attacked the autocratic reactionary governments. It never showed up German or Italian intrigue, or the danger of reaction in America—how could it, when it would have to name as the chief agent of reaction none other than itself? Although dedicated to fighting "subversive activities" on all fronts, it heard no evil, saw no evil, spoke no evil, concerning Nazism, Fascism, or its equivalents in Japan, Portugal, and Franco Spain. Its propaganda has run into millions of words, but never is there an unkind mention of the Ku Klux Klan, Coughlinism, vigilantes, the plot between Legionnaires and Wall Street bankers to get General Butler to seize the capital, the Christian Fronters, or the dozens of other "patriotic" groups. The Chamber of Commerce specializes only in attacking men and institutions which might harm dividends and profits. It attacks everything liberal, pro-labor, intellectual, and reformist, as well as socialist and communist. It is out for the money; and for money everything that is against the vested interests is subversive.

The proof of this is to be found in the literature of the Chamber of Commerce itself. Its most important publication is entitled *Safeguards Against Subversive Activities; a periodical summary of published material, organization action, legislation, and other measures to combat subversive activities.* The first issue (June 1935) begins with resolutions of the Chamber and the Junior Chamber. The former says:

> The spread of propaganda and activity by numerous subversive groups is increasing, their common goal being violent overthrow of the existing economic and social order in the United States.
> So serious has the situation become that it is imperative that public opinion be aroused in an effort to rind effective ways of combating and counteracting this movement whose purpose is to bring about revolution by force.
> We accordingly urge that Congress . . .

There follow the usual anti-liberal, anti-alien, anti-radical ideas which are introduced in the form of bills at every session of Congress by the agents, private and congressional, of the C. of C. lobby.[2]

The bulletin also reprints in its first issue the eight-point petition of the Benevolent and Protective Order of Elks, seven of the points being directed against subversive activities in general and one "to prohibit entry of Communists." There is no mention of Fascists or Nazis, apparently because such elements are not subversive to Elkdom.

The largest part of the eleven-page bulletin is taken up with a list of gag measures, all of which apparently have the Chamber's approval. These are the redbaiting bills which come up annually and which sometimes are passed, frequently to be later called unconstitutional by the United States Supreme Court.

The last part of the monthly report is usually devoted to recommending magazine articles and books dealing with subversive activities, and here again, almost without

---

[2] The best book on the subject of the property lobby versus the public welfare is Kenneth Crawford's *The Pressure Boys* (Julian Messner, 1939).

exception, only those attacking communism, Russia, radicalism, aliens, labor leaders, and liberals are mentioned, whereas literature exposing and attacking fascism and reaction is left unmentioned.

In its first issue, Isaac F. Marcosson's article, "The Alien in America" (*Saturday Evening Post*, April 6, 1935), is recommended. The Chamber quotes Marcosson as saying that crime and subversive activities in their most revolutionary forms are to be found among aliens who are illegally in America. (So far as crime is concerned, the Wickersham report has amply disproved the charge.) Marcosson concludes with an attack on the "undesirable alien" as an agitator. Reputable organizations of the best citizens in America have denounced this sort of innuendo as propagandistic misrepresentation.

In issue No. 2 (July 1935), redbaiting organizations which have passed appropriate resolutions, such as the Reserve Officers' Association, the Constitutional Protective League, the Kiwanis International, and the Sons of the American Revolution, are highly praised—as are Nicholas Murray Butler of Columbia and James R. Angell of Yale, for attacking the theory of the class struggle. The reports of the Lusk, Fish, and McCormack-Dickstein investigating committees are summarized and approved, although it is a fact that the Lusk reports have been completely discredited and today generally serve only the lunatic fringe of which Mrs. Dilling is the high priestess; the Fish reports are little better and contain even more glaring falsities; while the most important item in the McCormack-Dickstein report is the proof of the fascist conspiracy which General Butler exposed and which the press soft-pedaled.

In the Chamber's bulletin No. 4, J. G. Shaw's article in *Liberty*, "Will the Communists Get Our Girls in College?" is recommended. This is the article which Mr. Shaw's daughter answered under the title, "My Father ls a Liar."

Generally the Chamber of Commerce attack on labor is camouflaged, but sometimes the artists in smear-words forget themselves. In the fifth issue, for example, there is a reprint entitled "Labor Relations and Radicalism," which is detailed in the sixth issue. Mr. Eric A. Johnston, under the mask of anti-communism, makes an attack on union labor on the west coast, notably San Francisco, Portland, Longview, and Seattle. Labor troubles, strikes, and labor's legitimate and legal exercise of its rights become subversive activities when recounted in the C. of C. report. Mr. Johnston, a director of this institution, urges fellow-employers to educate their workmen against the wiles of labor leaders whom he calls Communists; he urges the "gradual evolutionary dissipation through education, training, sound reasoning, of the fallacies of that devastating, destroying theory that might is right," apparently forgetting that that is in fact the employers' theory, that the employer has the police, militia, gas bombs, machine-guns, and the press on his side, and uses this might to make the world safe for dividends.

In the January 1936 issue the Chamber quotes G. M. Godden, of the Christian Protest Movement, the same Godden who is quoted by Coughlin in *Social Justice*, except that the Chamber does not quote the anti-Semitic lies.

The issue of June 1936 is devoted mainly to a speech by Roger D. Lapham, president of the American-Hawaiian Steamship Company, at the C. of C. annual convention. It deals entirely with labor, there is almost no mention of reds or Communists, but it is the chief item in a bulletin devoted to attacking subversive activities. The natural conclusion is that labor itself is subversive. Strike leaders are termed radicals and left-wingers, but it is mentioned that when the San Francisco strike was over, the men obtained wage increases of 12 percent or more, which was a great pain in the pocketbook to the employers. As for Harry Bridges, the speaker is careful not to repeat the charge that the Pacific Coast leader is a Communist, but he knows how to employ smear-words and innuendo. The situation is intolerable, what with labor getting better money and shorter hours, and the Wagner Act giving workmen more power. "Power inevitably leads to abuse," concludes Mr. Lapham. It is a sad picture—for commercial patriots.

The anti-red booklets published by the Associated Farmers are recommended; the Kiwanis and the Hotel Greeters of America, who promise to combat radicalism, are applauded; and so are the Student Americaneers and the Better America Federation.

Among the redhunting tidbits the C. of C. monthly report picked up for August 1936 are a Mormon (Church of Jesus Christ of Latterday Saints) resolution warning against communism and a Loyal Order of Moose ditto. Both actions are against communism, and there is no mention of Fascism, Hitlerism, etc., although the Moose speak of "every other movement."

In issue No. 15, April 1937, among the pamphlets recommended is *Is It Happening Here,* published by *Our Sunday Visitor,* Catholic weekly, which says fascism is preferable to communism, one reason being that it is friendly to religion, meaning the Catholic Church. Also recommended is a pamphlet by Reverend Joseph F. Thorning, S.J., who has spread more misinformation and propaganda about Spain than any other person besides General Franco. Altogether a score or more of pamphlets are okayed, all of them published by the Paulist Fathers, the Jesuits, and other Roman Catholic institutions. It is obvious from an inspection of the entire output of propaganda of the Chamber of Commerce that it is working closely with the Roman Catholic hierarchy in the redbaiting campaign.

The first item in the next (June 1937) issue is devoted to the nice work of the Knights of Columbus. Supreme Knight Martin H. Carmody is quoted. Carmody attacks not only communism but socialism and social-democracy, all of which he accuses of wanting to banish God, subvert orderly government, and spread fanaticism and hate. (This will be news to the numerous Protestant preachers who are

Christian Socialists and Social-Democrats.) Supreme Knight Carmody is followed by Pope Pius XI. Also recommended: a. pamphlet published by the *National Republic.*

In November 1937, the first item in *Safeguards Against Subversive Activities* is under the heading, "National Chamber Program. What Helps Business," and continues to say that "what helps business helps you." The inference is plain: the Chamber attacks what it considers subversive; that helps business, and it helps you—if your chief interest is the welfare of big business. The hero of this issue is none other than Walter Lippmann—the former socialist, the former liberal.

In 1938 and 1939 considerable space is given to backing and fighting for the Dies committee. The national hero this time is J. B. Matthews. Every renegade is lionized. Mayor Hague is listed as a fighter against communism in those issues of the bulletin preceding the decision of the Supreme Court that Mayor Hague, in denying the C.I.O., labor, and liberals their right of free speech, violated the Constitution of the United States.

In February 1940, the Chamber bulletin quotes extensively from Dies and gives his list of organizations labeled "Communist Party fronts." Among them is the League of American Writers, of which I happen to be a vice-president and therefore may be allowed to say that the Dies statement is a lie, and, like the similar inclusion in the list of "Communist fronts" of the North American Committee to Aid Spanish Democracy and the Friends of the Abraham Lincoln Brigade, is an outrageous action which only congressional immunity makes possible.

The technique of half-truths that are more dangerous than lies, the Chamber also knows how to employ. When Dean Landis of Harvard University Law School reported to Secretary of Labor Perkins that the charges against Harry Bridges were unfounded, he concluded by saying that, since he had established the fact that Bridges was not a

Communist or affiliated with that party, he did not take evidence on the policy of the party itself. And this paragraph is the only one the bulletin reprints. It suppresses the entire report in which Dean Landis brands as falsifications, forgeries, and perjuries considerable evidence offered against Bridges by some of the professional and commercial patriots who had been approved in the Chamber's previous publications.

The usual three or four pages of alien-baiting in the first 1940 issue are followed by the usual pages of reprint of patriotic resolutions, in this instance by the American Coalition, the American Legion, the Disabled American Veterans of the World War, the Veterans of Foreign Wars, the Military Order of the World War, and the American Federation of Labor. In 1940, after five years of redbaiting, the words Fascism and Nazism begin to creep into the professional patrioteers' budget of anti-labor, anti-alien, and anti-liberal resolutions—and into the pages of the Chamber of Commerce bulletin.

In addition to the monthly report, the Chamber has distributed throughout the United States a booklet, *Combating Subversive Activities in the United States*, as fine a sample of half-truths, whole untruths, perversions of truth, rumors, misstatements, and propaganda as even Father Coughlin has ever written or uttered. To begin with, there is a repetition of the notorious distortions which Medill's Chicago *Tribune* published in 1886 and later, regarding the Haymarket explosion. Next there is the story of the assassination of President McKinley by a man named Czolgoscz, for which the anarchist doctrines of Emma Goldman were blamed—by the Hearst papers. (If there was any subversive influence involved, it was that of the Hearst press, which, attacking the President, predicted a bullet was speeding his way; and the Chamber forgets that Hearst was hanged in effigy at that time, as the inspirer of the murder.)

The booklet then rushes on headlong to describe the "subversive activity of the Communist International" in all parts of the world, items presumably culled from the Hearst press. In the United States, subversion consisted of the following:

> Communists [in 1932 and 1933] . . .stirred up trouble in connection with the so-called bonus army in Washington; attracted notoriety through agitation in connection with the Scottsboro, Ala., negro case; organized the "Hunger March" on Washington; staged a protest before the Japanese Embassy in connection with military activities in China; and instituted rent, anti-eviction, and unemployment demonstrations in various cities. The fomenting of bank runs in 1932 was also charged to communists.
>
> During 1934, the communists have participated in a number of strikes held in the United States, endeavoring to take the leadership of strikes out of the hands of organized labor and utilizing such demonstrations for the promotion of unrest and the arousing of the spirit of antagonism against the government, the recognized labor unions, and other institutions of American character.
>
> Prominent among such subversive activities during 1934. was the communist entry into the longshoremen's strike and the general strike on the Pacific Coast, where the communists, under the leadership of an alien communist organizer, pursued obstructive tactics which prevented agreements, arrived at with government help by employers and recognized labor representatives, from being adopted. The strike lasted 84 days, from May 9 to July 31; was marked by extreme violence; and resulted in deaths, bloodshed, and an estimated money loss of $300,000,000.

These are the statements of the Chamber of Commerce, the organization of the leading business men of America, not the statements of yellow journalists like Hearst, or redbaiters like Easley, or the free-lance artists who invent fantasies to sell to wealthy men trembling over their bank books. According to the safe and sane gentlemen who represent the fine flower of present-day big business, participation in a strike is a subversive activity.

The redbaiting propaganda of the Chamber of Commerce is sent to all the local chambers in the United States and to a special "Subversive Activities Mailing List" of the leading reactionary citizens of the country. Among them, for example, are: Harry A. Jung, aforementioned distributor of the forgeries known as the *Protocols of Zion;* William Randolph Hearst, of whom the less said the better; Colonel R. R. McCormick, publisher of a daily no intelligent man could consider "the world's greatest newspaper"; Horner L. Chaillaux, chief redbaiter of the American Legion; and Jasper E. Crane and Edmond E. Lincoln of the Du Pont company.

The Associated Farmers are on the mailing list; so is J. E. Campbell of the Constitutional Protective League; Fred Clark, national commander of the Crusaders; John B. Trevor, president of the American Coalition; Silas Strawn; the Industrial Association of San Francisco; Walter Steele, editor of *National Republic;* W. H. Oldham of Republic Steel; Margaret Kerr of Better America Federation; Admiral Standley; Admiral Sterling; L. R. Custer, general manager of Bethlehem Steel; and scores of bank presidents, steel corporation presidents, professional patrioteers, police officials, and public utility men. Scores of persons on this mailing list have been publicly named as enemies of labor unions and organizations defending civil liberties. Many on the list have been exposed by die La Follette committee as the users of spies and thugs, the buyers of poison gas and machine-guns for use against their employees.

The Chamber of Commerce of the United States and the hundreds of local chambers which it influences constitute one of the most important anti-labor forces in America. For them redbaiting is as profitable a weapon as the gas and guns, spies and thugs, which the same 2500 employers have used on another front.

* * *

The main difference between the United States Chamber and the local chambers of commerce, so far as this investigation is concerned, is one of method and degree: the national body does things in a big way, openly, and yet with a certain amount of finesse, whereas the local chambers of commerce are not above underhand methods, espionage, skulduggery, and terrorism. It has already been noted that the local chambers have usually been rated second only to the American Legion in the annual reports of the Civil Liberties Union on fascist forces in America; the local chamber members are also frequently the leading Legionnaire redbaiters.

The chief business of the local chambers of commerce is the diligent pursuit of strike-breaking, redbaiting, the promotion of company unions, and the capture of "runaway" factories. New Jersey and Connecticut chambers of commerce angle for New York state manufacturing plants, and the South appeals to steel, textile, and other businesses to quit the unionized North. In their advertisements they speak of "a plentiful supply of loyal labor"; to their prospective customers they promise to break the "alien and subversive" labor union movement.

The Jersey City chamber is the backbone of the Hague campaign against the C.I.O., and it therefore shares with Hague the shame of being caught in unconstitutional activities by the United States Supreme Court. Only a few weeks before that notable decision was handed down, the Jersey City chamber had adopted a resolution supporting Hague for his "courageous" stand in his fight against radical labor. It thanked him in behalf of the "business and industries of New Jersey"; it deplored the "invasion of our city by . . . elements from the outside whose manifest purpose is to illegally disturb and hamper and destroy. . . ."

Chambers of commerce frequently subsidize the National Guard when that organization goes into action against labor. For example, A. J. Horn, executive secretary of the Toledo, Ohio, chamber, told the representative of

People's Press, the labor weekly, that the Toledo chamber raised a fund of $4910 for the local militia units, and admitted that the chamber had been subsidizing the militia for seventeen years. The Cleveland chamber also helped, its quota being $20,000.

The organization of company unions is another popular pastime in which local chambers indulge. The Brooklyn Chamber of Commerce organized and fostered no less than three hundred of them, according to the testimony of Mrs. Elinore M. Herrick, New York regional director of the National Labor Relations Board, in a complaint against the Atlas Bag and Burlap Company.

The same Brooklyn chamber was accused by a committee favoring a municipal lighting plant of taking money from the Brooklyn Edison Company at the time the issue was being forced by Mayor La Guardia in 1935. The committee charged that payments of about $7500 a year were subsidies, not dues.

Again, in the case of the labor board against the Hopwood Refining Company, it was charged that L. L. Balleisen, industrial secretary of the chamber, encouraged the company to escape paying union wages by running away to Hague's Jersey City scab utopia. The Board ordered Hopwood and thirty other companies to cease and desist from using the Balleisen plan.

The New York State Chamber of Commerce is another typical commercial-patriotic redbaiting-for-profit organization. It once had a liberal branch—a committee on education—which tried out a few intelligent ideas, but its proposals were overwhelmingly defeated by the chamber. At the time the Albany legislature was proposing that all school buses be painted, like barbershop poles, with red, white, and blue stripes, to confound the reds, that state support be withdrawn from schools "permitting subversive teaching," and that other superpatriotic and meaningless legislation be passed—the education committee went on record as disapproving.

The Chambers of Commerce

Immediately, none other than Captain John B. Trevor, who runs one of the many professional patriotic outfits which Mrs. Dilling calls upon for heavy support, denounced the education committee report as "one of the most sinister documents . . . [which] makes the Chamber of Commerce a part of the united front presented by the Communist Party." He called upon the red-blooded men of the chamber to destroy the red proposal.

Some time later the American Committee for Democracy and Intellectual Freedom, headed by Professor Franz Boas, was forced to brand the report of the New York chamber's special committee on economical and efficient education as "advancing a fascist conception of the state and of culture." The chamber report states that public schools are founded for preserving and strengthening the state, and have nothing to do with culture because "a review of history indicates that as culture arises, morals and physical well-being go down and often the destruction or disintegration of the State has followed."

In Chicago, the word *liberty* "is a stench in the nostrils of big business men," according to the statement made by the Chicago Civil Liberties Committee after interviews with three representatives of the Chicago Association of Commerce. The Civil Liberties Committee had asked the association to endorse its stand on freedom of speech, press, and assemblage. But the business men countered with a proposal that the committee change its name from Civil Liberties to Civil Rights "because there is confusion in the minds of business men that liberty means license, whereas the protection of civil or legal rights is a more legitimate purpose and accurate statement of the work." The three business men who made this suggestion were Lucius Teter, investment banker; Chester Creider, secretary of Butler Brothers (noted for underpaying its girl workers); and Jesse Jacobs, executive secretary of the Chicago Association.

In California, the State chamber of commerce has,

according to Governor Olson, "operated solely as a 'front' for special private interests whose sole object has been to thwart the will of the people." It is also guilty of "unethical, secret political activity." In asking for a state legislative investigation, the governor appended to his message photostatic copies of inter-office correspondence of the chamber, marked "strictly confidential," in which members were urged, in fighting proposed tax and pro-labor legislation, to keep the chamber's identity secret and to say nothing in writing which could be used against it.

Of all the California local chambers, that of Los Angeles is the most rabidly anti-labor. Even conservative *Time* reports that "in Los Angeles no one damned as a liberal can count on the all-powerful support of the red-hating Chamber of Commerce and the Merchants' & Manufacturers' Association."

The Los Angeles chamber is also one of the backers of a Washington, D. C., vigilante organization calling itself America First! Inc. The Industrial Association and the steamship lobby are joined in this enterprise; and Robert B. Armstrong, vice-president of the Los Angeles Steamship Company, is also vice-president of the Los Angeles chamber.

The California State Chamber of Commerce, according to a boastful address made by Charles Mariner, "spent $50,000 in labor disturbances framing organizers when evidence was not sufficient to convict them, and using physical violence when necessary. . . . California locals have won a lot of credit for their anti-union, strike-breaking, redbaiting methods. The San Jose chamber has done its part in winning for Santa Clara County, of which it is the capital, the name of 'cradle of American fascism.'"[3]

When miners were locked out in Amador County, California, an organization calling itself the "Mother Lode Vigilante Committee, Local 84," composed of members of

---

[3] Speech before the Hi-Twelve Club, San Jose. Reported by Evelyn Seeley in *The Nation*, April 15, 1936.

the chamber and the Industrial Association, distributed the following bulletin:

> We are pleased to find that most of the pickets have learned that the best place to spend the night is in bed and not on the picket line where they might endanger their health and their lives. . . .
>
> This local climate is none too good for the health of union officials or Mr. Brown would not have left our community. Automobile rides these cold nights are liable to give one pneumonia—IF NOTHING WORSE. . . .
>
> FROM NOW ON THE VIGILANTE COMMITTEE WILL BE KNOWN BY ITS DEEDS AND NOT BY ITS WORDS. Advise your red friends to leave the county so that the committee will not have to take action.

The Tacoma, Washington, Chamber of Commerce purchased submachine guns, tear gas, and nausea-gas bombs, which it presented to the police department "to use against gangsters." Actually, everyone concerned knows this is pure euphemism: machine-guns and gas are to be used by a "red squad."

The Washington chambers frequently assume new names when they go in for strike-breaking and similar activities: in Tacoma they are the Citizens Emergency Committee and the Committee of 200; in Seattle, the Committee of 500; and in the state, the Washington Industrial Council.

There are hundreds and hundreds of similar examples of local chamber of commerce activities. Every citizen of a small town who has had any dealings with this organization or attended its meetings knows that behind all its patriotic camouflage is nothing but an organized effort to increase and safeguard capital and profits. With this avowed purpose no one can find any fault. But it is also apparent that in fighting for its investments and the interest therefrom, the chambers of commerce engage in every activity from legal smearing to illegal and frequently murderous vigilantism.

A word must also be said about the International Chamber of Commerce. Its chairman is Thomas J. Watson, one of the wealthiest employers and the recipient of the second largest salary in America. He was the first American to receive the swastika decoration from Adolf Hitler. In return, the head of the International Chamber of Commerce gave the Nazi salute, a gesture not without its significance, though in June 1940 Watson returned the swastika. But the swastika mentality remains.

Chapter 17
The National Association of Manufacturers
Power and Corruption

The Congress of American Industry, which is the annual convention of the National Association of Manufacturers, has been called the "greatest aggregation of white-tied wealth and power ever assembled under one roof." The late Paul Y. Anderson, one of the greatest Washington correspondents, wrote of the N.A.M.:

> Once [it] bribed Congressmen and page boys; now it seeks to bribe whole communities. The old device of a thousand-dollar bill in the palm has been replaced with an elaborate program whereby business men, taxpayers, professional workers, and school children are told by radio, screen, billboard, cartoon and canned editorial that their existence depends on peace in the mills. To put it more bluntly, they are told the only way they can get along is by keeping the damn labor agitators out. . . . With more than 4000 members its policies are dominated by 207 corporations, whose officers in 1936 drew aggregate salaries of $88,750,000. . . . Sixty percent of all the tear gas sold to industrial concerns in recent years was bought by these 207 companies, and 55 of them paid $2,225,000 for espionage in the years 1933 to 1937. . . .

They also employed George E. Sokolsky.

The N.A.M. was the subject of the first of the series of congressional lobby investigations, owing to an exposé by Colonel Martin M. Mulhall, chief lobbyist of the business organization. A committee headed by Representative Finis Garrett established, among other facts, the following:

(3) The N.A.M., through Mulhall, obtained advance information on proposed and pending legislation from certain members of the House, including McDermott and Republican Leader John Dwight. . . .

(5) The N.A.M. and N.C.I.D. [National Council for Industrial Defense, its lobbying branch] "took an active interest and vigorous part in Congressional campaigns . . . for the re-election of members whose views were in harmony with their legislative program . . . and resorted to questionable and disreputable means to bring about the defeat of members who had not approved their policies."

(6) The N.A.M. and N.C.I.D. expended "large sums of money in these campaigns . . . and extended their activities into various districts throughout the country, where the methods employed were secretive, reprehensible, and deserve the severest condemnation by the House."

In addition, the N.A.M. engaged in antilabor activity. The committee found that Mulhall frequently had been sent by the N.A.M. "into sections where strikes were in progress, evidently for the purpose of trying to break them." That union-busting was, in the eyes of the Garrett Committee, one of the principal objects of the N.A.M., is evidenced by the mass of testimony and documentary evidence compiled on this point. The committee in its report to the House remarked: "We have set forth these instances with considerable detail because they appear to be typical of the mental attitude and purposes of the N.A.M. and the N.C.I.D."[1]

In the House committee minority report, Congressman William McDonald called attention to a phony organization called the Workman's Protective Association, also operated by the N.A.M. "It seems ridiculous . . ." he wrote, "to ask anyone to believe that the so-called W.P.A. was anything but the flimsiest cover for Mulhall's operations in corrupting, by the use of money, union labor

---
1 Summarized by Kenneth Crawford in *The Pressure Boys.*

men of some influence with the fellows to wantonly betray these fellow-workmen." Of the N.A.M., McDonald wrote:

> The naïve effrontery shown upon the witness stand by officers of the N.A.M. in assuming that the committee would accept at face value the bald denials and ridiculous evasion and perversion of the meaning of actions all too plainly corrupt and sinister . . . cannot be permitted to pass without mention.
>
> Their plainly shown attitude was that the American Congress was considered by them as their legislative department and was viewed with the same arrogant manner in which they viewed their other employees, and that those legislators who dared to oppose them would be disciplined in the same manner in which they were accustomed to discipline recalcitrant employees. . . . The evidence convinced me that Mulhall, Emery and his associates, with the enthusiastic approval of the responsible officers of the N.A.M., did influence legislation; did prevent the enactment of laws; did force the appointment upon committees or subcommittees of certain men believed to be necessary for the carrying out of their schemes, and prevented other men whom they believed to be inimical to their interests from being placed thereon.
>
> They did, by the expenditure of exorbitant sums of money, aid and attempt to aid in the election of those who they believed would readily serve their interests, and by the same means sought to and did accomplish the defeat of others whom they opposed. In carrying out these multifarious activities, they did not hesitate as to means, but made use of any method of corruption found to be effectual. They did not hesitate to use the employees of the Government in the very Capitol itself. And, as is shown by literally hundreds of items in the Mulhall expense accounts, by the purchase of organization labor men to betray their fellows in election campaigns and strike-breaking activities, they instituted a new and complete system of commercialized treachery.

So much for the bribery of congressmen and page boys; as for the bribery of whole communities, the La Follette committee discovered that the N.A.M. spent as much as $750,000 on publicity and advertising and conducted "America's biggest propaganda network." The annual sum, it may be noted, is only one-thirty-third as large as that once spent by the National Electric Light Association, but it would be erroneous to assume that the resulting amount of corruption in the press was therefore proportionally fractional. The N.E.L.A. was forcing its stuff into print for a special branch of industry, whereas the N.A.M. did not have to use the same amount of bribery and pressure to get publicity. Representing as it does the same big business which does practically all the advertising in America, it received free space for its propaganda—at least as much as the N.E.L.A. paid millions to obtain.

The La Follette committee discovered, for example, that 268 radio stations accepted the N.A.M.'s anti-labor propaganda in something called "The American Family Robinson"; 246 stations accepted its "George Sokolsky program"; 6252 newspapers accepted its "Industrial Press Service"; 270 newspapers accepted a feature called "Uncle Abner Sez"; and 1812 movie houses showed a reel called "Let's Go American." The only expense involved in getting this material to the public was the salaries of a few of the best brass-check journalists in America. According to the La Follette committee, academic participants in this N.A.M. campaign were: Professor Gus Dyer of Vanderbilt University; Professors Clarence W. Fackler and Walter E. Spahr of New York University; Professor Eliot Jones of Stanford; President Thomas of Clarkson College of Technology; and President Ernest M. Patterson of the Academy of Political Social Science.[2] Their stuff was sent

---

2 According to the weekly, *Labor*, the N.A.M. employed the following professors also: Harley F. Lutz of Princeton, Erik McKinley Eriksson of the University of Southern California, and Dean J. E. Le Rossignol of the University of Nebraska.

free to the press as the "Six Star Service," and the press, knowing the source, published these articles without informing the American public that it was part of the plan "to bribe whole communities."

Redbaiting has been an important activity of the N.A.M., dating back to the time when there were no reds, but merely labor union leaders of the old school. Years ago the N.A.M. announced that it

> is not primarily a labor-busting organization. It is true we have done much preventive work along that line, but we claim to be and are a boosting organization. We are not opposed to good unionism, if such exists anywhere. The American brand of unionism, however, is un-American, illegal and indecent. . . . Our government cannot stand, nor its free institutions endure, if the Gompers-Debs ideals of liberty and freedom of speech and press are allowed to dominate. . . .

In its official publication, *American Industries*, the N.A.M. thus went on record against radicals and free press:

> We must co-operate—we must get together and stick together to uphold our honor and honesty, we manufacturers and merchants, or rampant labor men, socialists and demagogues will be our undoing. All of these new-fangled ideas about the initiative, referendum and recall, and all these attacks on capital, no matter how honestly obtained, are for the sole and only purpose of putting more power into the hands of the papers and politicians. In fact, I think the greatest menace that our country has today is a so-called "free press" bidding for popularity with the thoughtless mob.

From its earliest times, the N.A.M. fought the eight-hour day, calling it "vicious, needless, preposterous"; it still opposes the abolition of child labor; and it always froths at the mouth over sympathy strikes and boycotts. By a curious coincidence, the newspapers in which the N.A.M. members are the heaviest advertisers do a similar frothing. It has been pointed out by Professor Clarence E. Bonnett that although the N.A.M.

> has not yet taken up the matter systematically, it has made, through its leaders, various attempts to influence the press, on the ground that the press molds public opinion and public opinion makes the laws.
>
> The Association has urged upon employers the patronage of friendly publications and the withdrawal of advertising from the unfriendly ones. In other words, it engages in a form of "boycotting."

Whenever *American Industries* found lists of persons or companies which unions called unfair and asked the public not to patronize, it republished them so that its membership could patronize those persons or institutions and advertise with them. A list of publications boycotted by labor was republished with the heading, "Papers for Others to Patronize."

Nowadays the redbaiting of the N.A.M. is done by aiding other redbaiters. Thus, in its booklet, *Labor Strife and the Third Party,* the N.A.M. recommended the notorious Mohawk Valley formula devised by James H. Rand, Jr., of Remington-Rand for breaking strikes, the first point of which advises manufacturers to pin the red label on the strike and thus turn public opinion against it. The N.A.M. also bought 10,000 copies of the libelous booklet entitled *Join the CIO and Help Build a Soviet America.*

Testifying before the La Follette committee, Reverend W. M. Tippy, federal organizer of the Churches of Christ in America, said:

> These religious organizations—the Catholic Church, the Jewish organization, and the Federal Council [of the Churches of Christ in America]—are charged with getting money from Moscow and being led astray that way. I have heard in the National Association of

Manufacturers men saying all of this nonsense. It is difficult for me to understand except to say that there is a fear being fanned by designing men and organizations. Apparently it is what you might call the "Red Network" crowd.

This is indeed the case. The N.A.M. itself concentrates on legislation and the mass molding of the public mind, but its members are also prominent figures in the Red Network crowd.

Ernest T. Weir is the fund-raiser for the propaganda fund. Among other leading union-fighters who have important positions in the N.A.M. are members of the Du Pont, General Motors, Standard Oil, Chrysler, Swift, U. S. Steel, Bethlehem Steel, Westinghouse, Remington-Rand, and American Smelting
corporations.

Money raised from these corporations was sent liberally to aid the vigilante movement in Johnstown, Pennsylvania, during the Bethlehem Steel strike. The N.A.M. also spent its money making 135,000 reprints of one of the Chicago *Tribune* stories headed "See CIO Drive as Communistic in Its Objects," and mailing them to that many influential persons.

And when the entire propaganda campaign of the N.A.M. was exposed by the La Follette committee, the N.A.M. selected editorials from the most reactionary newspapers in America—the New York *Herald Tribune*, the Baltimore *Sun*, the Chicago *Journal of Commerce*, *Newsdom*, and a dozen others—all critical of the La Follette committee, reprinted them in a booklet, and mailed them to every daily newspaper editor in America. The editorials of these pro-N.A.M., labor-baiting newspapers deplore the exposure of the $750,000 fund for discrediting unions. One general contention was that the exposure was itself propagandistic, to which La Follette's *Progressive* replied that "if it is (propaganda} for the civil liberties committee to inform the American people how the newspapers and other agencies that mold public opinion are influenced to carry the message of the big corporations . . . the committee can plead guilty with good grace. . . ."

One word more about the N.A.M.: at its 1937 convention God was named for honorary membership in the manufacturers' outfit. God was fitted for membership, explained Dr. George B. Cutten, president of Colgate University, in all seriousness, because "God is a reactionary." Dr. Cutten ridiculed as "twaddle" all this talk about "the more abundant life" spread about by radicals. Tom Girdler of Republic Steel presided. Dorothy Thompson and George Sokolsky also spoke.

Chapter 18
Associated Farmers
Tom Joad, That Red

In New York, the film version of *Grapes of Wrath* included the following conversation:

> Tom Joad: Say, what are those "reds" anyway?
> Another Oakie: A "red" is anyone who wants thirty cents an hour when they're paying twenty-five.

In Connecticut, the question was left suspended in the air; the answer was cut out—and cut badly, because there was no connection between the question and what followed.

In Steinbeck's book the matter of "reds" was part of a statement: "What is these goddam reds? . . . A red is any son-of-a-bitch that wants thirty cents an hour when we're payin' twenty-five!"

The Joads in California vaguely realize that the "farmers" for whom they work are in reality corporations, owned and controlled by banks and other corporations. The millions of Americans who have seen *The Grapes of Wrath* on the screen and watched armed vigilantes, aided by the forces of "law and order," terrorize migrant workers may, however, wonder how the law is broken with impunity.

The answer is that the Associated Farmers, the members of which own the rich valleys of California, also own the state legislature; they control the banks and the money; they control the press—they are the economic and political bosses of the state. In short, they are not what Americans ordinarily mean by farmers.

Who are the Associated Farmers? The Simon J. Lubin

Society of California, sponsored by Governor Olson, Congressman Jerry Voorhis (of the Dies committee), Bishop James C. Baker, Father Charles Phillips, Professor Robert A. Brady, Chester Conklin and John D. Barry of the San Francisco *News,* and other notable Californians, has investigated and has reported that, as farmers, the Associated Farmers are pretty much of a hoax. The A.F. is an organization of big business men, and its controllers are:

Bank of America (Giannini)
Southern Pacific Railroad
California Packing Corporation ("CalPak")
Libby, McNeil & Libby, packers
Charles McIntosh, president, Bank of California
A. J. McFadden, president of the state chamber of commerce
Mortimer and Herbert Fleishhacker, bankers
Herbert Hoover

When the La Follette committee dug into the files of the Associated Farmers, it discovered the real big interests that supply the money for this anti-labor, redbaiting organization which terrorizes the Okies and the Arkies. Some of the leading categories of financial backers are:

Railroads (including Southern Pacific, Union Pacific, Western Pacific, A.T. & S.F.), $17,170
Utilities (including Pacific Gas & Electric, one of the firms in the Tom Mooney frame-up; San Joaquin Power & Light; Southern California Gas; and Southern California Edison), $6175
Oil Companies (including numerous Standard Oil subsidiaries), $4519
Canners League (including California Packing Corporation), $13,700
Dried Fruit Associations (including Rosenberg Brothers, Balfour-Guthrie, Ltd., a British firm), $14,350
Citrus, Walnut Associations (largely C. C. Teague), $9869

Cotton, Oil, Ginning Companies, $7941
Can, Box, Lumber Companies, $12,975
Banks (including Bank of America, California Bank), $1290
Employers Associations (San Francisco Employers Association, Southern Californians, Inc., etc.), $22,056
Sugar Companies, $10,650

The La Follette committee, which unearthed this evidence, proved conclusively that the Associated Farmers were largely a big business organization; they were bankers, canners, packers, jobbers, and "industrial farmers." The La Follette committee discovered which of these "associated farmers" were responsible for murders, lynchings, vigilante violence, and the general terrorism in the fruit and vegetable valleys; it disclosed the bribery and corruption of the forces of law and order, the police and sheriffs; it showed the connection between corruption and politics, and generally furnished enough sensational material to fill the front pages of any honest and independent newspaper for weeks.

But the press of America did not publish the story. In Southern California, according to Carey McWilliams, the press was most active in suppressing the story; in San Francisco, the *Chronicle* and the *News* were fair but the *Call-Bulletin* and the *Examiner* "viciously distorted the testimony, encouraged the defiance of the Associated Farmers, and editorialized headlines and news stories"; in Los Angeles, the *Times* "joined in the attack, denouncing the [La Follette] committee as 'impudent and illegal,' praising the sheriffs for their defiance and in general doing all in its power to hamper the work of the committee."

In Chicago and New York and other cities it was about the same. Most newspapers published nothing. The New York *Times* buried a few paragraphs on an inside page now and again. But at the very same time, the entire American press published hundreds of thousands of words on the

Dies committee hearings. Much if not most of the Dies testimony was biased, prejudiced, unfair, and a large part of it falsehood, propaganda, and outright lies, but the press published it and played it up.

An illuminating incident in one of the Dies hearings corroborates the volumes of testimony in which the La Follette committee showed that the activities of the Associated Farmers exactly parallel the conspiracies of the associated manufacturers of Italy and of Germany. When Dies called Major-General Van Horn Moseley, U.S.A. (retired), who was the choice of the Christian Fronters, the German Bund, the Knights of the White Camellia, Reverend Gerald Winrod, and William Pelley to co-ordinate all fascist activities in America in preparation for taking over the country, Moseley arrived direct from a visit in the Imperial Valley, California. A letter introduced in evidence, from George Deatherage, head of the Camellias, told Moseley of an arranged meeting of "leaders of groups on our side of the fence," including Colonel Walter E. Garrison, former president of the Associated Farmers of California and president of the Associated Farmers of the Pacific.

The Associated Farmers, as such, naturally does not go in for violence, lynching, and terrorism; it only creates the proper atmosphere and its members, and the officials they bribe, do the rest. The A.F. itself goes in largely for political pressure: it is hailed as a new force against labor unionism by *Business Week;* it is one of the biggest fighters against the Wagner Act; in Oregon, according to Richard L. Neuberger of the *Oregonian,* it put over the most drastic anti-labor law in America's most progressive state; in California it nullified Governor Olson's liberal legislative program.[1] All this comes under the A.F. platform "to protect, preserve, and maintain American institutions and

---
1 This summary was made in August 1939 by the Institute for Propaganda Analysis, which publishes a monthly bulletin exposing corruption, propaganda, and redbaiting.

ideals, to preserve the Constitutional form of government . . . to oppose and combat any and all doctrines or practices which imperil the maintenance of these constitutional liberties . . . to fight against the infiltration of subversive doctrines . . . to combat the dictatorship of individuals or groups."

There are two studies of the California agricultural labor situation: one made by the Lubin Society at the request of Senator Wagner, the other made by Assemblyman John Phillips at the request of the California Chamber of Commerce, State Department of Agriculture, and other bodies. The latter report favors the A.F. and speaks of "communistic agitators," "radicals," "troublemakers," while the Lubin report's keynote is labor's search for a better living through better wages and working conditions. The Associated Farmers was actually formed following the Phillips report, for the purpose of fighting the reforms which the Lubin report recommended. Carey McWilliams, journalist, writer, and now Commissioner of Immigration and Housing, has a stenographic account of the first meeting, at which "it was decided that farmers should 'front' the organization, although the utility companies and banks would exercise ultimate control."

The three presidents of Associated Farmers have not been the big shots, the 2 percent who own 35 percent of the farms and reap 32 percent of the crops of California; they have been "medium" farmers: S. Parker Frisselle, manager of the University of California 500-acre farm, director in the Sunset Oil Company, and director of the California Chamber of Commerce; Colonel Garrison, owner of a 240-acre vineyard; and Holmes Bishop, a 20-acre farmer. But one of the real directors of A.F. is C. C. Teague, director of Security First National Bank of Los Angeles, head of California Walnut Growers Exchange, which owns Diamond brand, and head of California Fruit Growers Exchange, which owns Sunkist brand; and another is

Joseph Di Giorgio of the $30,000,000 Di Giorgio Fruit Company.

Fred Goodcell and Harper Knowles, secretaries of A.F., are professional redbaiters, Knowles being particularly active through the American Legion, and especially in the fight against Harry Bridges. A.F. itself engaged in "anti-Semitics," in particular, the dissemination of a forgery purporting to be a marriage license of Mme. Frances Perkins described therein as a Jewess and given a name ending in -*sky.*

> Examination of Associated Farmer propaganda [explains *Propaganda Analysis*] leaves the impression that the organization tends to represent discontent among agricultural workers as largely due to communist agitators. Wages and working conditions are glossed over (though leaders will admit that they are a source of dissatisfaction), and the rank and file are told simply that if it were not for "the reds" farm workers would be happy and contented. . . . The Associated Farmers explain the apparent contradiction between their constant disavowals of enmity to labor unions and their strike-breaking activities by emphasizing always that farm labor unions are "communist dominated." The cry of "communism" is their chief propaganda stock-in-trade. Of 375 items published in their monthly bulletin, the *Associated Farmer,* 190 were devoted to Communism, the *Rural Observer* reports. . . . Actually, the definition of Communism which the *Associated Farmer* seems to hold is rather loose, and covers anyone who might want to organize farm labor.

The Joads who want thirty cents an hour, and anyone who tries to organize the Joads to get it, are red-smeared by the A.F., and then violence begins.

Colonel Garrison, according to an N.L.R.B. decision, "asked that members send him pictures of labor leaders, of 'radicals,' and said he would 'see they were handled,' that the organization had a very effective system of undercover men working in the union, and that they had handled the suppression of a strike in Orange County." Carey McWilliams accuses the A.F. of maintaining an index file of one thousand "dangerous radicals which is merely a blacklist against labor union leaders."

When there is violence—riots, murder, and lynching—the instigators are not labor leaders but so-called patriots, vigilantes, and police authorities; and the atmosphere of violence is generated by the propaganda of the big business men who own the fertile valleys.

When the Department of Agriculture, the Department of Labor, and the National Labor Relations Board sent General Pelham D. Glassford to California to make an impartial investigation, he studied the situation for months and reported that it was his conviction

> that a group of growers have exploited a "communist" hysteria for the advancement of their own interests; that they have welcomed labor agitation which they could brand as "red" as a means of sustaining supremacy by mob rule, thereby preserving what is so essential to their profits—cheap labor; that they have succeeded in drawing into their conspiracy certain county officials, who have become the principal tools of their machine....
>
> Spread upon the pages of recent Imperial Valley history are certain lawless and illegal events which have not been investigated by officials who are charged with that responsibility....
>
> I strongly recommend a thorough grand jury investigation and the indictment of those who have been guilty of law violations in connection with an apparently organized campaign of terrorism and intimidation....
>
> The lawlessness and intimidation is directed not only against alleged communists, but also against those professional and business men of the community who, by word or deed, oppose the political aims of a small but powerful group engaged in exploiting a "red" hysteria, for the promotion of their own interests. The immediate

responsibility for action and results rests with the elected officials of Imperial Valley. It is time Imperial Valley awakens to the fact that it is part of the United States.

It is impossible, in this short chapter, to say anything about the many strikes, the acts of terrorism, the violence which the members of Associated Farmers caused in the California valleys. Paul Y. Anderson once noted that when the Migratory Workers Protective Union was formed in 1936 it had to act underground, in much the same way the Communist Party functions in Germany today, and for the same reason: fear of sudden and violent death of its members. Its governing body called itself the Committee of One Hundred. Between July and October of 1937 exactly thirty-six of this group of a hundred were run down and killed in what the coroners called "automobile accidents." One of the dead might have been a Steinbeck character: He was Alexander Templeton, a Baptist lay preacher from Oklahoma, and a rabid prohibitionist. The sheriff reported him as having been run over while lying drunk on the road. When George Brett demanded an autopsy, he was taken to jail in Fresno and kept four days; when he returned, he found that the authorities had cremated Templeton's body.

This is how members or hirelings of the A.F. have done their work in California. *Grapes of Wrath* and McWilliams's *Factories in the Fields* tell some of the story; so does the *Rural Observer* (published by the Lubin Society, San Francisco), particularly in an article by Helen Hosmer in the September-October 1938 issue.

Chapter 19
The Johnstown Plan
Big Business as Vigilante

Shortly after the Chicago police guarding Tom Girdler's Republic Steel plant murdered ten workingmen and seriously wounded sixty (only to be found "not guilty" later, after the workingmen had been labeled reds), "citizens' committees," "law and order" groups, and other vigilante organizations sprang up in the steel towns and cities of America. From Johnstown, Pennsylvania, there was launched a national pro-vigilante movement to which "our best citizens" subscribed. For a while there was a hysteria compounded of redbaiting and Roosevelt-baiting, to which the press gave tremendous publicity.

Today we know that that movement was initiated by the Chamber of Commerce; that the big money came from corporations (notably Bethlehem Steel) and individual enemies not only of labor but also of the Democratic administration; and that what we had witnessed was nothing less than big business engaging in open vigilantism. Even such a conservative big business organ as *Life* reported that "the Johnstown assemblage adopted a set of resolutions whose preamble was a perfect definition of vigilantism. . . . Vigilantes always consider themselves patriots preserving the national welfare against radical masses and weak officials. So do fascists. . . ." Nevertheless the press, notably the New York *Times*, continued to cheer for Johnstown vigilantism and to publish the press-agent propaganda releases regularly on Sunday mornings.

Eventually, the whole undertaking was exposed by the National Labor Relations Board and the La Follette committee, and the sordid motives came to light—but not in the regular commercial and venal press.

ORIGIN OF COMMERCIAL VIGILANTISM

After John L. Lewis of the C.I.O. and Myron C. Taylor of U. S. Steel had made a peaceful settlement, the former moved to unionize Little Steel. Here he came face to face with such men as Eugene Grace, successor to Charles M. Schwab; Tom Girdler, on whose head lies the blood-guilt of the Memorial Day massacre in Chicago; Ernest Weir of Weirton; and other steel company heads who had already been exposed as the employers of spies, stool-pigeons, agents-provocateurs, strike-breakers, thugs, murderers, and machine-gunners—in short, the men who, with their predecessors, had kept effective unionism out of the steel industry for fifty years by force and violence.

When trouble began in Johnstown, Pennsylvania, the mayor, a hysterical man named Shields, expected the usual action: that the city and state officials, the police, and the National Guard (aided by American Legionnaires and other strike-breaking agencies) would be mobilized, and labor would be driven back, defeated, to the mills, even if it were necessary to shoot a number of them to accomplish this end. That has always been the history of steel strikes in Pennsylvania.

But Governor Earle refused to shoot.

Troops were sent, but for once they *did* preserve the law—by permitting strikers and pickets their constitutional rights. The frantic Shields thereupon telegraphed President Roosevelt:

> Personally I am convinced that it [the C.I.O.] is a Red Russian organization gaining prestige by the use of your name. Confidential information in my hands warns me of certain dynamite explosions now planned. . . . Warnings have been received by me and my family will be destroyed. . . . Mr. President, I fought for you. . . . Now are you going to fail me by allowing this reign of

The Johnstown Plan

terror to continue?

Tom Girdler wrote to his employees: "Must Republic and its men submit to the communistic dictates and terrorism of the C.I.O.? If America is to remain a free country the answer is No."

This line became the basis of Johnstown commercial vigilantism. First there was the Citizens Committee and then the national movement, or Johnstown Plan, officially known as the Citizens' National Committee—all stemming from the Johnstown Chamber of Commerce, and liberally subsidized in secret by big business, especially Republican Party big business.

Two other important groups joined this attack on labor and on the liberal Democratic administration: a number of the clergy and a large part of the press. Protestant ministers and a Jewish rabbi supported the Johnstowners—although none was as violently fascistic as the Catholic leader, Coughlin. Reverend John H. Stanton, who was elected to head the national committee, was a notorious redbaiter.

Other committee members included the secretary, Lawrence Campbell, who was also secretary of the chamber and is noted for his attacks on aliens, unions, and reds; George C. Rutledge, a banker; Reverend Rembert G. Smith, one of the pro-fascists who participated in the National Conference of Clergymen and Laymen at Asheville, and an associate of the anti-Semitic Reverend Gerald Winrod, of Kansas; Donald Kirksley, editor of the *National Farm News*, which had been bought by the Pews, of Sunoco and of Pennsylvania Republican politics.

"Thank God for Tom Girdler," exclaimed the delegate of the Massillon, Ohio, Citizens' Committee, after the Reverend Mr. Stanton had opened the organizational meeting; "I think we ought to send him a telegram congratulating him for smoking out those Communists, John L. Lewis, Madame Perkins and President Roosevelt." There was a tremendous outburst of approval and applause.

Professor Gus Dyer of Vanderbilt University hailed the meeting as the "rising sun for the protection of American liberties." (This was shortly before Dyer was exposed as one of the six professors taking money from the National Association of Manufacturers.)

Big business plus armed force equals fascism. Mussolini, the employee of the Industrial Association of North Italy, and Hitler, with the backing of Thyssen and company, have proved this. But Johnstown was not yet quite ready to put armed force into its vigilante program; it first had to prepare the public mind; so it went into the advertising, publicity, and propaganda game. A $60,000 fund was proposed and John Price Jones, whose specialty is raising money for institutions, was engaged to do the advertising. He is a member of Thornley & Jones. George H. Thornley, the senior partner, is a close friend of Henry Ford and was formerly vice-president of N. W. Ayer, one of the big advertising agencies and representatives of Ford.

The Johnstown vigilante movement had no sooner been launched than Clinton S. Golden, Pittsburgh steel-worker organizer, charged that it was financed by the Bethlehem Steel and National Steel corporations, which had pledged $50,000 for the advertising campaign.[1] Senator Wagner said that "private citizens sponsoring anti-union 'citizens' committees' and vigilante groups may be violating the [Wagner] Act." But the newspapers of the nation (with few exceptions) did not print these statements and went along playing up the Johnstown Plan and boosting it editorially.

All the redbaiters in America enlisted under its banner. All the American fascists, reactionaries, labor-baiters and labor-haters, all the enemies of liberal and progressive ideas and movements, all the obscurantists in the country helped it along. When the La Follette committee exposed the Johnstown Plan, 90 percent of the press of America—which is on the side of the aforementioned elements—did not give any publicity to the exposé. The interested reader

---
1   La Follette's *Progressive*, July 31, 1937.

The Johnstown Plan

should get the sixteenth volume of the La Follette reports, from which the following facts are taken.

REDBAITORS AND LABOR-BAITORS

Among the letters seized by the La Follette committee is one which brands Boake Carter, the well known redbaiter, as a labor-baiter. The exhibits speak for themselves:

> Exhibit 3787-F, No. 18
> New York, June 25, 1937

Mr. Boake Carter,
c/o Station WCAU,
Philadelphia, Pa.
Dear Mr. Carter:

We are taking the liberty of enclosing a check for $25 which we would ask you use at your discretion in the fight against the C.I.O. This act was prompted by the newspaper appeal from representative citizens in Johnstown, Pennsylvania, for funds to carry on their work in behalf of the people of Johnstown who wished to work but were prevented by the C.I.O.

Your radio comments in behalf of the average American as against the trend of the present Administration toward dictatorship are much to the point. We sincerely hope you will carry on.

> Chain Deliveries Express, Inc.
> (*signed*) R. C. Bennet, President

> Same exhibit, No. 50
> 1622 Chestnut Street,
> Philadelphia, Pa.

Chairman
Citizens Committee of Johnstown, Pa.
Dear Sir:

Enclosed you will find a letter addressed to me, attached to which is a check for $25. The letter is self-explanatory.

I trust that you will acknowledge the beneficence of this American citizen, who believes in law and order.

Sincerely,
(*signed*) Boake Carter, per E.[2]

Dozens of the seized letters deal with newspapers, magazines, and other publications. One magazine was revealed soliciting $2500 with the promise to kill an article favoring the C.I.O. and to publish instead an editorial attack on the same organization.

Here is the letter from J. C. Monama, president and editor of *The World: An International News Weekly* (Philadelphia):

> Dear Mr. Rutledge: The World has just received an article, for publication, signed by 100 prominent liberal ministers, who take the side of the C.I.O. in the present controversy. That article is being distributed to all the newspapers and magazines in the country.
>
> The World will *not* publish said article. We are definitely against the policies and tactics of the C.I.O. Our Next issue will carry editorials against the sit-down strikes. . . .
>
> Our proposition is this: We are all with your Citizens Committee. We are ready to print 10,000 extra copies containing a boxed editorial against the article of the 100 liberal (communistic-minded) ministers referred to here above, and distribute same to the 10,000 protestant ministers of Pennsylvania, sending advance releases to the daily press all through the country—if your committee or other interests will foot the bill, which will amount to some $2500.
>
> Please answer this at once. If you or your committee cannot handle this, please take the matter up immediately with officials of the Steel Corporation, or others. Our time is very limited.
>
> (*signed*) J. C. Monama[3]

Arden S. Turner, national president of the Student

---

2 La Follette reports, (*"Citizen's" Committees*) Part 16, pp. 7275.
3 *Op cit.,* p. 7310, No. 182.

Americaneers and publisher of its official organ, *The Americaneer,* wrote that "as early as August 1936 [we] did not hesitate to call the C.I.O. communistic. Later events have proven our pioneering correct." Mr. Turner offered to exchange ideas and a personnel trained "in subversive research."

Glidie Cobb, publisher of the Pittsburgh *Crusader: Voice of the Negro,* asked for a conference and enclosed marked copies of his paper, friendly to the vigilante committee, evidently in forgetfulness that the K.K.K. was also part of the vigilante idea.

Guy L. Harrington, vice-president of Macfadden Publications (*Liberty,* various love confession magazines, etc.), was "in hearty sympathy with work."

Dr. J. E. Hodges, publisher of the Maiden, North Carolina, *News* wrote: "My paper endorses your work."

Kirkley of the *National Farm News* was afraid that capital correspondents were "not well informed" about the outfit, he proposed sending a press release to 12,000 papers.

John L. Rogers, editor of *Marine News,* offered "to publicize" the committee in his sheet.

John Price Jones was doing his bit in Johnstown, but John M. Eynon of Barrons Advertising Company also wanted to help work on the public mind. He wrote:

> As publicity and advertising counsel for The Citizens Protective Council and The Emergency Committee for Law and Order we have been spectacularly successful in moulding public opinion here to resist the very determined efforts of the A F L and C I O to organize workers in a dozen different industries. . . . We have made The Right to Work the popular theme with our newspapers. . . .
>
> We have had twenty years experience in moulding public opinion on behalf of management in labor difficulties; on behalf of utilities in legislation difficulties. Our relations with midwest newspapers have

become developed to a degree of greatest value in any emergency.

But the "insiders" seemed to believe that Bethlehem Steel was putting up the money for the advertising. Here, for example, is one of the letters which points out that such a disclosure would ruin the "spontaneous citizens movement." Albert C. Lord of the Cosgrave Coal Company wrote:

> . . . the obvious cost of the advertisement gave rise to considerable suspicion that perhaps it was being financed by the Bethlehem Steel Company.
>
> This, I am sure, is not a question which has arisen in my mind only, because various friends of mine have mentioned it, and I have also seen the doubt about the source of these funds referred to in the daily press. It would be unfortunate, it seems to me, if all the money had been supplied by Bethlehem, and I hope this is not so. . . . If it became known, or if there is any widespread suspicion that the whole movement was initiated and financed by the company, I think the value of it will be very seriously reduced. . . .[4]

All the professional redbaiting patriots of America flocked to the Johnstown colors. Royal Scott Gulden of the Order of '76 sent the following letter:

> Congratulations for the real old-fashioned all American stand that you and your committee have taken to protect your homes and country from the Red aliens and the renegade politicians and traitors now in political power.
>
> We have been organizing for several years for just the emergency that now is before us—as we have seen the situation developing right before our eyes and smelled the unwashed, while they wailed for human rights, as a blind—for their criminal activities.

---

4 *Op. cit.*, pp. 7307-08.

> Experience has taught us that the vigilance committee idea is the best one to handle the situation in an hour of trouble. It is thoroughly American. . . .
> Vigilantly yours[5]

Ralph M. Easley of the National Civic Federation suggested a union and the formation of a National Committee of One Thousand on Civil Rights to fight not only the sit-down but the closed shop, the check-off, the right to picket, and relief. E. P. Gaston, commander of the Patriot Guard of America, wanted to assist. Harry Augustus Jung suggested co-ordination with all "independent workers unions." Numerous letters from plain redbaiting crackpots were also found. Alice Foote MacDougall wrote permitting use of her name as a sponsor.

But most of the letters supporting the movement were from chambers of commerce and from big and little business men, almost all of them from employers and labor-haters. H. M. K. Gryllis, president of the East Chicago Chamber of Commerce, sent his endorsement on Du Pont stationery. Merwin K. Hart of the New York State Economic Council sent in the names of others who might help. Gordon Brown, salesman for Bakelite, supported the movement against "C.I.O. gangsters." Mrs. John A. Denholm of Bronxville, New York (that hotbed of Wall Street gentlemen where the assassination of the President and some of his cabinet is a regular subject of discussion), wrote: "Must combat subversive tendencies even though difficult to do so with Roosevelt, Lewis, Farley & Co. in power. Country being wrecked by the crookedest, most insincere visionary we have ever been cursed with." John A. Norris of 1 Wall Street (perhaps a man with a sense of honor, perhaps a cynic) wrote: "Would like to come, but do you think it advisable that economic royalists openly espouse your cause?"

When the list of financial backers was made public, the

---

[5] *Op. cit.*, pp. 7298-99.

newspapers generally did not publish it. *Steel Labor* (October 29, 1937) gave the following names of contributors: Ernest T. Weir of National Steel; Mesta Machine Company of Pittsburgh; George Ketchum, whose firm is advertising representative of National Steel; numerous officials of Bethlehem, including S. D. Evans, R. E. Hough, and C. E. Ellicott; Frank Altschul; Rex Beach, the writer; Joseph M. Cudahy of Chicago; Merwin K. Hart; Jerome H. Loucheim of Philadelphia; Spencer Penrose; Mary Roberts Rinehart; the University Society of New York; George D. Widener of Philadelphia; Owen Wister, the writer.

The American press, which has a strike-breaking organization of its own (as well as a growing C.I.O. union of newspapermen) was on the side of the vigilantes. Said the conservative and unsensational New York *Times:*

> "JOHNSTOWN PLAN" WINS WIDE BACKING
> Groups in Many Other Cities Aid Movement to Protect Right to Work
>
> JOHNSTOWN GROUP FIGHTS REDS HERE
> Drive Launched on National Scale to Oust Racketeers in Labor Unions
>
> EMPLOYER'S PLAN COUNTER-PICKETS
> Johnstown Group Backs Step Here to Get the Message of Businesses to Public

The facts, brought out at N.L.R.B. hearings and the La Follette committee investigation, forced the *Times* to play a different tune within a few weeks. However, neither the *Times* nor the rest of the press published the real story of the conspiracy of big business against the interests of labor, a small part of which is told in the foregoing pages. Could anyone expect the Johnstown *Tribune*, which had twenty of its staff in the Chamber of Commerce, to publish the truth? Or the labor-baiting Johnstown *Democrat?* The American press lionized the Reverend Mr. Stanton, originator of the Johnstown Plan, and Professor Dyer nominated Mayor Shields for governor of Pennsylvania.

The N.L.R.B. conducted hearings to find out who really backed the vigilante movement, whose money was in it. At first the "patriots" spoke of nothing but spontaneity and voluntary contributions. The first clue to dirty work was given by Michael J. Sewak, burgess of Franklin Borough, where most of the strike trouble was centered. He swore that Bethlehem Steel through its representatives, whom he named—Ralph Hough, assistant general manager, and Albert Bergman, who he believed did police work—offered to "take care of" a $7500 real-estate obligation and supply him with enough "pocket money" to go into business. All he had to do in return was to swear in, as special officers, the private army of strike-breakers, police, and thugs employed by Bethlehem. He said no. Then Ellicott arrived, the burgess testified, and said: "I will double the offer, but you have got to go along with us." The burgess again said no. Then, he testified, Ellicott said: "You will be sorry and you will pay damn dear for this." Testimony was also given that Mayor Shields of Johnstown had sworn in a number of special police to help the company.

The final sensational disclosure was made by Francis C. Martha, chairman of the Johnstown Citizens Committee, when the N.L.R.B. confronted him with damaging evidence: he admitted he had received $10,000 in cash from Sidney Evans of Bethlehem Steel and had turned the money over to Mayor Shields. He had received three packages, $30,000 in all, which he had given the mayor.

Did our free press at this moment speak out editorially about its recent hero? It did not. Only the liberal weeklies had something to say, as for example La Follette's *Progressive*, which declared that:

> When the Johnstown strike was in progress, the press of the country carried lurid stories about alleged

"violence" on the part of the strikers. The "Citizens Committee" was pictured as a group of public spirited gentlemen desirous of keeping law and order and safeguarding labor's "right to work." Johnstown's ex-bootlegger mayor and his strong-arm cops were called impartial keepers of the peace.

Now it appears that the "Citizens Committee" through its chairman was a collection agency or intermediary for obtaining strike-breaking cash from the steel company, that the police were paid salary and expenses from steel company funds dispensed by Mayor Shields, and that the "violence" was most likely inspired by the employer-paid deputies and police.

Some time later Senator La Follette concluded the record with evidence that members of the National Association of Manufacturers had contributed $36,000 of the $60,000 advertising fund of the Johnstown vigilantes. The Civil Liberties Committee revealed the fact that Mayor Shields had received $35,450 from the citizens' committee and "shortly thereafter was able to liquidate $23,485 worth of personal obligations, paying off three mortgages and back taxes." On the witness stand Shields admitted that all records of expenditure were destroyed, but he claimed that $5300 of this vigilante money was paid to Federal Laboratories for gas. However, La Follette presented proof that the Bethlehem company itself had paid for the gas supplied to the police.

On November 19, 1939, the count in the mayorial election in Johnstown showed that Daniel Shields, running on the Republican, Socialist, and Prohibition tickets had been defeated for re-election. Shields blamed the "red" and "communistic" C.I.O., but it was evident that the corporations had not put in a slush fund for their previous puppet.

The Johnstown Plan died of exposure.

Chapter 20
The Liberty League and Its Offspring

Of all the movements in the world to protect dollars and cents, to defend property values at the expense of human values, the most obvious has been that organized under the hypocritical name, the American Liberty League. In this instance the money motives of the men of wealth and power became known because the organization made a great stupid blunder. Instead of remaining non-partisan in politics, as it outwardly claimed to be, it identified itself with one major political party—and therefore it became to the advantage of the opposition major party to expose the methods and purposes of those who, in the name of liberty, were fighting for loot.

The Liberty League stated that its purpose was to protect the American liberties of any man. Its counsel, Raoul Desvernine, and other lawyers issued public offers to do so, but in each and every instance when a case of violation of civil liberties was offered this group, its hypocrisy became apparent. It was organized to defend solely the liberty of accumulated wealth—and to fight radicalism.

Another of its tactical errors lay in tying up the defense of money too much with attacks on liberal ideas. It came out against the New Deal of President Roosevelt and the Democratic Party at a time when the entire American people was behind them and before the American press had prepared a solid anti-New Deal front. Thus we find the true motive—the dollar motive—of the Liberty League exposed by no less an organization than Roy Howard's United Press and by hundreds of newspapers. Here is a sample exposure. The New York *World-Telegram* headline and story of

January 9, 1935, read:

> Liberty League Controlled by Owners of
> $37,000,000,000
>
> Giant Corporations
> Revealed as Pushing
> Fight on "Radicals"
>
> U.S. Steel, General Motors, Standard Oil, Chase Bank, Goodyear Tire, Etc., All Have Men on Council Crusading for "Liberty"

Washington, Jan. 9.—The American Liberty League, a non-partisan society created to oppose "radical" movements in the national government, was shown today to be under control of a group representing industrial and financial organizations possessing assets of more than $37,000,000,000.

A United Press survey of the league's new executive committee and advisory council disclosed a close connection between members and some of the nation's greatest business enterprises.

League directors were shown to have affiliations with such organizations as the United States Steel Corp., General Motors, Standard Oil Co., Chase National Bank, Goodyear Tire and Rubber Co., Baltimore and Ohio Railroad, the Mutual Life Insurance Co. and scores of others.

A study of corporation and financial statistics showed that of the twenty men and women who will constitute the league's executive committee, thirteen are officers or directors of organizations with assets of more than $14,000,000,000.

On the executive committee are Alfred E. Smith, former Presidential candidate and Governor of New York; lrénée du Pont, head of the huge Delaware powder concern; John W. Davis, former Democratic Presidential nominee, and A. A. Sprague, Chicago industrialist.

The Liberty League and Its Offspring 259

Among the 156 founders of the Liberty League, in addition to Messrs. Smith, Davis, and Du Pont, were Grayson M.-P. Murphy, Elihu Root, John J. Raskob, Alfred P. Sloan, and James W. Wadsworth. When the list of contributors was made public it was found that among the chief subsidizers were:

Sewell L. Avery, Chicago	$5,000
W. S. Carpender, Jr., Wilmington	2,500
Robert Sterling Clark, New York	4,900
W. I. Clayton, Houston	1,000
S. B. Colgate, Orange, New Jersey	5,000
Countess Frieda Frasch Costanini, Paris	800
S. T. Crapo, Detroit	1,000
S. H. Curlee, St. Louis	1,000
Archibald M. L. Du Pont, Wilmington	2,500
Irénée Du Pont, Wilmington	5,000
Lammot Du Pont, Wilmington	5,000
H. B. Earhardt, Detroit	4,000
Edward F. Hutton, New York	5,000
George M. Moffett, New York	5,000
Rufus L. Patterson, New York	5,000
A. Hamilton Rice, New York	2,000
Hal E. Roach, Culver City, California	2,500

In addition, the Delaware branch received $10,357 from: Ernest, Eugene, Eugene E., Irénée, and Mrs. Pierre S. Du Pont, and Crawford Greenewalt, Ernest May, Mrs. May, and Mariana Du Pont Silliman.

The Liberty League, from any and all viewpoints, turned out to be nothing more than a commercial organization of big business men, similar to the Chamber of Commerce and the National Association of Manufacturers. A liberal writer (Herbert Harris) called it

> . . . a smokescreen for protecting the privileges of Big Business. . . . For the only liberty the League fosters is the liberty to water stock, rig the market, manipulate paper, and pyramid holding companies to the

stratosphere. It is the liberty to mix alum with the loaf and weight pure silk with lead. It is the liberty to pay starvation wages and break strikes with hired thugs. It is the liberty to fire men at forty and hire younger help. It is the liberty to warp the minds and bodies of children in textile mills and on "sharecropping" farms. It is the liberty to buy opinions of the pulpit and the press. It is the liberty which leads to death.

Grayson M.-P. Murphy and Robert Sterling Clark, respectively treasurer and large donor, were two of the leading figures mentioned in the exposure by General Smedley Butler of the fascist plot to capture the American government, and in the testimony in which it was stated that Clark was the millionaire who was willing to give half his fortune to save the other half.

Senator Schwellenbach, the "hatchet-man of the administration," has assailed the Liberty League and the "leeches, rascals, crooks and bloodsucking lawyers" who, he says, control its politics. Evident beyond any doubt is the fact that the Liberty League includes in its membership some of the worst redbaiters, enemies of labor, anti-Semites, pro-fascists, and pro-fascists in America. Some of the work a little too dirty for the white-ties of the Liberty League was delegated to the Crusaders, the Sentinels of the Republic, the Minute Men and Women of Today, the Defenders of Democracy, Farmers Independence Council, Paul Revere Society, Southern Committee to Uphold the Constitution, America First! Inc., and other "patriotic" organizations which Jay Franklin called "not bona fide popular organizations but propaganda stooges for powerful financial and business organizations."[1]

When the Black lobby-investigation committee seized the records of the Sentinels of the Republic it discovered some letters exchanged by W. Cleveland Runyon of Plainfield, New Jersey, and Alexander Lincoln, the

---
1   For the activities of these Liberty Leagues children, see *You Can't Do That*, Chapter 13.

investment banker of Boston who is also president of the Sentinels. Runyon attacked Roosevelt for bringing "the Jewish brigade" to Washington; he predicted the fight "for Western Christian civilization" could be won, that "the enemy is world wide and that it is Jewish in origin." To this repeater of Hitlerite phrases, Lincoln replied: "I think, as you say, that the Jewish threat is a real one." Runyon replied saying, "the New Deal is Communist . . . Tugwell has stated the real issue. They are planning a breakdown, which is necessary for the Communist dictatorship. The people are crying for leadership and not getting it. Our leaders are asleep. The Sentinels should really lead on the outstanding issue. The old-line Americans of $1200 a year want a Hitler."

The active group in the Sentinels, it was shown, was the Pitcairn family of Pennsylvania, notably Raymond Pitcairn, who supplied $91,000; Reverend Theodore and Mr. Harold F., who supplied $10,500; Mrs. Raymond, who gave $1000, and Mrs. Harold F., $500. Other financial backers were: J. Howard Pew, president of Sun Oil Company ($6000); A. Atwater Kent; and Nicholas Roosevelt of the New York *Herald Tribune*.

It is most interesting to note that the Sentinels supplied editorials to more than thirteen hundred newspapers, "urging a return to American principles."

WHERE THE MONEY COMES FROM—AND GOES*

Contributor	Corporate Affiliations	Organizations to Which He Contributed
Addinsell, H. M.	Pres., Chas. Harris Forbes Corp., Dir., Cities Service Power & Light Co., Phillips Petroleum Co., United States Electric Power Corp.	Crusaders, American Liberty League
Allen, E. M.	Pres., Mathieson Alkali Works, Dir., Austro-American Magnesite Corp., American Refractories Co., International Cement Corp.	Crusaders, American Liberty League, American Taxpayers League, National Economy League
Ames, Theodore		Crusaders, American Liberty League
Baker, George D.	Partner Boody, McLellan & Co. Treasurer, Chalis Realty Corp.	Crusaders, American Liberty League, American Federation Utility Investors
Bamberger, Clarence	Officer and director of nine corporations, mostly mining and oil, and stockholder in 20 other similar corporations.	Crusaders, American Federation Utility Investors
Du Pont, Irénée	Vice chairman of the board of E. I. Du Pont De Nemours & Co. Member finance committee and director General Motors Corp.	Crusaders, Sentinels of the Republic, American Liberty League, Southern Committee to Uphold the Constitution, Minute Men and Women of Today
Du Pont, Lammot	Pres. and dir., E. I. Du Pont De Nemours & Co. Chairman and dir., General Motors Corp. Dir., General Motors Acceptance Corp. and three banks.	Crusaders, American Liberty League, N. Y. State Economic Council, Economists National Commission on Monetary Policy, Southern Committee to Uphold the Constitution, Repeal Associates, Farmers Independence Council

* From the *New Republic*, September 2, 1936.

Contributor	Corporate Affiliations	Organizations to Which He Contributed
Echols, A. B.	Vice pres. in charge of finances and dir., E. I. Du Pont De Nemours & Co. Dir., Wilmington Trust Co., Gasselli Chemical Co., Du Pont Building Corp., Hotel Du Pont Co., Du Pont Viscoloid Co., Du Pont Film Mfg. Co.	Crusaders, Sentinels of the Republic, American Liberty League, American Federation Utility Investors, Economists National Committee on Monetary Policy, Taxpayers Research Council, Farmers Independence Council
Emery, Joseph H.	Member advisory board, Chase Nat'l Bank. Trustee Union Dime Savings Bank.	Crusaders, American Liberty League
Erickson, A. W.	Chairman of the board and dir., McCann-Erickson, Inc. and Congoleum-Nairn, Inc. Pres. & dir, Newskin Co., dir. Bon Ami Co., etc.	Crusaders, American Liberty League, N. Y. State Economic Council
Greef, Bernhard, Jr.	Partner, Greef & Co., brokers.	Crusaders, American Federation Utility Investors
Houston, George H.	Pres. and dir., Baldwin Locomotive Works, Standard Steel Works Co., and others.	Crusaders, American Liberty League, National Economy League
Hutton, E. F.	Former chairman of the board, General Foods, Inc. Chairman of the board, Zonite Products Corp. Dir., Manufacturers Trust Co, and Chrysler Corp.	Crusaders, American Liberty League
LaBoyteaux, W. H.	Pres., Johnson & Higgins; Wilcox Peck & Hughes; Elimar Trading Co. Dir., Grace Nat'l Bank, Merchants Ass'n, Curtin & Brockie, Albert Wilcox & Co.	Crusaders, American Liberty League, American Taxpayers League, National Economy League, Economists National Committee on Monetary Policy, Citizens Budget Commission

Contributor	Corporate Affiliations	Organizations to Which He Contributed
McCall, S. T.	Vice pres. and treas., Am. Brake Shoe & Foundry Co., Am. Manganese Steel Corp., etc.	Crusaders, American Liberty League, American Federation Utility Investors
Merrick, F. A.	Pres. and dir., Westinghouse Electric and Mfg. Co., Westinghouse Electric Elevator Co., Westinghouse Electric Supply Co., Laurentide Mico Co., Ltd.	Crusaders, National Economy League
Moffett, George M.	Pres. and dir., Corn Products Refining Co. Dir. six other large corporations.	Crusaders, American Liberty League
Montgomery, E. W.	Dir., two cotton mills and two cotton corporations.	Crusaders, American Liberty League
Morris, E. M.	Pres., Associated Investment Co., Morris Finance Co., Motor Indemnity Ass'n, Motor Underwriters, Inc.	Crusaders, American Liberty League, Economists National Council on Monetary Policy
Morris, John A.	Member Gude, Winmill & Co. Pres., Gude, Winmill Trading Corp.	Crusaders, Sentinels of the Republic, American Liberty League, American Taxpayers League, American Federation Utility Investors
Pew, J. Howard	Pres., Sun Oil Co. Dir., Sun Shipbuilding & Dry Dock Co., and Philadelphia National Bank.	Crusaders, Sentinels of the Republic, American Liberty League, American Taxpayers League, National Economy League
Purnell, Frank	Pres., Youngstown Sheet & Tube Co.	Crusaders, American Liberty League
Rosenthal, Benjamin	Executive vice pres., U. S. Playing Card Co. Pres., Russell Playing Card Co.	Crusaders, American Liberty League, American Federation Utility Investors, N. Y. State Economic Council

CONTRIBUTOR	CORPORATE AFFILIATIONS	ORGANIZATIONS TO WHICH HE CONTRIBUTED
Sams, E. C.	Pres., J. C. Penney Co.	Crusaders, American Liberty League
Schiff, John M.	Partner, Kuhn, Loeb & Co. Member of the executive committee of Western Union Telegraph Co.	Crusaders, N. Y. State Economic Council, National Economy League
Sloan, Alfred P.	Pres., General Motors Corp. Dir., E. I. Du Pont De Nemours & Co., Pullman, Inc., and others.	Crusaders, American Liberty League, N. Y. State Economic Council, National Economy League
Strauss, Lionel F.	Director of eleven street railway companies.	Crusaders, Sentinels of the Republic
Van Alstyne, J. H.	Pres., Otis Elevator Co.	Crusaders, American Liberty League, N. Y. State Economic Council, League for Industrial Rights
Weir, E. T.	Pres., National Steel Corp., Weirton Coal Co., Weirton Steel Co., and others.	Crusaders, American Liberty League, National Economy League
Woodward, Wm.	Honorary chairman of the board of Central Hanover Bank & Trust Co. Dir. of seven other corporations.	Crusaders (sound money comm.), American Taxpayers League

Part V

Marching as to War

Chapter 21
The Triumph of Dies

As the writing of this book was drawing to its conclusion, the drive for America's entry into the Second World War mounted to a frenzy. The administration, the press, the professional patriots, the munitions-makers, the Dies committee, and most of Congress climbed on the war bandwagon. The New York *Herald Tribune* came out for an immediate attack on Germany. Public opinion was being driven into the totalitarian groove which is so necessary for a modern, or totalitarian, war.

Signs appeared in ordinary commercial factories telling the workingmen to shut up. Theirs was not to question why, theirs was but to work for low wages and say nothing, while big business again took advantage of the war situation to make its enormous profits.

The move to emasculate the Wagner Act, defeated in Congress in May 1940 through labor pressure, was revived, and with it came the proposal to abolish all the reform measures of the New Deal, notably the W.P.A., the National Youth Administration, and the Wages and Hours Act.

Redbaiting, which had been growing tremendously during the past year, began to reach the hysterical stages of 1919-1920, when A. Mitchell Palmer, hoping to be the 1920 Democratic presidential candidate, violated the constitutional rights of tens of thousands of persons through raids, arrests, violence, and brutality.

The Dies committee, which had been denounced as vicious by all men of intelligence and reason, became more and more the weapon for silencing all opposition to reaction and warmongering. President Roosevelt had once said that "the Dies Committee made no effort to get at the truth. . . ."[1] Not once, but a hundred times, it had been proven beyond question that the Dies committee was listening to and propagating falsehood. But, in wartime hysteria, when truth is the first casualty, the value of the committee's obscurantism was recognized.

Inasmuch as the hearings are still going on at the time of this writing, it is impossible to write a complete account of the developments, but certain significant facts may be pointed out.

First, it is evident that the power to investigate is the power to destroy. Thus, the La Follette committee, by its exposure of the private detective agencies which employed professional murderers, crooks, thugs, and hoodlums to break strikes, drove the worst agencies out of business and forced the others to reform. As a result of the La Follette committee's activities, industrial espionage, vigilantism, labor violence, the use of gas bombs and guns against labor, the interstate transportation of strike-breakers, and other criminal actions were to some extent checked, if not eradicated.

It must be noted, however, that in all instances the La Follette committee attempted to give every man and organization a fair hearing. It listened to the defense, it always permitted counsel to represent the accused, and it conducted its hearings in an atmosphere of honesty and fairness.

The Dies committee, however, has used its power to attack every liberal and progressive organization it could lay its hands on. Moreover, it did not permit the accused to defend themselves, but allowed unsubstantiated statements to be spread on the front pages of all the newspapers of America. By these means, and in the face of the growing hysteria brought on by the preparations for totalitarian war, many individuals were frightened into silence and many organizations destroyed.

One of the anomalies of the situation was that the war

---
1 White House press conference, October 25, 1938.

preparations which President Roosevelt began so feverishly in May 1940, when the Germans erupted into Holland, Belgium, Luxembourg, and France, were aimed against Nazi Germany, whereas the redbaiters of America, from Coughlin to Dies, had either protected and favored the Nazis or, at most, made feints at Nazism as a concession to public opinion while they really went after groups that were essentially anti-fascist.

Neither Dies nor J. Edgar Hoover of the F.B.I. so much as slapped the wrist of Father Coughlin although he was overtly the father of Christian Front activities (which might or might not have been directed toward overthrowing the government by armed revolt, but which were certainly un-American in the sense that the Dies committee was supposed to be investigating).

Earlier, Ambassador Dodd had warned America, from his post in Berlin, that an American billionaire was helping prepare a fascist coup in this country. Dies did not take this tip. He was also given evidence that members of the National Association of Manufacturers were "aiding Nazi and Fascist movements in this country." He informed the N.A.M. that one of his agents would look into the matter—and there the matter has rested.

Another important fact was the amazing change that took place in the attitude of the press toward the Dies committee. At first Dies was a joke, and a bad joke at that; he was called a fool and a clown by the best citizens and the newspapers quoted them with delight. But by the time his appeal for a second appropriation came up in Congress, it was evident that the Democratic Party was no longer afraid of his smearing the New Deal, and that reactionaries in both parties had realized how valuable a weapon they had in the redbaiting committee.

In October 1938, when the Dies committee was still attacking the Roosevelt reforms and before it became an aid to the war hysteria, the President, who had himself denounced the representative and his methods as sordid and untruthful, suggested that the Washington correspondents who covered the hearings be asked if they thought Dies was fair or unfair.

John O'Donnell and Doris Fleeson, who write the column "Capitol Stuff," acted on the suggestion. They asked eighteen correspondents and only two voted that Martin Dies was fair. These two men represented the most reactionary papers in the country.

Liberal journalists not only voted Dies unfair, but said so in strong terms. Paul Y. Anderson said: "Some congressional committees smell, some are foul, and some stink. The Dies committee stinks." Richard L. Strout of the *Christian Science Monitor* compared Dies and La Follette, pointing out that everything La Follette did was decent, whereas Dies "publicly sifted hearsay evidence."

Strout also took the occasion to comment on a fact that is damning to the press of the United States. He said: "The Dies committee gets more attention, more headlines and more newspaper space in the average week than the La Follette committee gets in a normal month."

O'Donnell and Fleeson try to excuse this by saying that "Dies obligingly operated his show during the dead summer months when the President was absent from Washington and the correspondents were panting for news." However, it is a fact that the La Follette committee held hearings in summer and winter, in times when there was other sensational news and in times when there was a dearth of it.

One of the worst instances of this press perversion was the handling of the testimony of a man named Frey, one of the bitterest American Federation of Labor enemies of the C.I.O. Frey tried to smear the latter organization with red paint. The procedure, Washington correspondent Kenneth Crawford later wrote, was ridiculous: "He repeatedly betrayed himself. At one point, for example, he accused John Brophy, a Lewis lieutenant, of communistic leanings and affiliations. It happens that Brophy is a devout

Catholic. His parish priest so informed the committee." But what did the press do with the nonsensical testimony? Even the New York *Times* gave it the front page and "unquestioned credence." Yet it was stale stuff; the *Times* and other papers had printed it almost word for word, not once but several times, because Frey had often made the same irresponsible statements before. The old and respected newspaper rule that news that has been printed is not news, was violated in the anxiety of these papers to harm the C.I.O. by red-branding it.

The *Herald Tribune* changed sides several times, but in the end returned to its reactionary redbaiting stand. On January 20, 1940, when Dies was a particularly nauseous stench in liberal nostrils, the *Tribune* editorial said: "We suggest that his well earned retirement in favor of a chairman equally in earnest but less vociferous would help matters." Apparently this was too much. So four days later, the *Tribune* editorial said: "Whatever mistakes Mr. Dies may have made it must be acknowledged that he has earned the right to continue as the committee's head, if his health permits."

The entire press, according to the American Committee for Democracy and Intellectual Freedom, suppressed the charge made in Congress by Samuel Dickstein that the newspapers themselves had intimidated members of the House to the extent that they were afraid to vote No on support of the Dies committee. Congressmen were buttonholed by representatives of the press and given to understand they would lose press support if they showed they could not support Dies. The only reference to this subject, part of a heated debate in the House, was this line, under "Day in Congress" in the New York *Herald Tribune:* "Heard Rep. Dickstein urge stronger action against subversive groups," implying that he supported instead of condemned the Dies committee.

The American Committee for Democracy and Intellectual Freedom announced that more than a hundred outstanding citizens, including twelve college presidents, six deans, and leaders in the scientific and cultural world had signed a petition to Congress requesting no further appropriations for Dies. The only major newspaper to mention the story, the *Herald Tribune*, gave it four paragraphs in an inconspicuous spot on page 3 immediately adjoining a large story headed "Dies Declares Radicals Try to End His Inquiries."

When, on October 25, 1939, the Dies committee gave the press the mailing list (containing the names of federal employees) of the American League for Peace and Democracy, a legal organization the committee had been smearing, so that the recipients of the League's news releases were by implication branded as "reds," the *Herald Tribune* condemned the action as the "worst" blunder Dies had made—but took the occasion to attack the Democratic administration, saying it was "a strange perversion of the function of a government agency." The same perversion also occurred in the *Herald Tribune*, however, for it published the list the next day. The Chicago *Daily News*, a liberal paper, did not publish this list, stating that "it was a smear effort aimed at the owners of the names on the list and also at the Roosevelt administration."

The Dies committee refused to hear the testimony of those men and organizations it had smeared. The only recourse left to the victims was to appeal to the press, which had been the agency for smearing.

Congressman Adolf J. Sabath, chairman of the House Rules Committee, said during the final debate on the Dies committee resolution that he had received petitions asking for a hearing from the following organizations: the American Federation of Teachers, Consumers Union, Committee for Peoples Rights, Professional League for Civil Rights, Public Affairs Committee, National Board of the Young Women's Christian Association, American Committee for Democracy and Intellectual Freedom, League of Women Shoppers, and many others. All of these

The Triumph of Dies

petitions, and replies to the distortions and falsifications of the Dies hearings, were issued to the press of the United States but, according to the American Committee for Democracy and Intellectual Freedom, none was published, and "the extent of the opposition to the Dies Committee [was] thereby minimized."

The same organization said that heavy pressure was brought on the Dies committee to investigate Father Coughlin, Pelley, the Ku Klux Klan, and Merwin K. Hart, but it predicted that the newspapers would not report these matters. Unfortunately, this proved true.

Pelley of the Silver Shirts not only endorsed Dies but announced that since the Dies committee was carrying on exceedingly well the work to which he and his organization had dedicated themselves (redbaiting and anti-Semitism) there was no longer a necessity for him to remain in business.

Coughlin in his editorial in *Social Justice* on December 11, 1939, proposed Dies for President. He said that Dies has made a great record in a "fight for clean Americanism."

The Institute for Propaganda Analysis, in its bulletin on the Dies propaganda machine, notes that the liberal journalists, Kenneth Crawford and others,

> look upon the committee as the soundingboard for every anti-labor propagandist in the United States, out to destroy the C.I.O., the New Deal, and, indeed, all liberal and progressive organizations by smearing them with red paint. Of course, says Mr. Crawford, this is the fascist technique: stampede the people by shouting "Communist!" And he believes that Mr. Dies is the hatchet man of "the native American fascist." . . .
>
> Day after day the charges—the wild charges as well as the plausible ones—have appeared in hundreds of newspapers. . . . The man in the street has seen only the charges, day after day; and, inevitably, some of them have begun to sink in. Adolf Hitler understands this well, this power of repetition: lies will become accepted truth

if repeated often enough, he wrote in *Mein Kampf*. As the old saying goes, "Sling enough mud, and some is sure to stick.". . .

When the committee's second report was issued, absolving the C.I.O. almost completely of the charges of "Communist domination," the one story which appeared in the newspapers could not possibly have offset in his mind the dozens of stories in which every leader in the C.I.O. was accused of communist sympathies. . . .

Similarly even though hundreds of liberal organizations were named by witnesses as "Communist front" organizations, the committee itself named only 11. It rejected at least 90 percent of the charges made before it, possibly more; but, again, the charges appeared in the newspapers, and they must have impressed themselves upon the minds of many newspaper readers. . . .

What has Dies accomplished? According to Martin Dies, he has scored many "triumphs." He listed them to a reporter of the *Sunday Star* of Washington, D. C. Here are a few:

(1) Paralyzed the influence of the left-wing faction of the Roosevelt administration. . . .

(2) Discredited the Congress of Industrial Organizations, making it "the most unpopular body in the United States."

(3) Dethroned John L. Lewis as dictator of congressional legislation. . . .

(4) Defeated Frank Murphy for re-election as governor of Michigan, through testimony representing him as condoning sit-down strikes. . . .

(5) Discredited Secretary of Labor Perkins for alleged laxity in enforcement of deportation laws.

(6) Offset revelation of the La Follette civil liberties committee as to labor-baiting practices of sections of big business. . . .

These are "triumphs" which damn the committee in the eyes of all fair and honest men. Paul Anderson summarized the "accomplishments" in mid-summer, 1938, before the Dies committee had made many of its more outrageous and unethical assaults upon liberal institutions and men. Anderson wrote:

> Thus far the committee has devoted itself mainly to the following:
> (1) attacking the only form of labor organization which the industrialists have been unable to tame;
> (2) smearing the Senate Civil Liberties Committee, as a means of disparaging the value of civil liberties in this country;
> (3) broadcasting scandal against the legitimate government of Spain, to appease American resentment over the German-Italian invasion of that country;
> (4) trying to soften American horror over the anti-Jewish atrocities in Germany by circulating the intimation that they were provoked by a "Jewish boycott" in this country;
> (5) smearing a list of New Deal officials who are on record in favor of peace and democracy.
>
> By what method [continued Mr. Anderson] does the Committee strive to achieve these ends? By applying the epithets "communist" and "communism" to every person and every principle which it hopes to discredit. How did Mussolini and Hitler justify their conquest of democracy? They never took a step without proclaiming that it was necessary to save their respective nations from "Bolshevism"! It is all old stuff—fabricated in Italy, finished in Germany, and now being peddled in Washington.

The Dies committee acted as if it were an agency of the National Association of Manufacturers, the chambers of commerce, Mr. Ford, Mr. Girdler, Mr. Weir, and other large manufacturers who want to kill the C.I.O. and the Wagner Act. It gave the Hearst and the Scripps-Howard brand of labor-baiting a forum, and it tried desperately to permit the Associated Farmers to "put over in a big way the communist-menace propaganda which is always the excuse for vigilante lawlessness" (Crawford). It refused to investigate Father Coughlin or to take notice of the 251 arrests of Christian Front hoodlums charged with violence and subversive activities. It failed to look into southern activities, such as Ku Klux Klan lynchings.

Finally, at the end of May 1940, President Roosevelt, whose administration had been one of the chief victims of the Dies redbaiting committee, and who had denounced it frequently, suddenly endorsed it. For almost three years the President had fought it courageously, but when he took command of the war hysteria he put a stamp of approval on the committee's work. Up to now it had been "shoddy"; now, Mr. Roosevelt told his press conference, the extent of subversive activities could be found in the Dies committee reports. The lies, half-truths, smears, the "backfence radical gossip . . . scandals, guesses and wild charges" which conservative *Time* reported had become part of the war hysteria itself.

CHAPTER 22
Who Are the Real Fifth Column?

In turning the Dies committee into a witch hunt directed against all who did not agree that the most immediate problem for the United States was the danger of foreign invasion, and in transmuting the resultant war-preparedness hysteria into a weapon against labor, liberals, and nonconformists, the national and local leaders of reaction applied to their victims the phrase *Fifth Column.* It replaced the word *reds;* it could also include Blackshirts and Brownshirts; moreover, it was comparatively new and had touched the popular imagination when the so-called Fifth Columnists had helped betray Norway to the Germans.

Actually the phrase *Fifth Column* is applicable only to reactionaries. It was first used by General Mola, who, when marching for fascist Franco against the Spanish Republic, said he was converging on Madrid with four columns, and expected help within the capital from a fifth—in other words, traitors to the republic who would knife the Popular Front democracy in behalf of fascism.

The use of the phrase by the real Fifth Columnists in America to fight the labor unions, pacifists, liberals, and leftists is a typical fascist trick. "Fascism," said Huey Long, "will arrive in America on an anti-fascist platform." Congressman Dies, who has tried to make the phrase synonymous for reds, has not only failed to prosecute American black and brown Fifth Columns, but has actually refused to use the evidence furnished him regarding Italian and German Fascists and Nazis in their American organizations. Had Dies been sincere in directing the House Committee on Un-American Activities, he might have gone after a Fifth Column revealed by the following episode:

Rhea Whitley, committee counsel, identified letters written by Oscar C. Pfaus, director of the Fichte Bund, Nazi propaganda agency, and Dr. Anna Bogenhold Sloane of New York City, regarding the establishment of a pro-Nazi newspaper to be called *The National American Patriot.* To the proposal to have it edited by James Philip Gaffney, Pfaus wrote the choice was ideal. In a letter to Pfaus, Dr. Sloane said:

> I want to have a council of twelve leaders of patriotic movements connected with it in the hope that this would link together all patriotic movements in the United States for the purpose of recovering our country from control of the Jews.
>
> I am in communication with the following who I hope would serve as such councilors in case I succeed to get this new paper started:
>
> 1. Dr. Hiram Wesley Evans, president, Ku Klux Klan;
>
> 2. Dr. Edward Hunter, president, Industrial Defense League;
>
> 3. Mr. Donald Shea, president, White Shirts, and Gentile League;
>
> 4. Mr. William Dudley Pelley, president, Silver Shirts;
>
> 5. Rev. Charles E. Coughlin, publisher, *Christian* [*sic*] *Justice;*
>
> 6. Mr. George E. Deatherage, president, Knights of the White Camellia;
>
> 7. Mr. James True, president, James True Associates;
>
> 8. Gen. Geo. Van Horn Moseley;
>
> 9. Mr. Geo. W. Christians, president, Crusaders;
>
> 10. Rev. Gerland [*sic*] Wvinrod;
>
> 11. Mr. Fritz Kuhn, president, German Bund;
>
> 12. Mr. Harry A. Jung, president, Vigilant Federation.

If Congressman Dies were really looking for a Fifth Column, a collection of the reactionaries of today, the

American Fascisti of tomorrow, he might also consider this handbill:

> GREAT PRO-AMERICAN MASS MEETING
> IN BEHALF OF FREE SPEECH
> AND
> AMERICANISM
> Wednesday, May 24, at 8:30 p.m., Carnegie Hall
> Speakers:
>
> Boake Carter, Radio's Fearless News editor, on the timely subject, "Free Speech and the News"
> John A. Matthews, Advisory Master of Court of Chancery of New Jersey, will speak on "Only one Ism—Americanism"
> John E. Kelly, brilliant, well-posted writer and lecturer will speak on "John L. Lewis—Public Enemy No. 2"
> J. E. McWilliams, Dynamic Young Orator, will speak on "Keep America out of War"
>
> Presiding—George U. Harvey, Dynamic, Capable Borough President of Queens, President of "We Americans"
>
> This meeting is under the sponsorship of:
> American Federation Against Communism.
> American Patriots, Inc.
> With the cooperation of The Christian Front, and twelve other Patriotic Organizations.

The Christian Front, under whose co-operative auspices these speakers, including a judge and a news commentator, were to spread patriotism, was not investigated by Mr. Dies, although the F.B.I. found several of its members practicing rifle-shooting with President Roosevelt's picture as a target.

The Christian Front is almost entirely Catholic but, as I have shown at greater length in my book, *The Catholic*

Crisis, there is no religious line with the reactionaries; Catholicism, Protestantism, and paganism have frequently united under the fascist banner and co-operated with reactionary Jews, Mohammedans, and perhaps infidels. Hitler, Mussolini, Franco, and the Mikado at one time threatened to unite to conquer the world; and Coughlin, Kuhn, and General Moseley have always worked on the same side of the social-economic fence in America. The pattern of fascism runs true, from Berlin to Burgos, from Tokyo to the Shrine of the Little Flower, from Bund Headquarters on Eighty-sixth Street to the Palazzo Venezia, and from Tompkins Corners, New York, to the Tribune Tower, Chicago, whence Judge H. W. Rogers (retired) and Harry Jung, respectively, mail the same "literature" which Goebbels distributes.

It is worth noting that the first treasurer of the Italian Fascists, the man who collected the funds for the Blackshirts of Mussolini, was a Jewish banker, Giuseppe Toeplitz of the Banca Commerciala, and that all the Jewish manufacturers of Milan and Turin supported Fascism and reaped its benefits: the smashing of the labor unions, the outlawing of strikes, the suppression of civil liberties, and finally the reduction of the standard of living in Italy to the lowest in Europe.

The American Liberty League invited Protestants, Catholics, and Jews to join. Al Smith got no blackball, nor did any rich Jews. All that was required was a contribution and a willingness to fight all liberals who wanted to change the *status quo* of the Big Money. For years attempts had been made to gather all reactionaries in America into one movement, but even the Liberty League did not succeed. Dies, however, gave them a rallying point.

The group which wanted Moseley to lead reaction into power consisted of the following heads of "patriotic" organizations: Moseley, Kuhn, Coughlin, Deatherage, Pelley, Robert Edmondson, Winrod, G. L. K. Smith, Senator Reynolds, Zoll, Christians, Henry Allen, Colonel

Sanctuary, and James True.

The same group met in a magazine called *Patriots Digest*, whose officers are: R. Caldwell Patton, president; Clarence M. Chauncey, secretary; Thomas J. Hallowell, treasurer; John E. Kelly, Gault MacGowan, Lambert Fairchild, Edward Curran Lodge, and Major William Lathrop Rich, advisory board.

The first issue of *Patriots Digest* gives an excellent picture of what the redbaiters of America, Catholic and non-Catholic, want; an article by Kelly advocates disfranchising millions of poor Americans because they are on relief; a reprint from the *Catholic News* repeats one of the most atrocious lies about the Spanish war; there are two reactionary items from the New York *Sun* and H. L. Mencken; a page of Hearst items entitled "Red Fist over America"; a cartoon of an oriental-faced person labeled "C.I.O. Threatens Labor"; a reprint from *National Republic* and from Spain, the Franco-subsidized propaganda sheet; an article by Father Curran repeating a story originated by the London *Times* of O.G.P.U. Slaughter; praise for Coughlin; approval of the Dies committee; kind words for Hitler; suggestion that the C.I.O. is following "the same bloody path" of the French Revolution and that Lewis may be a Robespierre; cartoon favorable to Kuhn; expression of regret that German Bund is attacked; attack on Mayor LaGuardia as a "little pink perennial, communist candidate"; and an article by MacGowan of the New York *Sun*.

The big money is always the fascist money, everywhere, and no questions asked about religion. In many of the pro-Franco organizations up to 1939 there were no Catholics at all. A group which signed a letter protesting an appeal to Franco not to murder all Loyalist prisoners included: James Emory Brooks, N. M. Crouse, Knowlton Durham, Ogden H. Hammond, Merwin K. Hart, John Eoghan Kelly, Irwin Laughlin, W. H. Loomis, A. Hamilton Rice, and Charlotte Churchill Starr. A pro-fascist

"Non-Partisan American Committee for Spanish Relief" was headed by Basil Harris, vice-president of International Mercantile Marine, and included Hammond, Leon Fraser of the First National Bank of New York, General Haskell of the New York National Guard, Joseph Grace, the shipping magnate, Kelly Graham, president of the First National of Jersey City, Thomas F. Woodlock of the *Wall Street Journal* and Frederick H. Prince, the banker. Only two are Catholics.

A word of caution must be said at this moment about the general impression among non-Catholics that the Catholics of America are reactionaries, pro-fascists, redbaiters, and anti-Semites. Nothing could be more false: the fact is that the majority of Catholics are not only anti-fascist but actually expressed themselves against Franco when he was proclaiming a Christian (Catholic) Crusade against the "reds" of Spain. Furthermore, they are the backbone of progressive organized labor in America. Unfortunately Coughlin, Lodge, Father Talbot, Father Thorning, and other Catholic reactionaries who get newspaper space, were for Franco (and his Moorish murderers wearing the Sacred Heart of Jesus embroidered on their uniforms). It is interesting to note that these same "leaders" and their publications denounced the C.I.O. when it was organized, although 65 percent of its membership is good Roman-Catholic.

Certain facts seem to lend credibility to the misconception that the Catholics of America are on the side of the Blackshirts and the Brownshirts: the outstanding fact that the Catholic who has the largest audience, Coughlin, is a fascist sympathizer, and is not curbed in speech or action by his bishop—whereas a Catholic liberal, Monsignor Ryan, seems to have been silenced; the facts that the majority of the Catholic press is reactionary; that three of the four cardinals were pro-fascist during the Spanish war, and that most of the hierarchy is reactionary. It is these reactionary Catholics who control publicity and get the front page, whereas Father Francis J. Haas, who appeared at the first convention of the C.I.O. and later proposed an annual wage of $2500 for labor, gets no front-page notice in the Catholic press (or elsewhere).

The trial of the seventeen Christian Front members on a charge of conspiracy to upset the American Republic is not half as significant as the support given them by the Brooklyn *Tablet*, which is a diocesan weekly. Representative Martin Kennedy of New York defended the Fronters in the House; Harvey of Queens praised them as Americans; Fire Commissioner McElligott of New York refused to investigate the Christian Front affiliations of his own men, and the Dies committee and the F.B.I. refused to take any action when Mayor LaGuardia of New York publicly declared that "some master mind, or minds not yet disclosed, were working on these young men . . . inducing them to wrongdoing, disloyal and criminal acts." Coughlin's name was kept out of the trial.

Significantly the *Protestant Digest* points out that:

> While Catholic prelates like the late Cardinal Hayes, politicians like Martin Dies, business reactionaries like Merwin K. Hart, were façading for the Franco Front, the Christian Front boys held forth for Franco on street corner meetings, sold *Social Justice* and *The Tablet*, pushed Jews into the gutter; were, that is, the Storm Troopers, the squadristi, the mass base of the Franco Front.
>
> Prior to the Franco rising, no Fascist cause has made any headway in the United States. The Italian Fascist and the German Nazi organizations were of little importance. In the Spanish venture, however, the Nazis and the Fascists were allied with powerful elements in the Roman Catholic Church, which had ready to hand in the United States all the necessary paraphernalia of propaganda: highly developed organization, speakers, press—and believers.
>
> It is fundamental to an understanding of the work of the members of the Franco Front to note that when they

used the word "Communist" about Spain, they applied it indiscriminately to Mason, Nineteenth-Century Liberal, Freethinker, Anarchist, Protestant, Basque Catholic, Republican, Catalan Autonomist, Socialist, Labor Union member and Democrat as well as Communist. In referring to the American scene, they used the same technique and the word "Communist" has been slowly widened to include Mrs. Roosevelt, John L. Lewis, Mayor LaGuardia, the Jews, the C.I.O. and President Roosevelt's personal advisors, or, in fact, anybody who will not be browbeaten by the pressure of the Franco Front into a denunciation of all international Isms (except *Catholicism*—naturally).

According to the *Protestant Digest,* the supporters of the Franco Front in America are: Dr. Alexander Hamilton Rice, Hart, Thorning, Scanlan, John F. Cassidy of the Christian Front, Dudley P. Gilbert, Deatherage, Curran, State Senator McNaboe, Zoll, and the following persons who helped the Sodalists of St. Peter's College prepare a symposium dedicated to the murderer Franco: Father Talbot, Ogden Hammond, Major J. O. Kelly, Professor F. X. Connolly of Fordham, and the Marquesa de Cienfuegos, of Atlanta, Georgia.

> Hart [concludes the *Digest*] was naturally the liaison between the Franco Front and Martin Dies, whose committee has been an effective alley of the Franco Front, not only in painting Loyalist Spain as "communistic," but also in widening the scope of the term "communist," thus increasing fears of a Communist putsch.

The German Bundists and the Mussolini organizations in America are small, unimportant, and generally impotent. The real danger of a Fifth Column is the danger of native American fascism disguised as better Americanism. The Franco Front is one of the real Fifth Columns. Its members possess that reactionary state of mind. They and their Tory forebears have always tried to make a desert of the Bill of Rights and call it patriotism.

CHAPTER 23
Conclusion: War of Words and Worlds

SUMMARY

It should be obvious from the foregoing massing of evidence that:

(1) Redbaiting is itself a big business.

(2) Redbaiting is a powerful weapon of big business.

(3) Redbaiting is also a political weapon. It is so powerful that it helped Hitler take power, obtained $300,000,000 in loans from Morgan, Dillon Read, etc., for Mussolini; became the main excuse for the Hitler-Mussolini-Franco-Mikado Axis.

(4) Redbaiting is conducted chiefly for profit. The profits may be paid in egotistic satisfaction, in the greatest power any man ever held, in psychiatric coin, sometimes; but, mainly, it pays in dollars and cents.

(5) The biggest redbaiters in America are the members of the chambers of commerce, the National Association of Manufacturers, the Associated Farmers, the Liberty League, and other purely commercial organizations, who redbait to preserve their wealth, the system which makes their holdings secure, the *status quo* of Big Money.

(6) Redbaiting is almost universally accompanied by, and is a screen for, labor-baiting, anti-Semitism, anti-Catholicism, and sometimes anti-Masonry and lynching hysteria.

(7) Redbaiters made the C.I.O. their main target for several years; in this they had the co-operation of the American press, many of whose workers are the C.I.O. men of the Newspaper Guild.

(8) Redbaiting is powerful enough to capture the control of a nation, and ridiculous enough to stop the use of red flags on dangerous highways (as in Salinas, California).

(9) Redbaiting is one of the important forces in present-day America.

First Aid for Reader and Reviewer

The foregoing summary may prove of some help to readers and reviewers—especially to reviewers who must read as they run, and who run at a terribly fast pace. I feel that there should also be, in a book dealing largely with name-calling, some statement about my own use of names.

First of all, I realize that I have often used the words *fascism* and *reaction* interchangeably. In this I follow as my authority Mussolini, who, though he did not invent the word *fascist,* gave it world-wide circulation. "Fascism," he wrote, "is not afraid to call itself reactionary, illiberal, and anti-liberal." He also summed up all the conflicts now going on in the world as the struggle between fascism and democracy, and concluded that "either we or they" will win. Since Mussolini made fascism what it is today, I follow him to the extent of accepting his definitions.

In much the same way the late Ambassador Dodd, one of the great American liberals, used *fascism* for *reaction* when he said, on arriving here from Germany after his resignation as American Ambassador there: "Fascism is on the march today in America. Millionaires are marching to the tune. It will come in this country unless a strong defense is set up by all liberal and progressive forces."

As for the term *red:* Heywood Broun deplored the fact that this three-letter word was being used as a smear-word by the press of the country, but explained that it was so easy to use small words in headlines that no copyreader could resist it.

However, there is a legitimate, ethical use of the term, and an unethical use. When, for example, the newspapers carried the streamers, "Red Army Attacks Mannerheim Line," it was a legitimate use of a synonym for Russian or Soviet; but when the Hearst editors wrote *red* in place of *loyalist* in referring to the army defending Madrid, it was a malicious attempt to smear the Spanish Republic which was defending itself against a fascist conspiracy and uprising.

The most unfair use of the smear is by association. This is the method of *The Red Network* and the *Spider Chart* which was current in the War Department in the 1920 red scare—and which will no doubt be revived at about the time this book is published.

When the C.I.O. was formed, redbaiting by association was
so common that the following story went the rounds: "President Roosevelt," said one of the enemies of labor, "shook hands with John L. Lewis; and Lewis shook hands with David Dubinsky; and Dubinsky [once] shook hands with Earl Browder; and Browder is a Communist; that makes President Roosevelt a red."

One of the best characterizations of the term redbaiting was that issued by the executive council of the American Federation of Teachers in answer to an attack by Major Charles S. Hart, the Grand Exalted Ruler of the Elks. Said the A.F.T.

> "Redbaiting is the hall mark of all who oppose the attempts of the American people to secure a more equitable distribution of the wealth their hands and brain produce."

All this may be over-simplification, but I prefer it to obscurantism.

WHAT THE AMERICAN PEOPLE REALLY WANT

And finally, an author is apparently expected to write a conclusion giving a formula by which the ills of which he treats may be cured. If he fails to do so, if he merely investigates a matter, produces the documentation, exposes the evil, on the assumption that "vice is a monster of so frightful mien, as to be hated needs but to be seen"—he is immediately branded a muckraker. *Muckraker* itself is a smear-word, a predecessor of the term *red;* it was first used by Theodore Roosevelt, who had encouraged the great Lincoln Steffens and others in their work, but who later branded them muckrakers when they got around to looking into his own activities. However, it is interesting to note that a comparatively unknown person aptly replied to the President: "Where there is muck to be raked, it must be raked, and the public must know of it, that it may mete out justice. . . . Publicity is a great purifier because it sets in motion the forces of public opinion, and in this country public opinion controls the course of the nation." The speaker is now Chief Justice Hughes.

But to me it seems perfectly obvious that the American people really knows what is wrong and what should be done about it. When not willfully confused by labels, it is remarkably progressive. It will be remembered that as a result of the tests conducted by Professor Hartmann, and referred to in the Foreword to this work, he concluded that "evidently most of these voters want the specific things for which socialism stands, but they do not want to have them labeled that way."

During the 1936 presidential campaign a Chicago high-school teacher made a similar test. On a straw poll, her class voted: Landon, 70; Roosevelt, 20; scattering, 10. The teacher then wrote out the Landon Republican Party platform, the Roosevelt Democratic Party platform, and a third platform such as Karl Marx might have written for the United States. When now the class voted again, the third platform got 54 percent of the votes, the Republicans and Democrats dividing the minority.

In the spring of 1940, the magazine *Fortune* made a survey which also showed that about 15 percent of the American people—and that means, of course, 20,000,000 persons—subscribe "to practically every point of public policy that a socialist platform usually embodies." Yet the vote for all parties with socialist platforms has never reached more than 1,000,000.

All these experiments and polls indicate two things most clearly: (1) that the American people want something better; (2) that they do not vote for something better because of the scare-words—the redbaiting, the use of names, of labels, of seemingly innocent things like three-letter words.

"The reactionaries," says John Dewey, the philosopher, "are in possession of force, in not only the army and police, but in the press and the schools."

THE IMMEDIATE OUTLOOK

Fascism is reaction armed with bayonets.

In the summer of 1940, at the time this book was concluded, the President was at one and the same time dropping his reform program, giving in to reaction, and, through the skillful manipulation of a war scare, insisting on bayonets. On the one hand he was reconciled with the Dies committee which he had previously repudiated; on the other he was making quiet-voiced but nonetheless panic speeches about the imminence of foreign bombers over our Midwestern cities. It bears repeating: Fascism is reaction armed with bayonets. And fascism is an attempt to retreat to the Dark Ages, and to slavery for the mass of men.

In the summer of 1940 there were already indications that the 1914-1917 hysteria was to be equaled if not surpassed. Aliens were being hunted in factories and fields, fingerprinted, registered. Our youth were to be drafted to protect them from thinking too independently for themselves. The Dies committee was already going beyond the stupidities and viciousness of the Overman committee. The witch-hunting days of A. Mitchell Palmer were being revived.

The immediate outlook was pretty black. The American people were still 95 percent or more against going to war, and many still remembered the disillusionment of 1918, but the American people were also in a great majority against Hitler and all foreign fascism, and it seemed possible for the war-makers to use this hatred of Hitlerism to overcome the desire to stay out of war. In the plan of conversion, the means of communication were of the first importance, and the anti-pacifist, anti-alien, anti-liberal campaign sought to inflame a great mob spirit that would once again wipe out the Bill of Rights.

A man named Milligan opposed the Civil War. He was arrested, tried, convicted, and sentenced to death for his opinions, but he fought his way through to the Supreme Court, and that august body—delaying the matter, it is true, until the war was over—wrote a decision in such plain English that no lawyer is necessary to interpret it, and no quibble is possible. Said the Supreme Court:

> The Constitution of the United States is a law of rulers and people, equally in war and peace, and covers with the shield of its protection all classes of men at all times and under all circumstances. . . . No doctrine is more pernicious than that any of its great provisions can be suspended during any of the great exigencies of government. That leads directly to anarchy and despotism. . . .

In our day, to fascism.

FINAL WORD TO THE CONSUMERS OF NEWSPAPERS

"Eternal vigilance," said Thomas Jefferson, "is the price of liberty."

Made in the USA
San Bernardino, CA
25 October 2013